ALSO BY MONA HARRINGTON

The Dream of Deliverance in
American Politics (1986)

Women of Academe:
Outsiders in the Sacred Grove
(with Nadya Aisenberg, 1988)

WOMEN LAWYERS

REWRITING THE RULES

WOMEN LAWYERS

REWRITING THE RULES

Mona Harrington

ALFRED A. KNOPF   NEW YORK   1994

THIS IS A BORZOI BOOK
PUBLISHED BY ALFRED A. KNOPF, INC.

Copyright © 1993 by Mona Harrington

Library of Congress Cataloging-in-Publication Data

Harrington, Mona, [date]
Women lawyers : rewriting the rules / Mona Harrington.
p.   cm.
Includes index.
ISBN 0-394-58025-7
1. Women lawyers—United States.
KF299.W6H36   1994
349.73′082—dc20
[347.30082]   93-18000
CIP

Manufactured in the United States of America

First Edition

FOR ELIZA, BENJAMIN, AND THOMAS

questioners, critics, advocates

Acknowledgments

MY THANKS GO FIRST to the dozens of women lawyers who were willing to talk with a stranger asking deeply personal questions, and who answered with thoughtfulness and amazing frankness. I have enjoyed their openness and humor, admired their lack of pretense and their desire to get to the bottom of things even on subjects that were hard to face, and I have appreciated their graceful generosity with time.

I know that they will not always agree with my interpretations of what they have told me. One, in fact, raised the issue of my privileged role as interpreter. Who would and who should, she asked, analyze the content of the stories I was hearing? Had I considered organizing some post-interview process by which the interviewees could reflect on the material I had gathered and speak about its meaning? The questioner was a law professor strongly concerned with issues of voice—more specifically, with the exclusion from policy-making of the voices of powerless groups affected by policy. Her implication was that if I, alone, did the interpreting of the stories women told me, *I* would be joining the ranks of exclusionary authorities by appropriating to myself the authority to speak for others—appropriating the text, as literary critics call it. This was a disconcerting thought, as I had seen myself doing precisely the opposite—gathering and publishing the stories of women whose voices were often not heard in a male-dominated profession. I worried about this question but decided that, as a practical matter, I could not organize rounds of self-interpretation by interviewees across the country. And finally, I concluded, I did not want to. I wanted to present the experience of a wide range of women lawyers by listening to them as attentively as I could, but I also wanted to speak myself about the relation of that experience to larger political questions.

Like my interviewees, I speak as a woman trained in the law, but, unlike most of them, as a woman who left the law for political science and who now speaks as a writer vitally involved with feminist issues and questions of equality generally in American politics and culture. This is the sensibility that frames my judgments about the stories I have heard. I have tried to make my voice clearly distinguishable from those of the women talking to me, and I hope that I have done justice to the multiplicity of views they have conveyed.

I also owe thanks beyond measure to all of those friends whose conversation is, for me, the medium that shapes ideas and sustains the spirit. To start at the beginning, Julia Budenz, the poet, convinced me to take on this project when it was proposed by Victoria Wilson, an astute editor at Knopf who knew that women lawyers were engaged in vital issues of wide-reaching significance. Nadya Aisenberg and Gillian Gill, indefatigable readers, helped me through the formative stages, Nadya supplying, throughout, illuminating connections between law and literature. Gillian provided patient instruction in French feminist theory when that became necessary and, with Russell Holmes and Lynda Boose, offered reflections on the psychology of fathers and daughters in the law. I hasten to add that none of these three is responsible for what I have finally said on that mysterious subject. Constance Buchanan helped to provide coherence to projections of a major revision, and also supplied trenchant commentary on the culture of powerful institutions. Ann Congleton, whose philosophic range extends from the ancient world to women's competitive sports, supplied close criticism of chapters on the mind/body split and on professional culture. Marguerite Bouvard, a poet–political scientist, read mounds of material and synthesized ideas in surprising language, a stream of small phrases that capture large meanings. Laura Meadows, my law school classmate and an early organizer of women lawyers' networks, conducted a continuing tutorial on the practicalities of the profession. Margaret Miles applied the frozen-yogurt technique to several rough spots, urging that I talk through confusions and blockages to a sympathetic listener and questioner who knew the territory. Madeleine Kunin joined me in orgies of agonizing over the writer's lot during her bookwriting year at the Bunting Institute.

By the end, Molly Shanley, acute analyst of women's legal issues, had read most chapters through two grueling drafts and had scoured the final manuscript line by line, an act of true friendship. Jane Garrett, my editor, had provided staunch support, cheerful confidence, and wise guidance at every step along the way. And Paul Gagnon had listened to travails, pored over language, and seen me through yet another intellectual venture.

Contents

WOMEN LAWYERS

REWRITING THE RULES

Introduction

NO-MAN'S-LAND

THE OLD ORDER OF THE SEXES is breaking apart, not quickly, not neatly, not logically according to some carefully phased program. It is breaking, as complicated social systems do, at points of particular pressure. Fissures appear in some places while other parts remain intact and yet others are in flux with old and new rules both operating, in uneasy tension.

The pressure comes from the surge of democratization that since the 1960s has been building and working change in arrangements of power throughout the society. Starting with the civil rights movement, groups outside the established circles of authority began to raise in new terms the old American issue of equality. The old measure of equality was the right to vote and to enjoy equal legal rights generally. The new measure is inclusion in all the places and institutions where people actually make the decisions that shape the way we live. What we are about now, outsiders and insiders both, is nothing less than the renegotiation of our entire social contract.

In the present system, insiders hold effective power to rule the country within a structure of overlapping elites—governmental, corporate, professional. Members of these elites run our corporations, banks, schools, universities, law firms, churches, farms, armed forces, medical and psychiatric institutions, science labs, news media, publishing houses, sports, arts, and entertainment, as well as our governments from the local to the national level.

The problem with this system from the viewpoint of the outsider is not that the insiders make up a vast conspiracy to protect and promote their own interests at the expense of others—although many surely do. Rather, the problem is that the elites have not represented the society as a whole. They have been almost all men, almost all white, and, to a lesser but large extent, from economically comfortable backgrounds. This means that in spite of their education, their experience, their hard work, and their good intentions, their decisions usually have not reflected the experience of women, or racial minorities, or the poor. But these decisions, cumulatively, affect millions of people daily, including the less privileged groups whose views fall outside the policy-making compass.

It is this socially centralized system of power that is increasingly subject to question and challenge and change by outsiders demanding a democratic share of effective power over their own lives. They are demanding that their voices be heard—in government, in the arts, in the media, in the canon of knowledge taught in the schools. They are demanding access to careful education, to previously closed job markets, to the top professional schools, and to high managerial ranks in the public and private sectors. Women are demanding that the rest of the society share in the heavy responsibility of caring for children and for the sick, the troubled, the incapacitated, and the elderly.

As a precondition for such social rearrangements, outsiders are demanding new respect, forms of public address free from demeaning stereotypes, rules of civility that preclude insulting or abusive language, and fair standards in the media for the depiction of women, minorities, and other frequently stigmatized groups.

Opponents find these demands for democratization—coalesced by the 1990s into the general issue of "multiculturalism"—outrageous. They seem like unearned claims to places of privilege and responsibility, claims that would displace the deserving, that would make race and sex rather than merit the grounds for inclusion in everything from jobs to law schools to college reading lists. Toni Morrison displacing William Shakespeare. Less qualified African-Americans or Latinos or women displacing white men in hirings and promotions. And—the focus of widespread fury—the insistence by outsiders on language they deem suitably respectful as the necessary currency for talk about these issues. For the infuriated, this last demand is thought control, a reign of linguistic terror policed by the politically correct.

Many issues that bubble up out of the furor over multiculturalism may be trivial—like the rancorous disputes in a wealthy Boston suburb over the refusal by school officials to allow the town's garden club to hang Christmas wreaths at the high school. But the conflicts that lie beneath the whole range of multicultural claims form the fundamental drama of American politics at the end of the twentieth century. Although sometimes coded and disguised, these conflicts have dominated every presidential election since 1960—with the possible exception of the Watergate-driven campaign of 1976. And they came into particularly bitter prominence in 1992, when speakers at the Republican National Convention openly declared a cultural war on groups seeking social change—feminists, homosexuals, single parents, working mothers, and obstreperous racial minorities.

It is within this large context that the old rules defining the power relations between men and women are breaking and re-forming. The premise of the relation inherited from past centuries was unequal power, without any question. Men were supposed to make the rules. They were supposed to govern the political, economic, and cultural affairs of the world, and to rule as father of the family at home.

The basic terms of the male-female relation were an exchange of protection for possession. Up to the nineteenth century in the United States, possession of a woman as wife included possession of her property, but by the twentieth century, the exchange was increasingly personal. By making herself sexually desirable, a woman would gain a husband, and in return for giving over her body and her domestic service to him, along with her acquiescence to his rules, she was to receive his physical and financial protection. Individuals might add in their own exchanges and variations, but the basic social rule made women subordinate to men in both public and private life and made women's sexuality the primary element of their identity and value.

The first major challenge to this design of inequality was posed by the nineteenth-century suffragists, whose successors won equal voting rights for women in 1920 and have tried from that point onward, so far unsuccessfully, to enact a constitutional amendment prescribing equal legal rights for women across the board. But starting in the 1960s, the current women's movement began to challenge the entire structure of the old relation. The attacks were wide-ranging. Women's proper roles should not be confined to those of wife and mother, or volunteer helper to the community, or adjunct to a male boss at work. Rather, women should be able to make their own work, suiting their own talents, the center of their lives, or a major part of them, if they chose. And domestic work should not fall on women alone but should be divided between men and women. Women should be able to decide whether or not they wanted children and whether or not they wanted to continue pregnancies they had begun unwittingly or unwillingly. In general, none of the old subordinating restrictions should apply. Women should be able to serve on juries, on the judicial bench, in elective office of all kinds, in the armed

services. They should be able to run marathons, go to the moon, fight
fires, perform surgery, and enjoy the same opportunities as males to study
or train for these pursuits.

Parts of this program, especially claims to education, open work
opportunities, and access to public life and decision-making, are similar
to the demands for inclusion put forward by other outsider groups. But
of all the new claims in all the new movements for change, those being
raised by women carry the most revolutionary implications. The simple
reason is that drastically changed relations between men and women would
change everything—every workplace, every profession, every political
institution, every judgment of social priorities, every budget, every family,
every love affair, every person, in every race, every class, every ethnic
group.

But in the early 1990s, the issues of this great drama, and certainly
their outcomes, are far from clear to the public at large because change
breaks through the surface of convention unevenly. We have a woman
Supreme Court justice with the same power as her eight colleagues to
formulate basic rules for the whole society. At the same time, we have
daily displays of breasts and buttocks—even in the *New York Times*—as
clothing, makeup, and perfume ads send women the age-old message:
"Make yourself sexually desirable or you will not be wanted, not be loved,
not be valued." We have women in unprecedented numbers assuming
authority in the administration of President Bill Clinton, while we have
pitched battles in the streets over the authority to control women's reproductive choices. We have in the film *Thelma & Louise* a woman shooting a would-be rapist, then, anticipating injustice, flouting the law with
her woman buddy in a mad dash for freedom in Mexico. But at the end
of the story, we have the lawmen, with boots and guns, surrounding the
outlaw women at the edge of the Grand Canyon, cutting off all escape
except death.

We have the new rules and the old operating at once. Women with
decision-making power and women confined to the old sexual identities
live in the same neighborhood. Some women push for change. Others
adamantly defend the status quo. And men are perpetually off-balance,
variously threatened by change, relieved by it, uncomprehending, pan-
icked, pleased, furious, welcoming, well-meaning, condescending, suspicious, defensive, anxious, abusive, violent. In short, the old order is
breaking but the new is not yet in place. We are in a period of moral and
political incoherence. And no certain rule of progress assures us that the
full logic of democratization will at some point take hold and reorder the

society, amicably, on terms of equality. Because the stakes are so large, forces of reaction operate strenuously to reverse the direction of change and to define some new order of inequality. This is what Susan Faludi documented in dismaying detail in *Backlash: The Undeclared War Against American Women*, and what Margaret Atwood portrayed chillingly in her dystopian novel, *The Handmaid's Tale*.

You may be wondering, at this point in a book supposedly about women lawyers, just when and where they are coming into the picture. I have talked first about the large political drama engulfing the society, because the issues and stakes it involves define the present place of women lawyers. I see them virtually at the center of the struggle, at a point of particular sensitivity and enormous tension, whether they choose to be actively involved in the politics of change or not. This is so because the law is powerfully implicated in the ordering and the reordering of the society, both as conservator of the old and formulator of the new. Whether on the large scale of interpreting the Constitution or the mundane level of interpreting business contracts, lawyers engage in rule-making that affects, in one way or another, all corners of the society. And women entering the law are necessarily claiming equal authority to make the rules—a claim flatly contradictory to the old order, which assigned that authority, in the law and elsewhere, to men. That is, women in the law, by their very beings, herald a new order even if they arrive with no personal revolutionary intent.

Embodying change in a profession at the epicenter of change, operating just at the point where the old and the new collide, women lawyers are on dangerous ground. They are, willy-nilly, pulled in both directions. Their sex connects them to the conventional roles of women, while their work connects them unconventionally to the professional roles of men. And in their duality, they are not fully part of either camp. Rather, they are mistrusted, often despised, by both.

By entering the male establishment and operating to some serious extent on its terms, women lawyers arouse the mistrust of women who are not helped by law, who are held in some state of disadvantage or even danger by laws and legal practices reflecting the old inequalities. And the briefcase-wielding women lawyers certainly arouse resentment among the great majority of women who work in the low-paying, low-status jobs traditionally assigned to their sex. But at the same time, by implicitly asserting a claim to equal power with their male colleagues, women lawyers disturb the older relation in place between men and women, threatening deep disruptions of the order that law is supposed to preserve. Vulnerable to mistrust by both male lawyers and by nonprofessional women, women lawyers cannot count on the support of either—in fact, they are likely to be betrayed by both.

This is what happened to Anita Hill, the black woman law professor who in the fall of 1991 testified to the Senate Judiciary Committee that Clarence Thomas, President George Bush's nominee for the Supreme Court, had sexually harassed her when she had worked for him ten years earlier. Assuming, as I do, that Hill's charges were true, Thomas had betrayed Hill's claim to professional respect and dignity by treating her not as a putative equal but as a woman he could symbolically or actually possess. But as the public reacted intensely to her shocking testimony, Hill was betrayed also by a large majority of women, who, according to the polls, refused her their kinship and sympathy.

Some women didn't believe her, accepting the argument that if Thomas had really harassed her, she would have brought a public complaint at the time or left her job and discontinued all contact with him— rather than following him, as she did, to another job and then staying in touch even after she had become a law professor. Others believed her but thought that since she had benefited from Thomas's backing and had ended up in a nice, tenured professorship, she should not have turned on him. A majority of black women stood against her for violating the race code—the requirement that black men and women suppress differences with each other and maintain public solidarity in a hostile white world. Many women, black and white, thought that Hill's complaining about sexual harassment was a kind of whining on the part of an incredibly privileged woman, a claim of victimization that was unseemly, not deserving of sympathy, given that most women face more serious employment problems of low pay, lack of medical insurance, lack of security, lack of day care—*along* with the nuisance of harassment. And furthermore, some said resentfully, complaining about harassment is a luxury unaffordable to women who can be summarily fired for displeasing a boss, and whose families depend on their jobs.

In short, a woman who enters the professions is no longer one with nonprofessional women, which is to say, most women. She has left the clan. Its members will no longer recognize her as one of their own. They will not extend their understanding and sympathy if she runs into trouble. Or some will, but the majority won't. And neither will the majority of her professional male colleagues. Witness the viciousness of the senatorial attacks on Hill for turning on her boss, and the lack of effective support provided even by those senators supposedly defending her. The professional woman in trouble is at home nowhere. She has entered a no-man's-land. She is a permanent exile.

Exile, my friends who teach literature tell me, is the classic fate of people whose trust has been betrayed. The reason is that a betrayed person is dangerous, a potential avenger, someone who must be gotten out of the way. The ultimate example is Medea, who helped Jason win the Golden Fleece only to be betrayed when he took another lover. She did exact a horrible revenge, but was, in any case, exiled, and spent her life moving from place to place, belonging nowhere, trusted by no one, not part of any community. Women moving into professional power are in just this situation. They cannot help it. Or rather, some can work out protections for themselves, but they must do it against this basic plot, and it is a plot that is likely to marginalize or exile the women in it, not provide them protections.

Yet the fate of women in the legal profession is by no means wholly bleak. The ground they occupy is dangerous, but also, as a place of shifting power, it is fertile ground for creativity. From their vantage point between two worlds, women lawyers may register painfully the pressures of change impinging on their individual lives, but they can also take a hand in shaping that change. They may do this as practitioners who see issues from a different angle of vision than that of their male colleagues, or who find or create ways of working outside the dehumanizing hierarchies and depressing work schedules of the major law firms. Others may seek change as theorists, analyzing inequalities in the profession and in the law and proposing new rules, new designs for equalizing power. Still others may pursue activist agendas, challenging the present content of the law on rape, or abortion, or divorce, or harassment, or sex discrimination in the workplace—to enlist the courts themselves in redesigning the future.

What is happening to women in the law and what is happening to the law as women practice it are key parts of the larger, society-wide upheaval that is reshaping all our lives. They are key parts of the central question of whether greater democratization will succeed or fail. My purpose in this book is to find answers to two specific questions within that large one.

The first question is, What stands in the way of equal professional authority for women lawyers? By "equal authority" I do not mean professional success as measured by income or positions of seeming status in law firms or corporations or government. Many women make successful careers in various areas of the law, but few gain professional power equal to that of their male peers. And that phenomenon is what I am examining.

I am tracing the ideas and practices that stand in the way of women's access to real authority—the authority vested in the legal profession to make the rules that shape the way the society runs.

I then raise the large question: How are women lawyers using the authority they have to advance the equality of women generally?

I have looked for answers to these questions in the details of the lives of the women dealing with them. To this end, I have interviewed over one hundred women lawyers in cities all over the country. The women ranged in experience from recent law school graduates to lawyers who had entered the profession a generation ago, in the 1950s. I conducted the interviews on the understanding that I would not use names, so I identify the women when I discuss their stories only by age or type of practice or whatever characteristic is relevant to what they are saying. I name names only when the information I cite is already public knowledge or when the woman in question has given her permission.

Almost all the women were working in the law at the time they were interviewed, which for most was between 1989 and 1991. Some were in large law firms, some in women's firms, solo practices, public interest agencies, small criminal-defense firms, corporate in-house offices, government agencies (municipal, state, and federal), or international organizations. Some were judges. Some were law professors, and some of these were teaching and writing about conventional subjects like property or tax or civil procedure, while others were pursuing women's issues in the law.

This last group, the law professors exploring women's issues, are of particular relevance here because they are the developers of a new school of legal analysis called feminist jurisprudence. They are a tiny minority among law professors and a minority even among women professors, but their work is becoming increasingly influential. It is they who have brought into the study of law the idea that unequal power between men and women in the society generally is an issue of great legal significance, that it touches every area of law that affects women, which means virtually every area of law, including such seemingly neutral subjects as contracts or torts. Their remarkable reformulations of established legal thinking appear continually in the discussions that follow.

In spite of the differences in age, region, and type of work among my interviewees, they are similar in one respect: most are graduates of the Harvard Law School. I limited my basic pool to Harvard graduates because Harvard is the nation's preeminent law school and a key influence in the legal profession. It is also one of the largest national schools, and its graduates are prominent throughout the country in both public and private legal arenas. The influence of Harvard makes it important to look at the ways in which the school itself has dealt with its women students and women's issues generally, and to take some measure of the views concerning women's inequality in the law that Harvard graduates—men and women—take from their training into their practice. Also, the experience of Harvard women lawyers provides a rough measure of the openness of the profession and of the law to change. If the resistances are strong against the graduates of such a prestigious school as Harvard, they are even stronger for others. And as the stories show, the resistances *are* strong.

One final reason for focusing on Harvard was personal. As a graduate myself of the Harvard Law School (class of 1960), I could bring my own experience to the project, particularly as that experience paralleled the democratizing movement I am examining. I attended the law school before the present women's movement began, when law schools were still almost all male and Harvard was notorious among them for its resistance to breaking the sex barrier. It was the last major law school to admit women, doing so only in 1950, seven years before I entered. I was one of twelve women in a class of about five hundred. And I think it is fair to say that none of us at that time had developed any feminist consciousness whatever—beyond rejecting the conventional 1950s route to the suburbs via marriage.

Sometime in the fifties, perhaps in law school, I read Simone de Beauvoir's *The Second Sex*, the first major statement of the nascent women's movement, but all it did was confirm my belief that women could choose equality if they wanted it. We didn't have to marry straight out of high school or college and stay at home with children. We could become lawyers simply by going to law school, as men did, and then we could become wives and mothers *and* lawyers.

I didn't think this would be easy. I was well aware that it would require an unconventional husband. And I knew it would mean overcoming along the way widespread disbelief in the intellectual capabilities of women. But I still thought—most of us thought—it was mainly a matter of our choice. We thought that if we opted for the new rules, the old ones would fairly readily give way, allowing us to be judged not by our sex but by our merit. And a degree from the Harvard Law School surely attested to our merit.

We had no idea how powerful the systems of inequality were or that the institutions we most respected, such as Harvard, were part of them, no idea that the prejudices we recognized in individuals were connected to large subterranean systems of belief and habit chronically undermining the choice of equality, no idea that some of those belief systems operated within ourselves at constant odds with our own professional self-conceptions. We had no idea that we were part of an inherited social contract that required our inequality.

PART ONE

What stands in the way of equal professional authority for women lawyers?

I

RULES

A GENERATION AGO, in the 1950s and 1960s, when women made up
less than 4 percent of the legal profession, the equal authority of women
lawyers wasn't even an issue. Presidential candidates were not asked
whether they would appoint a woman to the Supreme Court. No one
wondered why so few women sat on any court, federal or state, or why
the partnerships of large law firms, and most small ones, included no
women. Certainly, law students around the country were not surprised
to find male professors in their classrooms. They would have been astonished, and probably dismayed, to find women there. And few found it
odd that in a representative democracy, almost all the elected lawmakers
in legislatures and executive offices were men. Male authority was the
norm. It was accepted as given, the more so as there were virtually no
women challengers.

In the 1990s, women have arrived on the scene of the law in considerable force, having made up about 25 percent of the nation's law
students by 1975 and nearly 50 percent by 1990. But in spite of these
numbers, the structure of authority in the profession has remained little
changed. As I write, about 90 percent of the judges on both federal and
state benches are men. Prosecutors and police at all levels are still almost
all men. Women make up only 10 percent or less of the partners in law
firms nationally, and the same low percentage of the tenured professors
on prestigious law faculties. As for the legislative side, when Anita Hill
faced the judgment of the United States Senate in the fall of 1991, that
body consisted of two women and ninety-eight men—or more precisely,
two white women and ninety-eight white men.

Why should this be so? What, by the 1990s, still stands in the way
of women's equal authority in the law? The answers to this question trail
through history, through economic, political, and cultural systems, and

through male and female psyches, in patterns of vast complication. The following chapters trace some of the hidden elements of the phenomenon—the belief systems, the cultural imprints, the unspoken interests, the concealed ideologies. This chapter looks at the barrier that is most immediate, most obvious and easily seen, and that is the operating structure of the legal profession, the rules that determine who gains authority and who does not.

Lawyers work in many settings throughout the commercial, charitable, educational, and governmental life of the country. But the authoritative center of the legal profession, the structure that designates the holders of serious professional authority, is the large corporate law firm.

This is so because the function of the large firm is, in fact, the primary function of the legal system. Young people entering the law often imagine themselves engaged in courtroom heroics, prosecuting or defending criminals, or protecting civil rights, but most lawyers most of the time are not involved in such struggles. Rather, their job is to supply the ordering expertise necessary to keep the nation's great economic machine running. Dean Robert Clark of the Harvard Law School has called this function "greasing the wheels of capitalism," and it consists of providing advice to clients about the myriad rules that order business affairs.

Lawyers advise corporate clients on the raising of capital by stocks or bonds or loans; the purchase and sale of real estate; the acquisition of other companies; the organization of funds for employee health insurance, workmen's compensation, unemployment, and retirement; the liability for harm done to other companies or individuals; the liability for taxes; and the procedures to protect the safety of employees and the public and the safety of the environment. And more.

In short, helping to organize the uses of capital through corporate channels is what lawyers mainly do, and they do it mainly in law firms, which is why the firms occupy a central position in the profession. And the partners of the firms that do the work of the biggest, most important corporations are the lords of the legal profession. It is they who effectively make the rules that govern the profession itself—its functions, methods, billing levels, personnel policies, ethics, and also, to a significant extent, its substantive readings of the law. That is, legislators pass laws and judges interpret them, but practicing lawyers apply them in hundreds of daily decisions so that the working shape of the law in many fields reflects their judgments and, behind their judgments, their perspectives and values. This is what their authority means.

Lawyers who gain substantial authority elsewhere, such as judges or high government officials or members of special community boards and commissions, generally move into such positions *from* partnerships in major firms. The partnership is the credential that testifies to their ability and responsibility. In other words, the authority that is built up within a large firm may spread out into other areas of lawyerly activity, but the important point is that it starts in the law firm. Therefore, it is the structure of the large firms, and the processes by which they admit some and not others to the inner circles, that are crucial to the question of women's status in the profession.

The literal rules of organization in the big firms have changed considerably under the economic impact of the economically explosive 1980s, but under the new variations, the long-established organizational system remains more or less in operation. Law firms generally consist of partners who are joint owners of the firm, and salaried associates who after a six- or seven-year trial period are made partners or let go. The big firms hire most of their associates right out of law school, sending interviewers to the schools in the fall of each year as the first step in recruiting, then bringing likely prospects to the firms for further review. Grades are important in the hiring process. The big firms seek top students, law-review editors preferably, law-review officers most preferably.

Generally, associates hired in a certain year form a "class" and move through the trial period together as first-year associates, second-, third-, and so forth, receiving training and reviews of performance as they go along. Associates may make lateral moves from one firm to another, but their identification with a class denoting the number of years each has been on a partnership track usually remains fairly stable. Some firms pay all members of a single class the same amount, even as partners; others base compensation, through various calculations, on performance.

Judgments of performance are necessarily subjective, but one critical measure of worth in law firm practice is the number of billable hours, or hours charged to a client, that an attorney maintains. This is a crucial figure because billable hours are the lifeblood of a law firm. That is, hours of service are all that law firms have to sell; the more hours sold per attorney, the greater the firm's profit. This fact of economic life translates generally into the rule that young attorneys seeking partnership are under pressure to put in long workdays, and not to make time-consuming and unbillable mistakes.

Until the 1980s—about which much more later—associates were generally hired on the expectation that they would be trained and nurtured through to partnership and that once a partner, they would remain part of the firm throughout their career. It was assumed that the apprenticeship period might be interrupted by emergencies, or special projects of various kinds, or military service, but it was not assumed that the normal seven-year trial would be chronically subject to interruption by pregnancies, heavy demands of child-rearing, or moves from city to city with a peripatetic spouse. That is, the training and partnership system assumed a consistently long workday and general continuity of service. And it assumed, too, a more ephemeral continuity—a commonality of spirit, a shared outlook, an ease of communication, a sense of membership in a club, a brotherhood.

Women, of course, were in trouble from the beginning on both logistical and social counts, and they still are. To achieve full authority in the legal profession, to be heard, to be able to make a difference if they choose to try, women must traverse the partnership track in the big firms. But the traditional partnership rules, in and of themselves, make it difficult for women to stay on the track. And this is true in spite of the fact that the rules, as they have been applied to women, have undergone several major permutations.

Before the women's movement surfaced in the late 1960s, the rules for entering and advancing in law firms simply did *not* apply to women in any clear way. The profession was so overwhelmingly male that there was little pressure and certainly little inclination on the part of professional leaders to think about how women would fit. In the most positive view, they could be seen generally as helpful subordinates of some kind, but not as full-fledged apprentices moving along the established path to partnership. For example, in the late sixties, one of my interviewees was told by a graying partner in a venerable Boston firm that his own daughter had become a lawyer but had left her practice when her first child was born, and it was because most women would do this that the firm routinely paid them less. He clearly found this system of temporary and lesser-paid work for women lawyers reasonable and was kindly explaining to a proto-daughter how it worked.

Thus, the women who entered the big firms in those years—and managed to stay—had to make up rules for themselves and negotiate them as they went along, usually moving one step at a time with no overall plan or guide. It is not surprising, under such conditions of unpredictability, that many who wanted to stay did not.

Looking more closely at that time, what stands out is the prevalence of overt, even crude, discrimination practiced by male lawyers with no apparent sense of wrongdoing—and accepted by the women with some disquiet but essentially with stoicism. It was simply the way things were. Interviewers in law schools or in firms would tell women politely that their firms did not hire women or, sometimes, that they did but already had one. Or they might say that they had once hired a woman but she had left, so they no longer risked it. Some firms posted "No Women" notices on the sign-up sheets for interviews at law schools.

If women did get interviewed, they would often be asked whether they intended to marry or have children. Some were asked how many children they planned to have. If a woman was married to a lawyer, she might well be told that she could not be hired because of potential conflicts of interest that could arise if her husband, or even his firm, had a case in which her firm represented the opposite side. One woman, on hearing this from an interviewer, was astounded. "I said, 'But New York law firms are full of fathers and brothers and uncles and cousins and all of that,' and he said, 'But they don't go home and get in bed together at night,' and I said, 'Well, you know, that isn't to say that when we get in bed together at night, we're going to talk about what we did at our law firms.' But it was hard getting hired." Another woman actually left her law firm in the mid-sixties when her husband's firm, on the other side of a piece of litigation, told him to tell her to quit—even though she was not herself working on the case in question.

Paradoxically, some women in this period made their way to partnerships through openings created by the *absence* of rules for women. A Harvard graduate in a mid-sixties class had lined up a government job in Washington, D.C., in her chosen field, land-use planning, but marriage right after graduation kept her in Boston, where she had not interviewed at all, and left her with no clear plans except to start a family. Then she heard from the law school placement director that one of the big Boston firms was looking for a woman to do estate planning. This was a field considered appropriate for women, even then, for several reasons. First, it was work done for individuals, not for corporations whose executives counted on representation by men. And second, the pace of the work was regular, not requiring the sudden late-night or weekend hours at the office that conflict with family responsibilities.

In any case, the prospective land-use planner jumped at the chance. "Looking for a woman!" she marveled, and called the interviewing partner immediately. Within days she was offered the job, but anticipating pregnancy, she said she would accept only if she could work part-time. The partner needed help quickly and agreed to the young woman's terms without asking for her reasons. They settled on three days a week and the fledgling lawyer was indeed pregnant by the time she started. "Because there were so few women," she says, "it was easier to set your own rules. They didn't have big policies approved by all sorts of committees. The lawyer who hired me ran his own fiefdom. . . . You know, in a funny way, when they were sexist, it was easier for a woman working part-time, because of course she's going to want to be home and cook dinner for her husband and take care of her family and her children." She laughs at this and adds that ultimately she had three children and took leaves of various lengths with each—a year and a half after the third. And she also became a partner in a major firm (not the one she first joined), but it took her seventeen years to get there.

The first significant shift in rules occurred in the seventies. The women's movement was in full swing. Anti–sex-discrimination laws were on the books. It was the equal-rights decade, the period in which women sought entry into the professions under the rules then in place, as if there were no differences that needed to be taken into account between their lives and those of their male competitors—as if the only issue were the exclusion of women from desirable work that they could do as well as men. The upshot was that women began to enter the law routinely under the conventional rules for male associates—the seven-year trial period and then a partnership decision.

The difficulties met by women operating under this regime are fairly well known, but I will include one story here to bring the general picture to mind. It is about a woman who played by the male rules and succeeded, and it is remarkable for its teller's honest reflections about the pressures she endured and her feelings about the value of her success.

On the surface, the story follows an ideal seventies script: The woman marries a supportive man, finds a firm open to women, has two children but continues to work full-time in spite of a constantly pressed schedule and some harrowing moments, and makes it—with marriage intact, children well, and interesting work continually unfolding. And she does it on merit alone—no fathers or other male relatives waving magic wands, no family wealth boosting her along, no special protection from a professionally powerful husband.

A college student in the late sixties, the heroine of this piece was immersed in liberal causes—urban issues, and human rights more broadly, throughout her student years. And in law school, where she did well, she was leery about entering a big corporate firm. "I thought I was going to have to do evil and immoral things. I figured I'd do it for a few years, for the training, and then leave." But she became involved, year after year, in the litigation of cases engaging her in "extraordinarily in-teresting," even "esoteric," questions of law, and her plans to leave kept receding.

Although few women entered her firm in the seventies—there were only four (out of sixty lawyers) when she arrived—and even fewer stayed, she decided at some point to try for a partnership and to do it in the normal time period, without a pause, in spite of the birth of her first child a year before the partnership decision was due. "I felt role-modelish," she says. "I came back after two months. I never for a minute thought of working part-time. I never considered it. I spent a lot of time thinking about logistics, how I would do it, would I have day care or live-in help, but I never thought of part-time. . . . It used to drive me crazy when women would come in and say they wanted to work part-time. I couldn't understand it. How could they do this? It seemed to me to be weakening the position of women. I was afraid the firm would stop hiring women."

As it was, she came up for partner with her billable hours about one hundred a year below average, which, in the early eighties, was about seventeen hundred a year in her firm. Even so, she says, her workday ran from 8:00 or 9:00 a.m. to 6:00 p.m., five days a week—a rate, she notes, that is now considered part-time in the big firms. She thinks that her lower-than-average rate of billable hours was an issue in the decision on her partnership. "The word used at the time was 'commitment.' There were questions about my commitment." But apparently her clear intention to work full-time was honored. In any case, she became the first woman partner in her firm.

She says that it was important for her at the time "to live up to the image of the professional woman" and not to let her family responsibilities intrude on her work. She used, at first, a day-care program that took children from 8:00 a.m. to 6:00 p.m. five days a week, starting at two months of age. She had complete confidence in the program but still suffered the guilt of the absent mother. "I don't know where my daughter picked up attitudes about what mothers should do, since she was sur-rounded by full-time working mothers, but some mothers of kids at day care worked part-time, and she would ask why I always got there at one minute to six. . . . One of my earliest recollections—I guess she must have been around three—was her not liking what she got for Christmas presents, and we made the mistake of asking her what she had wanted, thinking she was going to say a Barbie doll or something, and she said, 'More time with Mommy.' Those things stay with you forever."

The tight arrangements were also physically exhausting to keep up, especially after the arrival of a second child. She says that her husband has always helped out a lot, but that she is in charge of such things as selecting day care, interviewing baby-sitters, finding schools, and locating summer camps, all of which has to be done during workdays, and all of which takes a lot of time.

When her older child started school while the younger was still at home, she and her husband switched for several years to live-in help, an experience, she says, that would make a book in itself. Wanting to do it legally, they brought in young women from the Midwest—South Dakota, Wisconsin, Iowa—who apparently were eager to try out life in the East. The system was to pay an agency one thousand dollars to locate a person, to sign a contract without an interview and with less reference checking than is usual for a secretary, and then to show up at the airport and hope it worked out. "It usually doesn't," she says resignedly, "and you don't get your thousand dollars back."

One of these recruits gave her the scare of her life. "I was at work, and I had a conference call scheduled for four o'clock on a settlement agreement that I had talked about with another business partner on the case. I had made comments on that agreement during the day, so he knew I had something to offer, and about quarter to four the telephone rang from a neighbor saying, 'Your live-in has disappeared. She's left and gone home. We have no idea where [the baby] is, and [your daughter] is at a friend's house. We don't know where but we think she's going to be dropped off at five-thirty. What do you want me to do?' And I go, 'I don't know!' And I hung up and called my husband and said, 'Go home. Find the kids!' And then I took this conference call at four, which was totally amazing because I'm trying to hold back tears, I'm looking through my schedule to see what possible days in the week I could take off, I'm going through a drawer, a file drawer I have on emergency sitters and also agencies, I'm doing this, and someone says, 'Now, what was the comment you made earlier today?' And I was making comments on this agreement."

This sounds like the classically heroic story of a superwoman. She's terribly upset. She's on the verge of tears. But she's conducting her business, and since it's being done by phone, no one even sees her distress. She is keeping her family problems out of the office lest they feed the never-quite-dispelled doubts about the ability of women to function at the pressured pace of the big firms. But this is not the moral she draws from her own story. She says she is held up, in her firm and elsewhere, as an example of a woman who has successfully combined fast-paced work and family, as proof that the rules of the game in the big firms are not an insuperable bar to talented women. But this, she insists with some heat, is a wrong reading of her experience. Rather, she thinks her story shows that the rules place nearly unbearable pressure on women and repeatedly force most of them out—while the rulemakers remain oblivious to the dynamics of the problem.

"I guess it's all tied up with this whole coping notion. I had thought fifteen years ago that all my peers . . . or most of them would be married to other lawyers, doctors, accountants, architects, et cetera, and the issues that are, quote, women's issues would not be just women's issues. And I had thought that most of my peers would be two-career couples with children. I am still totally amazed that that has not happened, has not happened at all. There are not more than, I don't think, a half a dozen, if that, men in my firm of two hundred lawyers who are married to women who work full-time with children. And what I saw among my female peers when I came, every one of us was married to a man in an interesting, responsible job, and two, three, four years later, as we all started having kids, without exception, every one of them has either quit or gone part-time. And in an environment in which you have no men coping with getting to a day care by six or dealing with what women have got to deal with, the millions of things, you have no basic understanding of what's going on with the women . . . and no impetus to change. The management of the firm now is different from what it was fifteen years ago but has people who are no more sensitive to any of these notions than the older generation because they're still not dealing with it. And you don't have cadres of bright young men coming up through the system confronting these issues. There aren't very many bright young men coming up through the system who are doing the coping."

She sounds discouraged but not despairing, and I say something of the sort as I turn off the tape recorder after a two-hour evening interview. I'm speaking casually, but my interviewee snaps to attention and declares in no uncertain terms that making it in a man's world isn't worth it. Astonished, as nothing she said previously sounded this negative, I turn the machine back on and ask her to repeat what she said, which she does:

"This notion of making it in a man's world, having achieved that, I'm not sure it's worth it. And I think that a lot of women today are drawing that conclusion, and I think that accounts for some of the statistics we see of women dropping out of the practice of law. I'm not sure that a man's world is all that wonderful and that we necessarily should go through all the contortions we have gone through and will continue to go through in order to make it in that world. I think changing that world so it's not a man's world is extraordinarily difficult, and I'm far less optimistic than I was that those changes will come about." Then she gestures definitively for the tape recorder to be turned off. It is late and she is tired.

Without question, the 1970s' rules for women lawyers were killers. They could not possibly allow women in any number to reach positions of real, substantial authority in the profession. As feminists have long been saying, what looked like a balanced equation—the same rules for women as for men—was actually grossly imbalanced because another set of rules assigned to women the heavy responsibilities of child care and family care, responsibilities that men did not carry. This is not to say that women lawyers without families had it easy, that the playing field was level but for the family issue. Other blockages, discussed in the following chapters, also stood in the way, but even if no other deflecting forces were operating, the rules of the 1970s alone would have pushed most women to the sidelines.

Then the rules shifted again. In the eighties, law firms and other professional employers began to recognize the import of two intersecting facts of life. One was precisely the fact that women had family responsibilities that conflicted with the established work structure of the legal profession. The other was that nearly half the law school graduates coming into the job market were women. To attract the most talented young lawyers each year, law firm recruiters could not ignore the women. Yet the firms could not keep their female associates long enough to profit from their growing expertise without taking into account the fact that many of them would want to have children and would then meet the question of child care. Something had to give, and it was the established system of work rules for law firm associates and, to some extent, for partners as well. Maternity leaves came into the picture, as did part-time positions, even part-time partnerships in some firms, along with the greater acceptability of lateral transfers among law firms, and greater flexibility in general toward the accommodation of personal choices and situations within the overall requirements of employment.

However, while viewing what looks like a line of progress for women in the professional workplace through the development of rules that take into account the reality of their lives, it is important not to lose track of the issue of authority. The new rules made it progressively easier for women to survive as lawyers, but what effect did these rules have on the access of the surviving women to positions of real authority? The short answer is: Not much. A longer answer requires looking at dramatic changes in the structure of the legal profession as a whole in the eighties, shifts in the placement of authority within the profession, and its greater centralization in hierarchies with women in the lower ranks.

Any story about the big law firms in the big cities in the 1980s must start with the fact of phenomenal expansion. Firms made up of 50 lawyers in the 1970s swelled to 200 or 300 by the late eighties. Many added branch offices beyond their cities of origin and abroad. Some megafirms hit the 1,000-lawyer mark. The fabled New York firm of Skadden, Arps, Slate, Meagher & Flom went from 160 lawyers grossing revenues of $30 million in 1979 to 1,000 lawyers grossing $400 million in 1989. This is definitely the high end of the scale. More typically, by the late 1980s, the big New York firms would comprise 300 to 400 lawyers and gross revenues upwards of $200 million, while the bigger firms in other cities—Boston, for example—would include 200 to 250 lawyers grossing between $70 million and $80 million. Ten years earlier, no firm in the country grossed as much as $60 million.[1]

Pushing this growth were vast organizational changes in the big corporations that make up the big-firm clientele. Increasingly, the mega-companies were remaking themselves: employing new technologies; moving routinely into international markets; dealing with new ranges of governmental regulation of health and safety in the workplace, employee pensions, hazardous wastes and other pollutants; raising capital with new kinds of financial instruments; building new or expanded quarters; and engaging in financial speculation through mergers and acquisitions, the purchase and sale of other companies. Structuring and organizing these activities, especially the last, required armies of lawyers, while the complexity of changed business forms produced a stream of dispute and confusion that was grist for the mill of litigation departments.

With the mushrooming of the big firms came a tremendously increased demand for young lawyers. Firms that used to hire ten new associates a year began scouting in law schools for thirty or forty. And because the top schools did not appreciably expand their student numbers, the firms began to compete for promising graduates nationwide with dizzying enticements, notably starting salaries that tripled from the beginning to the end of the eighties. By 1990, a new associate was making more than a new partner typically had made ten years before—in New York, $82,000 to $83,000; in the other big cities, between $55,000 and $70,000.

1. Steven Brill, "Joseph Flom," *American Lawyer*, Vol. 11, No. 2 (March 1989), p. 66; "Survey: Law Big Business," Boston *Globe*, July 13, 1989.

Obviously, this was an advantageous environment for women. From a small and defensive minority in the big firms, women began to make up 40 to 50 percent of the entering classes of associates. And with the increased demand for their services came considerably increased bargaining power. This was the point at which the firms had to confront the employment issues that had troubled women so seriously in the seventies—particularly maternity leave, support for child care, and part-time workloads. But at the end of the eighties, it was clear that women's gains were more apparent than real. Along with wide-open entry, sky-high salaries, and a new responsiveness to family issues, the new job structure included demands for huge increases in billable hours.

The prior norm of 1,600 to 1,700 billable hours per year was, by the late eighties up to 1,900 or 2,000 hours for associates, with the curve breakers going up to 2,200 or higher. And the billables were topped, as always, by a substantial load of nonbillable time, which produced workdays that could not dip below nine hours and that often went up to ten hours or more, with late nights and weekends frequently added on.

The gargantuan demand for hours on the part of big firms fell on men and women alike, but as men and women are not alike in their responsibilities outside of work, the hours crunch of the eighties became especially severe for women. Here is a typical description of the kind of life the new work system dictated for young women with children: The speaker is a third-year associate in the litigation department of a big West Coast firm. She was a top student at the Harvard Law School, a law-review editor, and she describes herself as adept at issue-spotting, analyzing the basic issues in a case, and figuring out how to get at them procedurally. She tells me that she finds these challenges fun. "I've always liked procedure," she says somewhat apologetically. "For some reason, and I don't think it reflects well on me at all, I always had a real feel for the federal rules of civil procedure. I can't help it. I did." But balancing work and family is not fun. She has two children, ages four and three, and her journalist husband's hours away from home, while not so bad as hers, are nevertheless somewhat unpredictable. The couple employ an at-home baby-sitter but not live-in help, as their home is not large enough. "I do make an obscene amount of money," she says, "but supporting a family on it, it's not difficult, but it doesn't pile up lots of savings to put down on a house."

The leitmotif of her story, like that of dozens of others, is constant planning, pressure, and guilt. "Every day I feel as if I don't spend enough time at work and I don't spend enough time at home. The only place I spend enough time is on the freeway. . . . I have to be very careful not running into partners at six o'clock at night, because at seven I have to leave and get home and that's hard. . . . I'm always pushing deadlines. I'm always in trouble because I turn things in late. Fortunately, they're not bad, so they don't need to be done four or five times. Anytime anything's wrong, I don't have time to fix it, because it was late to begin with, that kind of problem. Then there's the tension of—you tend to think that if you're just sitting around the yard with the kids that you're wasting time. I *don't* feel that way. I'm very militant about not feeling that way, but if I have work that's not done Friday night, I frequently just refuse to go in. When I really think I have to go in, what I tend to do is not go in anyway but get real depressed about it, my life and all that, so I'm not much fun at home, either. It's hard to force yourself not to get caught up in this idea that you oughta be here working on a weekend if your work isn't done. I regard my time with the kids at home as just as important as my time here, if not more so. It's mandatory, at any rate, but that creates a lot of tension when things don't get done here, I don't put in enough hours or whatever. This firm is really a very relaxed firm as firms go. Billable hours' target is about nineteen hundred hours for associates, which I think is much less than any firm you could throw a rock at from here, but it's still—billing nineteen hundred hours, doing a little pro bono and some firm administration and maybe keeping up on periodicals, that's more hours than—that's too many hours. I don't have that much time. I try to work from, I guess I'd say, nine to seven. I try and bill every minute. I usually work through lunch because I'd rather go home at night than go out at lunch . . . and I always plan to be here earlier than nine, I just don't get here. If the kids wake up, then I get them breakfast and I get here by nine. If they don't wake up, then I miss 'em, so—ordinarily, they wake up. . . . I feel I can't do the best possible job here and at home at the same time, and I'm certainly not willing to do an even worse job at home than I'm already doing so that I can do a better job here, so I'm never satisfied with the way I'm balancing it. I mean, it's not that you can keep all the balls in the air if you're careful. You have to live with screwing it up all the time. And that's difficult.''

This is a scenario that, with minor variations, I will hear over and over again, even from women without children but with various interests they cannot pursue while devoting most of their waking, functioning hours to the business of their firm. On the other hand, some women actually like the pace—for example, a sixth-year associate in a prestigious eastern firm, who is married and plans to have children but has none yet, and who exudes energy and apparent happiness. A litigator, she says she likes being in a big firm doing the kind of corporate law that appears in the business section of the newspapers. She also likes her salary, which is around $150,000, likes dealing with clients, and, as others have said, likes the camaraderie of the office—"being around really smart people all the time." In addition to her regular practice, she writes for law journals— not philosophical articles such as those in academic law reviews but short, practical pieces on specific points of her practice. She also enjoys giving presentations on business subjects to the litigation department of her firm and elsewhere. This all adds up to about 2,200 billable hours a year, with another 700 to 800 hours devoted to writing articles, doing bar-association projects, and recruiting for the firm. Putting in that many hours while taking four weeks of vacation, which she says she and her husband always do, means working nine-hour days five days a week just on billable tasks, and another fifteen hours weekly for the extras.

This smiling, easy-talking young woman does not seem at all frantic in the midst of the schedule she describes, but rather delighted to be engaged in a variety of projects that she enjoys and to be paid well for it. Of course, she acknowledges, she has not yet added children into this picture, but she hopes to be able to do so without dropping out of law altogether or even down to part-time. In fact, she fears that stories I may hear about the agony of some women who are trying to put together work and family may feed the belief that women shouldn't have careers, or that they are not desirable employees.

Still, for most of the women I interview, schedules that keep them away from home, or wherever else they may want to be, ten to twelve hours a day—adding in commuting—are not desirable. And many insist that such a system is not necessary, that the firms impose inordinate hours in order to sustain an unnecessarily high rate of profit. A partner in a small, newly organized firm trying to construct a humane system of practice for its members calls the reigning work rules in big firms "crazed." What is basically wrong, she thinks, is the assumption by partners that they have to make more money each year. "That's crazy. If they're making enough money, they're making enough money. They don't have to make more. . . . You don't have to have twice as much as a comfortable living." She and many others say that the high-hours system is driven not by unstoppable economic forces but by managerial choice, and that the choices being made are driven by greed.

However, most of the partners I ask about this disagree. They think that their firms have had little choice but to pile hours on associates—

and, increasingly, on partners as well—because the high costs of their operations can be sustained only by high billings. First, they say, the cost of associates' salaries alone is astronomical and cannot be cut substantially because even with slowed growth in the nineties, the big firms must compete nationwide for the best young lawyers from the best schools. Moreover, they point out, the expanded firms, having outgrown whatever quarters they were in as the eighties began, and finding it important to present themselves to clients impressively, relocated to the new, marble-swathed office towers all the major cities now boast—so their rents went up, to put it mildly. Another new and expensive item for law firms of the eighties and beyond was electronic equipment—computers, printers, faxes, and other communications hardware—along with the necessary training programs for those who use them.

And then there are the rainmakers. In a business world requiring constant and costly legal service, companies have abandoned their traditional practice of using one law firm, year in and year out, for all their needs, and have begun shopping around for the best service and the best deal on particular projects. So law firms cannot simply count on institutional business but must court clients continually—and lawyers who are especially good at such courtship, the rainmakers, are highly prized and highly paid. That is, as partners they can command a large share of profits because they will themselves be constantly courted by other firms. This, too, marks a change. Partners used to stay with their firms for life, for better profits when times were good, and for worse when they turned bad. But with client companies moving their business around, law partners have taken to moving around too, and those with a golden touch must be bid for. And in boom times, even less productive partners have come to expect returns well beyond the old measures. In the seventies, in New York, a senior partner might have taken home $150,000 to $200,000, whereas in the late eighties, the return might have been anywhere from $200,000 to $1 million. So income to partners, although technically a division of profits after costs, is also itself an increased cost due to increases in the partners' expected—and in the case of rainmakers, demanded—rate of return.

The bottom line, as the partners say, is that the extraordinary hours required of associates are necessary to bring in the income necessary to cover extraordinary costs. The only way to reduce hours would be to reduce associates' salaries and partners' incomes, and, the partners say, competition holds both those rates up. That is, if a firm were to break ranks and lower associates' salaries in return for fewer hours, they would lose the best associates, and if they lowered partners' income for the same trade-off, their most productive partners would move to other firms. At least, that's the fear.

The shorthand expression for the sum total of these changes is that the practice of law has been transformed from a profession to a business. It means that competition and maximized profit are shaping the structure and practice of the big firms to a far greater extent than they did when gentlemen lawyers regarded themselves primarily as professionals providing service for a fee. It also means that a cash nexus now defines the relations between partners and associates. That is, the position of associates in the firms has come to be defined primarily by more complex and urgent profit considerations rather than profit *plus* professional concerns about grooming succeeding generations of partners.

For women, the transformation from law firm to business means that the new openness to women comes at a time when new constraints are also operating. When fewer associates (and very few women) were hired, firms selected them carefully, reviewed their work closely, and guided their development with a view to bringing most of them along to partnership. With great numbers being hired, now including women, the prevailing processes and expectations have changed radically. No one expects the thirty or forty new associates in the first-year class of an expanded firm to move eventually into the firm as partners. That's not what they are there for. They are there, as one woman says, "to drive the revenue train"—not in their first or second years, when they are barely if at all profitable, but in the fourth, fifth, and sixth years, when they know what they are doing and put in prodigious hours. Some will make it all the way to partnership, but most will not. What firms want to do is to keep associates long enough to be maximally profitable, but not to draw them into the circle sharing the profits.

The consequence for women—which they do not seem to be focusing on—is that the bargaining power they have to gain conditions of work that they want is commensurate to their value as employees for a limited period of time, not to their value as lifelong partners. They have the bargaining power to make arrangements that will keep them, once trained, in a position to contribute a substantial number of hours to the firm, but—in the scheme of things in the early nineties—little power to effect change beyond that.

How, then, have women entering the law in the eighties approached the issue of gaining new rules to work by in the midst of sea changes sweeping through the big firms? The politics of their position have been, indeed, curious and hard to pin down. To the women from earlier classes they can appear to be heedless radicals. A late-seventies graduate, now a partner in a Chicago firm, was taken aback when she spoke to a group of recent Harvard Law School graduates to advise them about making it in a big firm. She says, "I talked a lot about finding a mentor, and developing business, and learning the ropes, and the younger women were much more activist! . . . How can you get a better maternity-leave policy, part-time policy, better this policy and that policy? . . . I wish them well, but it was just so alien to the way I did it. I never thought about what the maternity-leave policy was. The maternity-leave policy was what they *told* you it was, and you didn't question it, because if you questioned it, you know, they didn't have to hire women, and they didn't have to hire you in particular, and you were just going to alienate people, and you just didn't think that way. It was just kind of a comical experience because these women were not that much younger than I in numerical age . . . but we obviously were thinking much differently." She adds that with law school classes approaching 50 percent women, firms should be thinking about family-support policies, but she still seems doubtful that women's militance will help. "I don't think I was ever hostile to people who were trying to change things. I just was never completely confident that they could do it. I'm still not. I'm still not."

A late-fifties graduate who worked full-time straight through marriage and the birth of several children to the partnership she now holds in New York had a similar encounter with eighties activism and was even more disapproving. She had traveled to a midwestern university to participate in a program organized for women law students. "They really thought that we should change the nature of the profession so that they could have child-care facilities at hand and have little ones running under foot, which to me suggested that they didn't really recognize that law was a service industry and you were there to deal with a client and it's his needs you're dealing with, not yours. And he's not terribly interested in your child-care problems. He's interested in his business problems, and properly so, and I don't see why the service industry should be remade to satisfy your particular needs. . . . It was kind of a fun day being *attacked* by the people you thought you were comforting. They were very militant about how we had 'finked out' to an all-male environment. And we finally said, 'Hey, we didn't do this for you. We did this for us. And this works for us. What works for you, you'll have to figure out.' It was kind of funny."

So the tactics have changed. The eighties generation is arriving at work demanding, with a militance that appalls their elders, maternity leaves, personal leaves, day care, and generous part-time policies. But their activism is oddly ungrounded in a clear understanding of the politics they are trying to play. The eighties graduates I spoke with fit well, for the most part, their popular designation as members of the postfeminist generation. Most of them had not, in college or law school, involved themselves more than casually in women's issues. Typically, they would say that they were grateful to the women who had done the pathbreaking in the professions, and that they were firm advocates of women's control over reproductive choices. But beyond that, they tended to distance themselves from feminism, associating it vaguely with shrillness, anger, and hatred of men. And while they were engaged in the profoundly political—and feminist—effort to redesign the work rules for women in one of the most powerful of professions, they tended to cast what they were doing in individualized terms. If they talked about seeking arrangements for maternity leave or emergency day care, they referred to "my firm" or "the partner I work for" or "a good deal they gave me" or "a bunch of old farts on the executive committee," rather than to the economic structure of the firm and of the profession and the place of women in them.

Certainly, most do not perceive the changes they seek as supports for short-term or continuing work as subordinates rather than long-term participation as equals in the profession. Two to three months' paid maternity leave, the availability of longer unpaid leaves, on-site emergency day care, part-time options for associates, part-time partnerships—most of the eighties graduates seem to think that changes along these lines are part of a continuum that could move them toward equality.

But almost all these programs provide women with support for periods of unusual need, times when the demands of child care are particularly intense, not systemic support over a long period of time. This distinction appears clearly in a comment made by the young woman who spoke of living with perpetual screwups at home and at work. She told of a lunch discussion at her firm about a change the partners were proposing in crediting the pro bono work of associates. Law firms have traditionally donated hours of time to worthy causes *pro bono publico*, for the public good—in effect counting the hours as part of the expected workload of their lawyers. The firm here had been crediting pro bono work as part of its associates' quota of nineteen hundred billable hours, but was proposing instead that the associates add any unpaid projects they wanted to do *onto* the nineteen-hundred-hour billable base. Simply put, they were proposing an increased workload. The young woman said she "groused" about this burdensome change, especially since the firm enjoyed a reputation of reasonableness about such things. "And the managing officer turned to me and said, 'Well, this has always been a good firm for taking into account and remaining flexible about people who have particular *problems*, who have children at home or a sick relative.' And I said, 'Well, excuse me, I don't have a *problem*. I have a family. I do not have a problem!' These are not idiosyncratic things like a wooden leg. . . . We all, by and large, have families. It's the norm, not the exception. But here, it's the exception. Whenever it impinges on the firm, it's an exception. . . . The fact that some people don't have children doesn't make it any less kind of what the species is about."

Treating family responsibilities as exceptional rather than normal often takes the form of individually negotiated leaves or reduced hours rather than a general policy specifying their availability. This means that a woman seeking reduced work time has only her own bargaining power to use. In some instances such an approach works well, but it is unlikely to work well systemically. As one woman says of her firm's "policy of no policy," "They say if they really like you they'll bend over backwards to keep you, but my suspicion has always been . . . that when someone they really like announces she's pregnant and she really wants the firm to bend over backwards, all of a sudden they won't like you anymore."

But whatever the mood or outlook of a firm, the major work/family issue is hours of work over the long term—not just in the months of care for a newborn baby, but in the years of raising a child to independence. The jumped-up norm for work time in the eighties leaves no room for long-term child-raising or any other significant activity outside of work. And yet the activist agenda does not touch this issue head-on. It does not question the sense or the necessity of the new norm but accepts it as "normal," then seeks exceptions to it for women.

And the exceptions consist of one form or another of part-time work, which, no matter how it is organized, carries serious professional disadvantages. A woman partner in one of New York's most prestigious firms speaks unhappily of "the male power group in firms using associates in general but part-time associates in particular to do the firm's lower-paid and less-interesting scut work, which is unpleasant in itself, but worse, often leads the associate doing it to a professional dead end—a track that never leads to partnership."

A young associate who had joined a big firm right out of school left within several years, although she did not yet have children, after watching the experience of two women on a part-time track. They worked from nine to four, without lunch, five days a week, and still had to cope with partners appearing at three-thirty with work to be done that day. The part-timers could either refuse the work or stay late and do it—for no extra compensation—*if* they could get their baby-sitters to stay late as well. And for this the part-time lawyers took a severe cut in salary from their full-time rates and were looked down on, besides, as people not serious about their careers. Said the associate, "I felt that was the worst of everything."

Other part-time arrangements may be three long days a week, five afternoons, or some other variation, but the disadvantages are the same. People who are not available full-time cannot do the kind of work that requires either constant attention, a fast response at an unpredictable time, a rapid timetable, or coordination with full-time people who become frustrated when they need to work something out with a part-time colleague who isn't there. With such work excluded, part-time assignments tend to be boring, and the people doing them not highly regarded.

Then there are the part-time or full-time arrangements, developed in the late eighties under various guises and names (including the "mommy track"), the point of which is to keep experienced people employed with a firm indefinitely but off the track to partnership. Sometimes called "income partners," who may or may not be eligible at some point for full or equity partnership and thus profit sharing, these people are actually permanent, salaried associates. And as the term "mommy track" suggests, they are often women who are willing to trade the rewards of partnership, including a voice in firm management, for reduced hours and reduced pressure. While beneficial to many women who prize livable work conditions at a good salary, the new tracks of the eighties and early nineties all lead the women on them to a status of permanent subordination.

The only way women who want lives outside of work could gain them with a hope of professional equality would be to challenge directly the heightened norm for work hours imposed in the eighties. They need to ask the feminist question of any norm—for whom is it normal? A required minimum of nineteen hundred or two thousand billable hours a year is obviously a norm for people without families (few men, some women), or people with families but without responsibility for them (few women, most men), which makes it mainly a norm for men. Clearly, instead of accepting the prevailing system, in which women who do family work are exceptions to a norm of high billable hours, women lawyers would do better to challenge the system's underlying values.

As their stories make clear, the problem for women lawyers is that the work rules currently in place tie into the social rules that so definitively assign the care of children to women that no dependable, systematic alternatives have been developed. Most important is the rule that divides labor unequally at home. Almost without exception, my interviewees with families say that they, not their husbands, have primary responsibility for home and children, and, further, that the great majority of their male colleagues have wives at home to provide household and family care. If this were not the case—if the social rules assigned home and family responsibilities equally to men and women—the effect on the workplace would be profound. If it were *normal* for men as well as women to leave the office at 5:15 to pick up a child at day care before 6:00, or to leave routinely at 3:00 on Tuesdays and Thursdays and to be unavailable for work on weekends, professional work rules would have to change. Law firms could not demand so many hours of their lawyers—men and women—during the years when they had children at home.

But even with reduced work hours and equally divided parental responsibility, working parents still need child care, and here the social tradition of mothers at home has had the further effect of blocking the development of widely available, reliable, professional child-care systems. This issue was startlingly dramatized early in 1993 when President Bill Clinton, attempting to break a previously untouchable male-only tradition, nominated a woman—Zoë Baird—for attorney general, only to have her withdraw during confirmation hearings before the Senate Judiciary Committee, after the public learned that she and her husband had employed an illegal alien as a live-in nanny.

Fierce public debate went on for days. How important was it that a prospective attorney general had broken a law that the Justice Department is charged with enforcing, when it is one that generally goes unenforced because the lack of child-care systems has set up a demand for home help that far exceeds the legal supply? Many women who disapproved of the illegality were nonetheless incensed that the issue of illegal domestic help, which had never been raised as a possible disqualification of any male candidate for any governmental position, had suddenly become a bar to the appointment of a woman. And they were the more incensed when the president's second choice, federal district court judge Kimba Wood, was forced to withdraw before being officially nominated because she too had employed an illegal alien as a nanny—even though when she had done so, hiring illegal aliens was not against the law. It seemed that the Senate Judiciary Committee had adopted a new ethical standard that would necessarily fall more heavily on women than on men.

Under the new standard, women *with* children, *with* onerous work hours, *with* the lion's share of family responsibility, and *without* reliable child-care options could be considered for top professional positions if, in the process of building their careers, they had never broken any rules. And while the literal rule debated in the Baird/Wood affair was the law against hiring illegal aliens, the actual rule in question for many debaters was the unwritten requirement that women take care of their own children unless economic necessity drives them into the workplace—which was clearly not the case for Baird or Wood.

In the end the president succeeded in appointing a woman attorney general, but only when he found, in Janet Reno, an outstanding candidate who, being unmarried and without children, could bypass the new family-ethics test. Clearly, it is the combination of the two sets of rules in play —professional and social—that must be challenged if women are to have open access to meaningful authority in the law.

And that challenge must extend as well to yet another set of rules blocking women's access to equal professional opportunity: the legal rules of sex discrimination. If women are ending up at demonstrably lower levels of authority than their male peers within their law firms, the laws against sex discrimination would seem to apply. Indeed, a landmark Supreme Court case in 1984, *Hishon v. King and Spalding* (467 U.S. 69), established that law firms could be sued for sex discrimination under Title VII of the federal Civil Rights Act. And several women have since sued their firms for discriminatory denial of a partnership and won, either through settlements or in court. But the extent of protection that Title VII and comparable state laws actually provide is quite limited, because the courts interpret sex discrimination to mean actions *intended* to bypass or exclude women on grounds of sex. That is, a woman charging that her law firm denied her a partnership due to sex discrimination would have the best chance of winning a lawsuit against the firm if she had evidence that partners voting against her said something like "I don't care how good she is, I just don't like working with women." She might also succeed if she had evidence that men with the same or lesser qualifications were made partners and she was not. In short, as the law stands now, discrimination means some kind of conscious, deliberate wrongdoing, an intentional refusal to judge a woman on her merits, fairly. It does *not* include a systematic negative impact on women of professional rules for advancement that do not take into account the social structure of women's lives.

Thus it is the crunching combination of three sets of rules affecting women's status in the big firms—professional rules, social rules, and legal rules—that places women in a perpetual and painful bind. Either they go by men's professional rules while shouldering the main burden of families and thus living under constant, punishing pressure, or they gain exceptions for themselves from men's rules and are thus not taken seriously as fully authoritative colleagues.

The consequence of this bind, and other dissatisfactions, is that the women leave. They flood into the big firms right out of law school, but in much larger numbers than their male peers they go off after a few years to do something else. A 1988 study and report by the American Bar Association's Commission on Women in the Profession (chaired by Hillary Rodham Clinton) documented this phenomenon thoroughly. Approved by the ABA's House of Delegates, the report called for deep changes in discriminatory and biased attitudes toward women in the male-defined professional culture and in family and workplace issues. A 1990 study by Deborah Holmes provided yet more confirmatory material on the same subject.[2] To check the numbers specific to Harvard, I did a rough count of the attrition from big firms, in New York City and in the state of California, of men and women of the class of 1980. I looked at their place of employment in 1982 (young lawyers frequently spend the first year out of law school in judicial clerkships or other special projects) and then again in 1989. In California, 79 percent of the men were in big firms in 1982, 75 percent in 1989. In New York, the percentage went up: from 70 percent in 1982 to 78 percent in 1989. Of the women in California, 81 percent were in big firms in 1982, only 50 percent in 1989. In New York, it was 54 percent in 1982, 33 percent in 1989. Statistics on the class of 1974 ten years out of law school were similar: only 33 percent of the women were in big firms by 1984.[3]

And this was in boom times for the profession. With the onset of recession in the early nineties, many big firms, particularly in the East,

2. Deborah K. Holmes, "Structural Causes of Dissatisfaction Among Large-Firm Attorneys: A Feminist Perspective," *Women's Rights Law Reporter*, Vol. 12, No. 1 (Spring 1990), pp. 9–38. The article includes an extensive bibliography.

3. Jill Abramson and Barbara Franklin, *Where They Are Now: The Story of the Women of Harvard Law 1974* (Garden City, N.Y.: Doubleday, 1986), pp. 301–7.

both slowed their recruiting and increased the "weeding out" of their less desirable associates—a process that could only heighten the pressure on women.

Furthermore, from talking with women law students in the Harvard graduating class of 1990, I gained the sense that many of the brightest and most imaginative of them would not go into the big firms at all. They knew what was out there, often from the direct experience of summer jobs in the firms, and many of them wanted no part of it. One woman in a group of students I met with remarked that the New York firm where she worked as a summer associate had more women partners than the other big firms but that only one of these women had borne and raised children. The others weren't married or had married men who already had children. Another student added that she had interviewed at this same firm, and that one of its women partners had referred to the deals she did as her children. At this, the others in the group all groaned, and one asked, "Didn't you want to say to her, 'Wait! Just for purposes of future interviews, you sound psychotic'?"

Yet another student recounted a chilling conversation she had had as a summer associate with a woman partner in her firm. "She was, like"—the student adopted, mockingly, a brisk, high voice—" 'I just don't understand why women today treat it as such an impossible thing to do it all. I mean, you know, for me, I wasn't going to get married, then I met X, and then I got married, and then I wasn't going to have kids, and oh well, and then we did. . . .' " The student then described what she saw as the older woman's obsession with work and, as a parting shot, imitated the woman again: " 'I didn't really *mean* to have children!' " The other students laughed, in horror.

Then another said of her big-firm summer, "A woman went on six months' maternity leave, then went part-time, and they spoke of her as if she was lost. A promising attorney, but . . . Her office was there, but she was hardly ever in it. It deep-sixed her career. It absolutely did. You can't do it. Not in corporate work. Maybe in trusts and estates. It's not possible, and you have to know that it's not possible."

Six of the women in the group were third-year students at the time of our meeting and had worked out various career plans. One intended to go to a major firm in New York solely to pay off her loans. She said that she would like eventually to work for a nonprofit corporation. Another was planning to join a big West Coast firm that, she said, valued the quality of life outside work. A third, on law review, said that she and her boyfriend would take New York jobs, but that she would specialize in trusts and estates, and that after several years they would move to a less pressured place and start a family. She expected that she would take time off periodically but that her husband-to-be would not, and she added that although her boyfriend is domestically inclined, they would not divide household work fifty-fifty—it would be mainly her responsibility. Two others, both on law review, were headed for judicial clerkships, from which one (she hoped) would go into government and the other would take up the position she had accepted in a small general-practice firm in Maine. The sixth had a job lined up in a medium-sized firm doing family law, mainly divorces.

In a way, it was heartening to hear these young women with wide professional choices open to them insisting on conditions of work that are essentially humane—that leave time for bringing up children, for developing emotional relationships generally, for donating time to community service, or for pursuing personal interests. But it was sobering, too, because by precluding careers in the big firms, these highly talented and energetic young women were moving themselves off the clearest path to professional authority and, perhaps, political power in the society as well.

Also worrisome is the fact that critical messages about the structuring of legal work are not being delivered loudly and clearly within the precincts of the big firms themselves. Women are voting with their feet and they are talking to researchers and interviewers, but they are not—at least as of the early nineties—forcefully carrying their messages of dissatisfaction into the big firms' executive committees.

It would be amusing to imagine a group of women lawyers presenting their firms with a manifesto declaring that law firms should recognize the men—and women—who work extraordinary hours as *exceptions* to a work norm low enough to allow a balanced life. The manifesto might urge that the firms, instead of penalizing lawyers who want to work reasonable hours, reward their obsessive workers with extra compensation as "money in lieu of life." And it might insist that no one billing more than a certain number of hours should serve on a firm's policy-making committees. The reason would be that a person consumed by work knows too little of life, thinks too little about the functions of law and its connections to the society, and has too dim a grasp of the individual views, needs, and interests of others in the firm to make balanced judgments about the common enterprise.

The manifesto might conclude with Virginia Woolf's stinging criticism, in *Three Guineas*, of the dehumanizing pressures that operate in the high professions. Woolf noted the professional work hours that occupy most of the waking day, and then declared: "[This makes] us of the opinion that if people are highly successful in their professions they lose their senses. Sight goes. They have no time to look at pictures. Sound goes. They have no time to listen to music. Speech goes. They have no time for conversation. They lose their sense of proportion—the relations between one thing and another. Humanity goes. Money making becomes so important that they must work by night as well as by day. Health goes. And so competitive do they become that they will not share their work with others though they have more than they can do themselves. What then remains of a human being who has lost sight, sound, and sense of proportion? Only a cripple in a cave."[4]

But the economic pressure to maintain high hours and a convenient division of desirable and undesirable labor is so great that raising even modest suggestions for upgrading part-time work seems risky to many women partners whose own status was hard won. I have heard frequently that women, including seemingly secure partners, resist banding together to push women's issues in their firms. "They don't want to alienate the men and become further isolated and undermined," says one woman partner who chafed for change. But even she is not sure whether acting together openly is a good or a bad thing to do. She fears the power base of the women is not big enough to go public on women's issues, that it's safer at this point to raise problems for women in her firm in one-to-one discussions. "Men feel threatened when women get together, and also the women are not unified in their view of what's going on," she says with a sigh.

In other words, the operating rules of the big firms not only place many women in them under great pressure and professional disadvantage, but they silence the women as well. Dissident speech will mark a woman more quickly than anything else as an outsider, someone who doesn't belong, not an equal. And wildly dissident speech, as in my imagined manifesto, would probably mark her as crazy. Knowing this, she will be very careful about what she says.

But the silencing of women in the law begins well before their service in the big firms. This is a story that the next chapter traces. It goes back to law school and to a philosophical and pedagogical tradition that strenuously resists the very concept of a woman's voice.

4. Originally published in the United States in 1939 by Harcourt, Brace & World, the essay now appears in a variety of paperback editions.

2

PROFESSORS

A YOUNG WOMAN who graduated from the Harvard Law School in
the mid-1980s recalls her first arrival at the school vividly. A southerner,
she had never been to Massachusetts, and she tells of landing at Logan
Airport in a state of excitement and anticipation, taking a cab to Cambridge—and not being able to find the school. Her cabdriver, a foreigner,
was apologetic and turned off his meter as they prowled the streets looking
for landmarks.

Their dilemma was understandable. For years, no major part of the
law school abutted on any public street at all. The main building, Langdell
Hall, faces an interior yard. The back of the building is at some points
visible from Massachusetts Avenue, a main thoroughfare, but is mostly
screened from public view by a gymnasium, a dormitory, and a Methodist
church. Austin Hall, the school's only other classroom building before
Pound Hall was erected in 1968, also fronts on interior space, and while
it can be seen from some street angles, it is set too far back to be identifiable
from a cab. A similar setback prevents the International Legal Studies
building, completed in 1958, from being identified, and a classroom and
office building rising in 1993 is completely invisible from the street. Pound
Hall borders on Massachusetts Avenue and its sign is—uncharacteristically—in full view, but nothing proclaims it to be part of the Harvard
Law School. Or rather, nothing known to the general public. Few cab-
drivers and few newly arrived students are aware that Roscoe Pound was
a longtime law school dean and an eminent legal scholar. The dormitories
and dining hall cluster around their own off-street yard, and several
nineteenth-century houses converted to office use do not catch the
eye. It is true that a HARVARD LAW SCHOOL sign, its large letters carved
into a granite block, sits by a driveway next to Pound Hall. But the sign

is easy to miss, as the block also serves as a bench and its letters are often obscured by the legs of people waiting for the North Cambridge bus.

The topographical message seems to be that if you don't know where the law school is, you don't belong there. The elusiveness of the place marks a distinction between outsiders—the southern woman, the foreign cabdriver—and insiders. Eventually, the young woman found her dormitory. She found the door that was her entrance to the law. But the uncertainty of her arrival signaled the range of trouble, of subtle and bewildering pitfalls, for outsiders entering new territory—not just at Harvard, but at any of the long-established schools of law.

For women, the trouble spins out, in a wide variety of forms, from a disjunction between a vision of the law that draws many of them into law school and the actuality of their experience once there. Women arrive at law school, my interviews suggest, thinking of the law, at its best, as a provider of evenhanded justice. They see it as a place removed from the pushes and shoves of the marketplace, from the temptations and taints of politics, a place where rational standards exist to define what is right and fair and necessary.

What particularly appeals to women in this concept of law, I think, is its promise to even out disparities of power and privilege. That is, women entering the law tend to think that even if its practitioners harbor prejudiced views of women, the law itself operates on a higher plane, overriding such attitudes. They see it generally as a shield for the vulnerable against the pressures of political power and economic interest.

A good third of my interviewees said their own purposes on entering law school were to use the law to promote social fairness through some form of public service. In classes of the late sixties and early seventies, that figure was as high as 50 percent. Some saw themselves as government lawyers helping to shape social services, rationalize public functions, protect the environment, prosecute wrongdoers, or build international institutions. Others focused on the threat of governmental power to the individual and wanted to work as protectors of civil rights and liberties.

Few end up making whole careers in these areas. Public and charitable funds to support such work run far short of the number of people who want to do it. And many who try find the demands of public service so great or the results so uncertain or the salaries so low that they drop out. But still, their vision of the law, the reason they entered it in the first place, rests on a belief in its profound fairness and protectiveness.

This vision may be personal as well. Many women speak of the appeal of the law for them as some difficult-to-define combination of the prestige that law confers and a sense that being part of the law enhances one's own control over life, a sense that the promise of the law to do justice throws a mantle of protection over its practitioners as well as its petitioners.

One woman, a mid-eighties graduate, speaks graphically in these terms. When she was growing up, she says, her family lived across the street from a lawyer who had been a state representative—a powerful, respected man in the community—and this lawyer had represented her father in legal actions following an automobile accident. The accident was a huge trauma for the family. Other people had been seriously injured, criminal charges were being brought, and the injured parties were threatening to sue. The woman was nine or ten at the time and didn't know what "sue" meant, but it was clearly terrible. In the end, the lawyer managed to avert criminal proceedings with a nolo contendere plea. "It was the first direct exposure that I'd had to the presence of the law," she reflects, "and that probably made a really deep impression on me—that lawyers were somebody who could come and save the day." Later, when she was about fourteen and her parents were being divorced, she persuaded her mother, who was going to sign everything in sight just to get out of the marriage, to hire a lawyer for advice and protection. Becoming a person who could embody such power was clearly an appealing prospect.

In some cases, the idea of empowerment through law is urged by a young woman's mother, although often in general terms of becoming self-supporting. Such advice is most common from divorced mothers or those who have had serious marital trouble and faced the prospect of living on alimony or income from whatever job they could get as middle-aged, untrained workers. What a number of such mothers teach their daughters out of this experience is the importance of not letting themselves become financially dependent on a man. And law seems to be a field that assures a good income while also arming a woman with weapons useful in a number of life's battles and harassments.

For outsiders, then, the desire to trust in the power of impartial law is immensely compelling. As the old order defining women's place breaks apart, as women are caught in the chaotic juxtaposition of old and new rules, as women lawyers enter the no-man's-land between the old worlds of women and men, as they claim ground there from which to become co-writers of the new rules, they want to trust in the protection of the law, the legal tradition we have inherited. They want to assume that the irrationalities they encounter concerning women's identities and proper roles derive from indefensible social attitudes, unthought-out and ill-informed. And they want to assume that such attitudes are not to be found in the intelligently conceived, carefully wrought principles making up the law. As much as they may more cynically expect unprincipled behavior in some corners of the law, they want to believe that the law itself and the profession itself stand for and deliver fairness.

What, then, do they find when they arrive at law school? The answer varies in different historical eras and in different law schools, but in all eras and in most schools—certainly the most prestigious schools, and most certainly Harvard—they find a strongly male environment. It wasn't until the 1980s that women made up so much as a third of the nation's law students. As one Harvard graduate from the early eighties recalls of her first law school class, "I sit down and look around, and there's a man in front of me, and there's a man behind me, and there's a man on my left, and there's a man on my right, and to meet any women, I'd have to, like, reach over these guys. . . . There was that sense of being in alien territory, in male territory." This was nothing, however, compared to the experience of the tiny band of women who entered the school each year in the 1950s—usually about a dozen to about five hundred men. "We were strange to the men of the Harvard Law School, we were strange to the professors," one of them begins. And then, her face stiffening, she goes on: "We didn't belong there. It was as if we had suddenly entered a man's toilet, you know. It wasn't our place."

Beyond student numbers, there is a question of atmosphere. Here, Harvard may be in a class by itself in the extremity of its male identification. A woman graduate of the early seventies describes it in terms that I heard echoed in comments from the earliest classes of women to the present. "It just seemed to be a place that did not wish women well, that wasn't happy they were there, that didn't want to see them succeed. It was misogynistic, it was just a big streak in a lot of those men, that they just didn't like women very much, just didn't like them. It was faculty and students both, but of course faculty are the power figures. They set the tone. . . . I remember that just in general you would be trying to talk about something serious or just speaking in class, and there would be a look. An actor who has tried to convey those things without words would know just what those expressions are, just what that body language is, and often it's . . . just evading a stare or crossing your arms across your chest. There are ways to do it that are even more subtle than that."

This woman is speaking of a time when the entire faculty of the Harvard Law School was male. It was twenty years after the arrival of the first women students that the first woman professor appeared in a classroom. And the omnipresence of male authority remained in place long after that. By the early nineties, the regular tenured faculty included five women—out of sixty-two. In other words, forty years after the first women students arrived, the faculty was still more than 90 percent male, and students could go through their entire three years without seeing a woman professor. A student in the group I spoke with from the class of 1990 talked about her astonishment and delight when a woman lawyer appeared in a classroom one day as a visitor to talk about some area of special expertise. "We hadn't seen a woman lawyer all year," the student said, "and she was attractive. She had painted nails, and she was tough and smart as a whip!" With a virtually all-male faculty, the message that femininity and authority can be combined is not one that women law students frequently receive.

And backing up the faculty as authority figures are the portraits. High on the walls of the classrooms, large oil paintings of legal luminaries stare down—bewigged English jurists, black-robed American judges, deans, professors, and other notable lawyers in three-piece suits, vests stretching across ample stomachs. Until 1988, when several students succeeded in a campaign to mount some portraits of women, this iconography of the law, which extends out of the classrooms, down long corridors, and around the high-ceilinged library, was wholly male.

Almost everyone mentions the portraits. Clearly, they haunt the imaginations of many alumnae. One graduate of the early sixties, now a partner in a major national firm, had loathed Harvard as a student, had not returned for over sixteen years, and then did so to attend Celebration 25, a conference commemorating twenty-five years of women at the school. But she left early. "I could just feel the atmosphere closing in on me again. I remember on Saturday night walking through Pound Hall, in which there are photographs of the faculty instead of oil portraits, and I was just struck by the total maleness of this place, and I said to my friend, 'Let's get a Magic Marker and draw boobies on all of them.' " She laughs. "But instead, I just left without vandalizing the law school, though they'd vandalized my brain for years."

In the early years of women's presence at the school, the message that women were interlopers in a male preserve was not simply semiotic. It was delivered annually to each class of first-year women by the longtime dean Erwin Griswold, a dour, truth-telling Quaker. One member of the first class of women remembers the dean saying that some faculty had opposed the admission of women, as he had himself, because each woman at the school was taking the place of a good man. Another woman remembers the dean's saying that the school was never going to take in so many women that they would keep out the best men.

Many women recall hearing remarks of this sort at an annual dinner the dean held for first-year women at his home. Most stories of the dean's dinner have him asking each woman, in turn, why she came to law school, a question underscoring the oddity of her choice. And in many if not all years, he reiterated his doubts about the wisdom of admitting women to the law school in the first place. It was because, he said, it was statistically certain that women would practice fewer years than men—an average of only two years, some recall his saying—and, therefore, women students would be wasting the exceptional resources of Harvard's legal education.

I remember the dean's saying this in 1957. I remember the dozen of us first-year women sitting in his living room, some on chairs, some on the floor, all decorously dressed. We had been at the school only a few weeks. And the dean said we shouldn't be there. I remember feeling a wave of astonishment, hurt, and anger, all mixed, inchoate, and thinking confusedly that learning about the law was an education. Maybe women wouldn't use it just as men did, but was that wrong? The dean couldn't tell people what to do with their education. Or could he? He didn't own the law. Or did he? To describe what I was thinking in this way makes it seem clearer, cooler, than it was. It was something like that, but I was too shocked and too unsure of myself to be able to evaluate the dean's words with any sense of certainty. They were so completely at odds with my expectation of welcome and praise for achieving admission that I had no place to put the news they conveyed. Nor did my classmates. We didn't challenge him, and we didn't even talk about it with one another, not for years. I think we simply couldn't fully process a concept so at odds with the belief we held that the law was fair, that we were in a place of fairness.

This sentiment appears clearly in the recollections of the dean's dinner of a woman in a class a few years after mine. "I can remember the room and everything. I can remember my shock. I mean, I guess I was angry because I was a Radcliffe graduate. I had gone to school with all these men [she means the dozens of Harvard graduates in the law school]. I had taken the same exams they had, and how was I different? How could my school do this to me? How could Harvard University—I mean, this was the epitome, you know, the smartest and wisest people in the world! How could they do this?"

Dean Griswold left the law school in 1967 to become solicitor general of the United States, and with him went the plainspoken assertion by school leaders that men and women were not on an equal footing in the law school or the profession. By this point, the civil rights and student movements of the sixties had shifted the terms of the nation's debate about equality. Discrimination by race or sex could no longer be accepted openly as the way things were. It was marked as wrong, illegitimate. Clear discriminations became targets for reform. And conventional attitudes about women's careers had also shifted. The idea that women leaving college would go on to graduate or professional school instead of straight into marriage became common. The consequence of all this ferment was a dramatic rise in the application and admission of women to law schools, starting in 1970.

At Harvard, which lagged slightly behind the national average in the percentage of women admitted each year, the figures jumped from 4 percent in 1965 to 11 percent in 1970, 25 percent in 1975, 29 percent in 1980, 37 percent in 1985, and 42 percent in 1990. But in the inner life of the school, at its intellectual center, a male identity persisted, a sense that the place belonged to men, a sense that women, even as their number rose dramatically, were still outsiders. It is a sense, not at all restricted to Harvard, that the presence of women is somehow out of keeping with the workings of the law.

The problem for women, the problem not solved by their increased number, is that long tradition connects legal analysis with intellectual traits generally ascribed to men: hardness, toughness, sharpness. And women are under perpetual suspicion of intellectual and temperamental softness. Recall the student who was gratified by the appearance of a woman lawyer who was "tough and smart as a whip" and who also had painted nails. What the student's remark reflects is the idea, lurking almost subliminally in legal culture, that women may be smart but they are not usually whiplike. Further, if they are feminine in manner and appearance, they are assumed not to be tough. And if they are not sharp enough and tough enough, they cannot learn to "think like a lawyer."

The reason that legal tradition prizes these mental qualities is that they are essential to the core principle of the Anglo-American philosophy of law—the principle of objectivity. This principle defines a rigorous, disciplined mode of thought based on generally recognized rules or values as opposed to individual preferences or prejudices. It requires that legal thinkers rise above personal interests and circumstances to analyze issues through strict processes of reason, using facts and logic as their only guides. The practice of objectivity is the very basis of the claim to fairness in our legal system, and yet it is the key to the suspicion that settles on women as soon as they enter their first classes. The unspoken question that greets them is, Do women, as a rule, possess the mental toughness to achieve and sustain objectivity? Or will they fall prey to softheartedness, faintheartedness, or reason-clouding appeals to emotion?

To an extent, the special pressure of these questions on women is masked by the immense pressure that law training places on law students generally. As anyone who has ever gone through the process is aware, law school provides an experience of learning like no other. The professors, particularly in first-year courses, are missionaries. Their mission is to reach into the skull of every student and reshape the mind inside to render it capable of thinking objectively, in traditional terms. And the classic teaching technique used for this purpose is the famous, or infamous, Socratic method.

Chronicled in Scott Turow's *One L* and John Jay Osborn, Jr.'s, *The Paper Chase* as a kind of coming-of-age ritual, the modern equivalent of battle with a fire-breathing dragon, the Socratic process, for most students, is a terrifying ordeal. And like knightly initiations of old, the process is supposed to be broadly, even grandly, empowering. Students are supposed to emerge toughened and tempered, clear-thinking, and ready for battle with the forces of unreason in the outside world. But since women enter the process under suspicion, the empowerment does not work in just the same way for them as it does for men.

How does the Socratic method work at all to change ordinary thinking into legal thinking? Picture, in its Harvard setting, a large lecture hall with raised, semicircular tiers of seats focused down into the well of the room, in the center of which is the professor's desk. The students—in most first-year classes, over one hundred of them—sit in assigned seats. The professor has a seating chart bearing the students' names. The students do not have a textbook explaining the subject of the day, nor does the professor usually deliver a general explanation by lecturing. Rather, the subject—for example, the doctrine of contributory negligence in torts—is derived from court cases, usually appellate court opinions presenting judicial interpretations of contested points of law. The opinions, collected in the fat casebooks the students lug around, may differ over time or in different jurisdictions. They may be vague or inconsistent. The professor, calling on a succession of students, provokes them through a relentless series of questions to clarify the issues at stake in a case, the relevant principles of law, and the reasoning that connects the principles to the particular facts.

The students learn by criticizing the judicial opinions before them, but their own comments are also subject to merciless criticism. Every vague or undefined or inconsistent statement must be explained, refined, or revised, and whenever a student comes up with a seemingly sound and conclusive resolution to an issue, the professor usually pounces back with a variation in the facts through hypothetical cases—or "hypos"—that are generally calculated to show up a flaw in the student's reasoning. Performing well in this setting depends less on reading and remembering reams of material than on thinking clearly and coolly, on the spot, with dozens of impatient classmates and an often taunting professor judging each remark.

Still, when the Socratic process is done well, it is, if frightening, remarkably compelling. The student is mesmerized by the sheer wizardry of the professor as he leaps from point to point, exposing gaps in what looked like solid ground. She is enthralled by the drama of moving from a universe in pieces to a moment of enlightenment when the fragments slide together. She rides a roller coaster of threatened attack from the demon-professor and release from danger by the savior-professor. "It was exhilarating, a little scary, like skiing too fast," says one of my interviewees. And another: "I just felt *swept away*. It was like entering a new world." Yet another: "I hadn't felt so immersed in something totally new since I was in fourth grade learning long division."

Even women who despise the method often accept its claims. They want to believe in the magic that will allow them, laserlike, to cut through the blurry confusion of normal thought to the lawyer's sharp-edged clarity. Most are eager to acquire the power to see clearly, to understand what others cannot, to become reasoners of the highest order.

But according to the professors, students, and former students I interviewed, as well as data published by other researchers, the Socratic method frequently has a double-edged impact on women. It teaches and encourages the logical analysis that is its purpose, but it can also, depending on how it is used, undermine the credibility of women students and effectively silence their voices.

From the stories told me by Harvard women of the early classes, before the women's movement, it is clear that a number of professors used Socratic dialogues to express their suspicion, if not contempt, of women students in ways that were completely open and clear. Some indulged in stereotyping remarks, such as "Miss X, could you give us a woman's definition of property?" or "How did you arrive at that conclusion, Miss X—intuition?" or "How do you know that? Are you a mystic?" Others had chronic trouble hearing women—one gave that as the reason

he never called on them. Another made a point of having women repeat
their remarks again and again as he advanced toward them, hand cupped
to the ear. Most simply ignored the women, rarely if ever calling on them
or passing quickly over their comments, not engaging them in sustained
discussion. Some made a point of complaining that they would have to
refrain from telling particularly good jokes about certain cases because
ladies were present. Some told the jokes anyway.

Then there was the notorious Ladies' Day. Eventually staged annually by several professors well into the 1960s, the event was initiated
in the mid-fifties by property professor W. Barton Leach, a former air-
force general. Leach was a tall, slim, handsome, supremely self-confident
man who, tipping back his chair or prowling the professor's platform,
owned whatever space he occupied. His sardonic wit did the rest. He
dominated the classroom completely. And according to one of the earliest
women graduates, he took "a fiendish delight" in putting down women
students. "He didn't make particular remarks," she says. "It was more
a matter of the arrogance of the attitude and what it conveyed, that sort
of surliness, seeming to say, 'Well, that's what I'd expect of a woman,'
although he wouldn't say it. It's hard to describe in words. I'm not sure
the men were aware of it."

Within several years, however, Leach had developed a special policy
for women of which everyone was aware. He would announce, early in
the semester—to classes that contained about 125 men and 4 or 5
women—that he was too much of a gentleman to call on his women
students without warning, and therefore he would designate a certain day
when the women alone would answer questions. Further, he would let
them know in advance the case that would be discussed so that they would
not have to think on their feet in the normal Socratic give-and-take but
would have ample time to prepare ahead. This was Ladies' Day, and on
the appointed day he would have the women sit at the front of the thea-
terlike classroom, where, he would say, their small voices could best be
heard.

The actual conduct of the Ladies' Day class was straightforward.
No one remembers trick questions, slighting remarks, or off-color asides,
but the selection of the case itself carried a belittling message. For a
number of years, Leach used the same one—something from the old
common law involving personal property. The opinion did not specify
what the property in question, the "chose in action," actually was, which
allowed Leach to divulge at some point, apparently satisfying to himself,
that it was underwear.

And what was the effect on women students of this none-too-subtle signal of disrespect? I wish I could say, of myself and my women classmates, that we refused to participate on Ladies' Day, rose in outraged revolt, denounced the whole procedure, and walked out to protest to the dean. In fact, we did none of these things. I know I simply sat there in a stew of terror and humiliation and answered the questions, hating Leach, hating the law school, but accepting silently the denigration being perpetrated by both.

In part, our silence came from the same stunned incredulity with which we responded to the dean's announcement that we were taking places at the law school that would be better used by men. But partly we were trapped by the stereotypes of women that the professors were expressing and perpetuating. According to the stereotypes, women were intellectually inferior to men. They operated through intuition, not reason. They did not think clearly and quickly. Their proper realm was the body (denoted by the underwear on Ladies' Day), not the mind. If we wanted to demonstrate our intellectual equality, we could not do it by identifying ourselves as women. But we would have had to do so in order to protest our treatment as women. That was the trap.

We didn't really think this through, imagining a protest by women, *as* women, and discarding the idea as unlikely to work in the face of the heavy prejudice around us. It was more that the idea of protest couldn't even form in the face of the prejudice. It was beyond imagining that in a place dedicated to the highest forms of reason, which we believed in and aspired to, that we would identify ourselves as a group of women when women, as a group, were associated with unreason.

So we were politically silent, but our silence extended beyond the political to our individual behavior in the classroom as well. Most of us were trapped there, too, between the desire to demonstrate our intellectual prowess by performing well in the classroom arena and the fear that if we opened our mouths, we would invite the contemptuous responses to women that we frequently witnessed. There were some exceptions, some brave, strong-voiced women, but most of us said nothing unless we were called on, which was rare. And our silence fed the stereotyping that produced it.

It was the great achievement of the women's movement in the late sixties and early seventies to open up the box of old stereotypes to public scrutiny and to release women professionals—somewhat, at least—from silent fear of them. In this period, the public surfacing of the movement had jolted many lawyers, women and men, into consciousness of the long-unnoticed unfairness in many areas of law that had been shaped by the old stereotypes regarding women. For example: A 1948 Supreme Court case had upheld a state law severely restricting women's employment as barmaids. Justice Felix Frankfurter, one of the most brilliant graduates of the Harvard Law School and a professor there before his appointment to the Court, wrote that the state law's restrictions on women's employment did not violate the Fourteenth Amendment requirement of equal protection because the purpose of the law—protection of women from insult and harm in bars—was reasonable. There was the stereotype: women had delicate sensibilities, were physically weak, could not take care of themselves, and needed protection, even if the protection kept them out of well-paying jobs.

But starting in 1970, a barrage of litigation identified and challenged—on the basis of the Fourteenth Amendment equal-protection clause—a wide variety of discriminatory laws that legislators and courts had regarded as reasonable under the old stereotypes. The cases contested, for example, an automatic preference for a husband over a wife when both sought to administer the estate of a child who had died; lower fringe benefits for female members of the armed forces; the effective exclusion of women from juries in some states; differences in Social Security and workmen's compensation benefits for widows and widowers; a veterans'-preference law for state employment effectively reserving the top civil-service jobs for men; and a wide variety of state laws that restricted women's employment for supposed reasons of health or safety.

In fact, the new doctrine of equal protection that emerged from this litigation is still far from clear, or stable, but it definitely rejects the premise used by Justice Frankfurter in 1948 that women's differences, weaknesses, and social roles justified virtually all kinds of unequal benefits or restrictions.

And in law schools, the new militant recognition of inequality based on sex made it possible for women students to understand and to consciously resist the stereotyping and overt denigration to which their predecessors had been subject. Across the country, women pressed their teachers for courses on women and the law, and on sex discrimination in employment. And the worst forms of sexist practice in the classroom, such as Ladies' Day at Harvard, faded into the past.

But the sources of sexism in law school training, the deep-rooted cultural suspicion of women's capacity to reason through analyses firmly guided by logic, did not disappear. Rather, it lingered on in the ghostly presence of the old stereotypes, now largely transmuted into an accusation of emotionalism. As noted earlier, one of the requirements of thinking like a lawyer—objectively—is rising above emotion, suppressing sympathy or antipathy for any of the parties involved in a particular case. And ancient conceptions of women as emotional by nature, as less able than men to control their emotions, have remained alive and active in law school classrooms.

One woman describes a Socratic sequence conveying this assumption with details fresh in her mind years after the event. It is a story of life imitating art, the art in question being the film version of *The Paper Chase*, in which a male student (Timothy Bottoms) in a Harvard Law School class is subject to persistent questioning by the ferocious Professor Kingsfield (John Houseman). In one tense scene, Kingsfield hands the thoroughly confused student a dime and tells him to call his mother to let her know he isn't going to make it at Harvard. In the real-life story, which occurred just after the film was released in 1973, the Kingsfield figure was the contracts professor Clark Byse, who possessed a hair-raising classroom reputation. The woman student in question was a small, soft-featured, red-haired recent graduate of a Catholic women's college. Now a law professor herself, she wonders whether Byse actually knew of her morally oriented, Irish Catholic, working-class background or just sized up her earnest innocence from her appearance.

"Around Thanksgiving time," she recalls, "Professor Byse calls on me. It was the case where a nice woman relative comes out and takes care of somebody and the contract says, If you take care of me, I will leave you Blackacre when I die. Well, of course what happens is that the older relative does not leave her Blackacre when he dies, and so there's a lawsuit. And I can't remember the exact legal point, but to achieve the equitable result, to give the woman Blackacre, the court had to get around a fairly straightforward law that would have gone the other way. She wouldn't have gotten the property, in spite of her hard work. Anyway, Byse called on me to recite the facts. I recite the facts.

" 'Well, what was the court's holding?'

"I said, 'Well, the court *said* a, b, c.' " (Emphasizing "said," she indicates that the court had found some language to get around the law that was going to produce the wrong result.)

" 'What do you mean, "The court *said* this?" Are you implying they didn't really mean it?'

" 'Well, the statute said—'

" 'What do you think law is? Nine men in black robes going in the back room and deciding cases by visceral reaction?'

"I was mortified. And of course I was in the last row, right in the center, where everyone could turn and look at me turning eighty-five shades of red. And he storms up the aisle and says, 'Miss X, here's a dime, go call your mother.'

"Well, of course everybody had seen the movie, and there I am: 'Oh please, just go away, just go away.' I'm sitting there. I'm shrinking down.

"And then he calls on a guy who says, 'Well, clearly, the court, blah, blah, blah,' "—she explains that the male student was presenting the court's opinion as rationally, not morally, justified—"and I was just sitting there mortified. And then five minutes later, Professor Byse says, 'How many of you agree with Miss X?' Nobody. 'How many agree with Mr. So-and-So?' And everybody's hands went up. At the end of the class, Professor Byse said, 'Of course, you realize Miss X was right.' But the humiliation—it was one of those things, 'I never want to see this man again, I want to get out of here, how could he do this to someone?' And here I am, the most innocent of the innocent at this place, afraid to say boo, and he had called on me."

What Byse had done was to perform a classic Socratic maneuver. He had thoroughly shaken up the class, not allowing it to take anything for granted. First, by playing off the sophisticated male student against the naïve woman, he manipulated the class into agreeing with the young man's faulty logic—that is, that the court *had* justified its conclusion rationally rather than viscerally. Then he announced that this was wrong, that the court had indeed followed its moral instincts rather than the clear requirement of the law. He had demonstrated to the class that they had not been sufficiently critical. He had also taught the lesson that courts are not infallible, that their pronouncements do not necessarily make sense. And he had driven home the point that the paramount value in the law of contracts is the integrity of the system of rules under which contracts are made, and not the moral question of fairness to the parties involved in a particular case.

But he had also done something else. In spite of the exculpation he offered at the end of class ("Of course you realize Miss X is right"), he implicitly connected the visceral (or moral, or emotional) view of the case with an innocent young woman, and condemned that view. That is what the drama of the dime accomplished. So he delivered a double lesson: The integrity of the system, not the morally satisfying result, is paramount; and, Think like a lawyer, not like a girl.

We don't know whether the young woman here favored the emotionally satisfying outcome of this case. Perhaps she might have thought that there was something wrong with a law of contracts that did not take into greater account the unequal bargaining power of the parties involved. The sick man in the case had property, and presumably, he was able to exploit his female relative because she had none. "Why should the integrity of a contracts system have such weight if its underlying values are biased toward people with property?" the student might have asked. But whether the woman student thought such a thing or not, the story makes it clear that she would be unlikely to say it. Rather, she was completely silenced by the spectacle of the professor storming up the aisle toward her and slamming the dime onto her desk. She was being taught, as women are generally taught, to be suspicious of her own doubts about such a case through the charge that she is given to emotional, not reasoned, response. She was being taught to doubt her own judgment and to remain silent.

This story is unusual only in the degree of grandstanding the professor permitted himself. Women in classes up to the present report incidents of a similar tenor. Here is one from a set of interviews conducted by a woman student at the Harvard Law School in the spring of 1988: "One morning in class, completely out of the blue, the professor asked us whether we thought evidence of a woman's past sexual history ought to be admissible in a rape trial. It was off the cuff like that—no preparation, or anything. This was actually a class in civil procedure. A bunch of hands went up. The professor proceded to call on seven men in a row, although there were women's hands up. The men said things like 'If a woman sleeps with a different guy three hundred sixty-four days out of the year, then don't you think it's likely that she consented to the three hundred sixty-fifth?' Another man said he believed women often say no to having sex when they really mean yes, and that women are masochistic.

"The professor wasn't doing anything to correct the misconceptions being thrown about. Then he asked if there wasn't anyone willing to stand up for the point of view that evidence of the victim's previous sexual history was irrelevant and shouldn't be admissible. Again, a number of hands went up, but again, he called on a man. The man said that if you flip a coin nine times and it comes up heads nine times, that this is not a predictor of how it will come up the tenth time. I was incredulous; a woman's choice about whether to sleep with a man reduced to the level of a coin toss!

"Another man the professor called on said that if someone broke into his house and stole his stereo, he'd want to know that person's history of stereo theft. At that point I waved my hand and got called on. I was very upset, and it showed. I said, 'There are so many misconceptions here that I need to correct. First of all, rape is a crime of violence, not a crime of sex.' At that point the professor just cut me off. He said, 'Settle down, settle down, and think about this like a lawyer.' The message was, If you're like this, you can't be a real lawyer, and real lawyers aren't women and real lawyers don't have emotions. I felt stifled and hardly ever spoke again in that class."[1]

Over and over again, this is the refrain I've heard: "I hardly ever spoke again." A chorus of stories from my interviewees, as well as reports from other studies, describe the same phenomenon. Even women who have been enthusiastic talkers at every prior academic stage, and those who have talked forcefully in other challenging settings—union meetings, debate competitions, community protests, fund drives, and business conferences—fall silent in law school classrooms. Not all women are silent, of course. Many participate in some way, and some speak readily and frequently, but both students and professors have told me that women still speak noticeably less than men do.[2] In fact, most of the law professors I interviewed had given a great deal of thought to the problem of getting their women students to speak, to develop a voice, in the classroom and outside.

The problem is to understand fully the source of the silence. Clearly, denigration and humiliation by professors has a profound effect, but the silence is too widespread, too persistent, for this to be its sole cause. Professorial badgering does not explain, for example, why many women are silent, or relatively so, in all their classes, even those in which the professors are benign, even those in which the professors are women. A more general explanation is the usual socialization of women, their long training in deference and passivity, which seems to result in their quietness in public settings by and large. But this does not explain why women who are talkers in other public spheres fall silent in the face of the law.

To some extent, I think that it is the hierarchical and adversarial

---

1. This story is taken, with the author's permission, from an unpublished paper by Katina Leodas titled "Women in Law School: The View from the Margins." The paper is on file at the Harvard Law School Library.

2. A Stanford University study of law and graduate students provides empirical data on this point. See "Gender, Legal Education, and the Legal Profession: An Empirical Study of Stanford Law Students and Graduates," *Stanford Law Review*, Vol. 40 (May 1988), pp. 1209–59. A qualitative study of women students at the Yale Law School comes to similar conclusions. See Catherine Weiss and Louise Melling, "The Legal Education of Twenty Women," in the same volume of the *Stanford Law Review*, pp. 1299–1359.

structure of the Socratic dialogue that many women react against. Starting with less social power than their male peers, they dislike engaging in hostile contests with a professor. They dislike being cast definitively in a powerless role, a victim's position. They dislike being manipulated by older men. All of this, along with their expectation of ridicule more extreme than that directed at men, feeds an inclination on the part of many women to remove themselves as active players of the game.

But there is a deeper source to the silence as well. It is signaled clearly in the story of the rape case. It has to do with the invalidation by the terms of the Socratic dialogue of what women see, *as women*, in legal issues. That is, the woman in the rape discussion was asserting ideas grounded in a woman's perspective on the crime of rape. She was speaking out of what she knew as a woman about a crime consisting (typically) of male violence against women. She argued, in effect, that the male students were speaking from a male perspective that limited their understanding of the issues involved. But to assert that a female perspective is different from a male perspective is to defy the principle of objectivity, which requires that legal thinkers leave their personal perspectives behind and use reason alone to analyze issues. Objective thinking must be perspectiveless. Therefore, the woman asserting a woman's view was squelched. The charge of emotionalism, readily available for use against women, was invoked, and the protesting woman put down as unreasonable.

But what if, on some issues, women *do*, by virtue of their experience of life as women, hold perspectives that *are* different from those of men? This is a question raised by a new generation of feminist legal scholars in work that has deepened the criticism of legal thought developed by the feminists of the 1970s. That generation successfully rescued women from the old stereotypes of inferiority, fighting off the idea that women's minds and temperaments fitted them for work in the family or in the helping or nurturing professions but not for the professions of high reason. That is, the work of the first wave of feminists in the present women's movement established the position that women were as rational as men and, in the law, as capable as men of thinking according to the rules of objectivity. The newer feminist critics start with this position of equal rationality, but they go on to explore the implications of women's differences and to question the concept of objectivity as it is traditionally understood.

The premise of this work is that women, in spite of wide variations in class and race and individual circumstance, generally share a range of experience in their lives at odds with that of most men—not totally at odds, but significantly so. Most important is the very fact that women *are* still outsiders to public power and authority—that, as a group, they hold less power than do men over the way society works. Certainly, it is clear in the big law firms, as in most other workplaces, that women gain less advantage than comparably situated men from the way society works. Also of enormous importance is the remaining force of the different social assignments women receive. Growing up, they share the expectation that they will take responsibility for people around them in need of care— children, the sick, the elderly, the unhappy. More often than not, they share the experience of giving birth and raising children, or expecting to, of fearing pregnancies they do not want, or, sometimes, wanting pregnancies they cannot have. They also share the experience of knowing they are prey to attack by men out of control, and they share the experience of chronically guarding against it.

And these differences in experience necessarily give rise to differences in perspective on a wide range of legal issues—concerning sexuality, concerning work, concerning family. For example, women are raising serious questions about such issues as the meaning of consent in rape cases, the definition and harms of sexual harassment in the workplace, the relation of hard-core pornography to male violence against women, the exclusion of women from workplaces for reasons of fetal protection, the unrestricted right of women to abort pregnancies, and the tangle of rights and obligations of parents—wed and unwed, biological and contractual, gay and straight—concerning the custody and support of children. On these and related issues, what many women see as relevant and important often differs from accepted precepts embedded in the law.

The problem in Socratic exchange is what to do with the differences. When women express them, as in the rape discussion cited above, their remarks are likely to be dismissed as unobjective. But very often, the sense of difference does not rise to an articulated position. Rather, in ways they can rarely identify while it is happening, many women hear the professorial voice against some kind of internal dissonance. What they hear does not entirely square with what they know. Still, not to accept the professor's authority, underwritten by the entire profession, is difficult, so they discount what they know. It must be wrong. It must be that they don't understand. So they censor their own questioning and, in confusion about what they really think, remain silent.

And here is the crux of the matter for the new feminist critics, the formulators of a feminist jurisprudence. They point out that if women's silence persists, women's knowledge, based in what is distinctly different in their experience of life, cannot enter legal thought and cannot influence the content of the law. They add that the same is true for the particular knowledge of racial minorities and other outsider groups. And the consequences are serious. If the voices of outsiders do not enter the ongoing formation of legal thought, the critics say, then the law cannot fulfill its promise of fairness to such groups. The reason is that without the perspectives of the less powerful in the discussion, the law will necessarily reflect the perspectives of the more powerful. In the entire history of Anglo-American law down to the present, this means the perspectives of economically privileged white men.

As Martha Minow, professor of law at Harvard, puts it, some groups in the society have "the power to treat themselves as the norm" but tend to lack the perspective to know they are doing it. Therefore, lawmakers and law interpreters, assuming their own objectivity, see law as applying in the same way to everyone, and do not see that it applies disadvantageously to groups without the power to establish norms themselves. As a corrective, Minow urges an approach to the law that would require lawmakers to look at issues from the point of view of those who are different. "The point," she concludes, "is not to find the new, true perspective; the point is to strive for impartiality by admitting our partiality." The key is to recognize that everyone sees from a particular perspective, and to bring to the law's judgments the perspective of the less as well as the more powerful.[3]

Mari Matsuda, professor of law at UCLA, calls this approach a methodology of "multiple consciousness" and argues eloquently for its adoption, and for recognition that it must encompass race and class as well as sex. "The multiple consciousness I urge all lawyers to attain," she writes, "is not a random ability to see all points of view, but a deliberate choice to see the world from the standpoint of the oppressed. That world is accessible to all of us. We should know it in its concrete particulars. We should know of our sister carrying buckets of water five flights of stairs in a welfare hotel, our sister trembling at 3 a.m. in a shelter for battered women, our sisters holding bloodied children in their arms in Cape Town, on the West Bank, and in Nicaragua. The jurisprudence of outsiders teaches that these details and the emotions they evoke are relevant and important as we set out on the road to justice."[4]

What is at issue here is nothing less than the traditional understand-

3. Martha Minow, *Making All the Difference: Inclusion, Exclusion, and American Law* (Ithaca, N.Y.: Cornell University Press, 1990), pp. 111, 376.

4. Mari Matsuda, "When the First Quail Calls: Multiple Consciousness as Jurisprudential Method," *Women's Rights Law Reporter*, Vol. 11, No. 7 (Spring 1989).

ing of objectivity that stands at the center of present mainstream conceptions of law. Theorists of the new feminist jurisprudence flatly dispute the very premise of objectivity, which is that it is possible for human beings to detach themselves from their social identities and to analyze issues through reason and logic alone. Feminists argue not only that this is impossible, that all thinkers carry socially shaped perspectives with them, but that thinkers seeking a high degree of detachment miss the concrete human detail that is a vital part of important issues.

The further charge is that in practice, the tradition of objectivity masks the very harms it is supposed to prevent. It is supposed to prevent bias toward powerful or favored groups, but instead it allows the perspectives of socially dominant groups to dominate the law. And it effectively silences those whose perspectives are different. As UCLA law professor Kimberle Crenshaw puts it with respect to law students of color, "To play the game right, they have to assume a stance that denies their own identity and requires them to adopt an apparently objective stance as the given starting point of analysis. Should they step outside the doctrinal constraints, not only have they failed in their efforts to 'think like a lawyer,' they have committed an even more stigmatizing *faux pas*: they have taken the discussion far afield by revealing their emotional preoccupation with their racial identity." They cannot speak out of their own experience, she says, "without risking some kind of formal or informal sanction."[5]

To break the silence Crenshaw describes requires displacing the tradition of perspectivelessness in legal thinking with a broadened concept of objectivity including multiple perspectives—the views of women, African-Americans, Native Americans, Asian-Americans, and others. It requires legitimating speech that expresses a point of view grounded in the particular experience of outsiders. The intellectual challenge in this project is to imagine a way of responding to differing and conflicting views and yet formulating laws that can apply to all groups fairly. But another, and yet more serious, challenge is political.

The underlying political question is, Who holds the power to make the laws? Under the traditions that prevail, the answer is, Elite white men. Under a system allowing multiple perspectives, that power would be distributed to outsider groups as well. In other words, the intellectual change would require a shift in rule-making power, and, as a consequence,

5. Kimberle Crenshaw, "Toward a Race-Conscious Pedagogy in Legal Education," *National Black Law Journal*, Vol. 11, No. 1 (Winter 1989), p. 1.

issues surrounding the call for change are marked by a wild mix of philosophy and political fury.

The sites of the debates are the nation's law schools, and the galvanizing issue is, in most places, faculty appointments. If it is necessary for the law to include outsider perspectives, then it is necessary for law faculties, where theorizing about law generally begins, to include outsiders. This is where philosophy meets politics. This is where the battle over change takes place—and nowhere more heatedly than at Harvard.

Tensions on the issue in the Harvard Law School faculty erupted dramatically in April 1990, when Derrick Bell, the first black professor in the school's history, went on strike—or more precisely, an unpaid leave of absence—which would last, he announced, until the school added a tenured minority woman to its ranks. At the time, the sixty-two tenured law professors included only five women, all of them white. Bell's protest followed a decision by the faculty not to offer a permanent post to a black female visiting professor who had been highly regarded by many students. If minority women's voices were absent from law school faculties, Bell insisted, so would their angle of vision be absent from the development of the law. And minority students would continue to suffer from the silencing of their views by standards that discount the importance of what they have to say. The response of the law school dean, Robert Clark, was that the school was committed to recruiting more women and minorities for its faculty, but that appointments had to be based on merit, not protests. "We do have high standards," he said, "and we aren't going to compromise them."

By the spring of 1992, no minority woman had been appointed to a tenure-track position, and Bell was up against a two-year limit to unpaid leaves. Under the rules, he would either have to return to his position or resign from the faculty. But he announced that he would do neither. Instead, he filed a complaint about the school's hiring practices with the federal Office of Civil Rights. He also appealed to the Harvard Corporation for an exception to the two-year leave limit, a plea the corporation rejected in August 1992, thereby terminating Bell's Harvard appointment.

In the meantime, a group of students had formed The Harvard Law School Coalition for Civil Rights and brought a suit against the school, charging that its persistent failure to hire minority women violated Massachusetts's antidiscrimination law. In March 1992, the students' suit went before the Massachusetts Supreme Judicial Court on the question whether the students had standing to sue over discriminatory hiring practices when they were not themselves employees claiming discrimination. The students argued that sex and race discrimination against professors meant that women and minority students were also "stamped with a badge of inferiority" and were deprived of role models available to white men.[6]

Shortly thereafter, the faculty-appointments committee announced its recommendations for tenure appointments for the following year. The list consisted of four white men. Anger erupted in student demonstrations. The civil rights leader the Reverend Jesse Jackson arrived on the scene and spoke to the students, urging their continued pressure for appointments of minorities and women. A small group of students staged a sit-in at the dean's office, while the dean continued to insist that the school's hiring had to be based on its own rigorous academic standards, not on popular demands.

But this is precisely the heart of the issue. What standards? Whose standards? What do the prevailing standards measure? A majority of the 1992 Harvard Law School faculty, and of most law school faculties, measures excellence in scholarly achievement according to the traditional standards of detached critical analysis. By these standards, scholars doing feminist jurisprudence or critical race theory do not look impressive. Their work is not usually published in the most prestigious law journals. It appears in the less-renowned law reviews or the half dozen or so feminist law journals established since the late seventies.

Certainly, students are well aware that women professors who teach and publish on the mainstream subjects gain respect from colleagues and students more easily than do those who pursue feminist work. To gain legitimacy, women professors have to do "the subjects with rules, macho stuff like civil procedure," one woman in the Harvard class of 1990 said. "The soft stuff isn't really regarded as scholarly or important to the law, so the women doing that aren't taken seriously."

This may explain Harvard's decision on the black female professor whose nonappointment in 1990 triggered Derrick Bell's initial protest. According to an enthusiastic student, an Asian-American woman in the group I interviewed in the spring of 1990, this woman's teaching was clearly nontraditional. "I had her for Advanced Torts, and she covered issues no one had ever talked about from a legal perspective—gang wars in L.A., vigilante actions burning down crack houses. That was different from what I thought law school was all about. I wrote a paper about black boycotts of Korean stores in New York City from a torts perspective. It

6. Dean Clark's remarks were quoted in the *New York Times*, April 26, 1990, p. A20. The students' argument before the Massachusetts Supreme Judicial Court was quoted in the *New York Times*, March 6, 1992, p. B8. The students' case was ultimately dismissed.

was the first time I had been able to bring in something from my own experience in a scholarly way and have it accepted as important." This student went on to note that the professor's scholarship in general focused on the relation of the law to outsider groups—"blacks, secretaries, assembly-line workers"—and that this work opened up questions and supplied insights not present in most treatises on torts.

But by prevailing conceptions of merit, work by women *on* women, or by minorities *on* minorities, looks like a kind of special pleading. It looks like subjectively based complaints about the integrity of social systems in place, rather than analysis of bona fide legal issues. It looks political rather than philosophical. It seems to violate the principles of detached objectivity, which form the bases of public respect and acceptance of law. It does not seem intellectually rigorous. In other words, in questioning the very concept of objectivity, feminist scholarship seems to fail the test of objectivity, and thereby often disqualifies its practitioners from recognition as serious scholars—unless they prove themselves by doing conventional work as well. Consequently, the voices of women professors doing feminist or other outsider-focused work tend to be silenced by the same intellectual standards that squelch the voices of women and minority students.[7]

A particularly ugly attack on feminist scholarship, this one on the part of law students, erupted in the midst of the already tense and angry atmosphere that prevailed at the Harvard Law School in the spring of 1992. As they do every year, the third-year student editors of the *Harvard Law Review* produced a parody of that year's volume for distribution at their annual banquet in April—an event to which all eighty or so of the *Review* editors are invited, as are faculty and past *Review* members.

I should note that membership on the *Harvard Law Review* is won by a competition that tests skills in legal analysis (judged by traditional standards), and that the twenty-five or thirty students in each class who are selected are marked for life as people of proven brilliance. Typically, the editors go on to clerk in the top appeals courts and the Supreme Court, and then to whatever professional plums they choose, including law school professorships. Few professors at prestigious law schools have not been editors of one of the prestigious law reviews. The reviews, therefore, tend both to reflect prevailing intellectual standards through their processes

7. For a thorough study of the experience of minority women in hiring decisions, see Deborah J. Merritt and Barbara F. Reskin, "The Double Minority: Empirical Evidence of a Double Standard in Law School Hiring of Minority Women," *Southern California Law Review*, Vol. 65, No. 5 (July 1992), p. 2299.

for selecting editors, and to perpetuate the same standards through the professional elevation of those selected. Certainly the *Harvard Law Review* has been, in the main, intellectually conservative in makeup and in the scholarship it has published.

Uncharacteristically, however, the March 1992 issue of the *Review* carried a radical feminist article about the reinforcement in the law of oppressive conceptions of female identity. The article was titled "A Post-modern Feminist Manifesto," and the circumstances of its publication were unusual. Its author was Mary Joe Frug, a feminist legal scholar and professor at the New England School of Law who had been brutally murdered, stabbed to death, on a Cambridge street near her home in the spring of 1991. The article was an essay she had left unfinished at the time of her death.

Like other postmodernist scholars (whose thinking I will discuss in more detail in Chapter 9), Frug was concerned with the power of language to shape thought. Her article urged feminists to challenge legal language that carries unacknowledged meanings subordinating women. And it suggested that lobbying efforts to change laws against prostitution might constitute such a challenge. The argument was that because the lobbyists were themselves sex workers (her term), their efforts represented the use of a female voice that refuses to accept conventional definitions of what a woman is or should be. Frug took no stand on the specific demands of the sex workers but, rather, applauded their implicit questioning of legal concepts that impose certain sexual and maternal identities on women without seeming to do so.

It was this essay that the *Review*'s third-year student editors satirized. They titled their parody "He-Manifesto of Post-Mortem Legal Feminism," cited as its author "Mary Doe, Rigor-Mortis Professor of Law," and stated that it was "dictated from beyond the grave." The text of the parody depicts a sex-crazed, hypocritical, intellectually frivolous feminist with "no sense of humor," who, after death, seeks admission to heaven. At first rebuffed because she does not meet the high standards of the admissions committee, made up of deceased members of the Harvard Law School faculty, she succeeds when the committee abandons selectivity and announces, "Heaven should be open to everyone. White, Black, Male, Female, Short, Fat, Bald, Talented, Untalented." The writing throughout the piece is clumsy, the humor crude, and the attack the more brutal as it extends, explicitly, to Mary Joe Frug's husband, a professor at the Harvard Law School. If he had been present at the banquet, as he might well have been, he would have found a copy of the parody at his dinner place. To make the matter yet more ghoulish, the publication of the parody coincided with the first anniversary of Frug's murder.

The shocking cruelty of the supposed joke rocked the law school and much of the university as well. Faculty groups exchanged tense statements about the significance of the incident and how the law school should respond to it. Central to the anguished debate was the question whether the vilification of a murdered woman over a piece of feminist work represented a deeply misogynist attitude that was pervasive at the law school and condoned by its leadership. Fifteen law school professors signed a letter connecting the parody directly to an environment of "sexism and misogyny" and calling on the administration to act quickly on the recruitment and appointment of more women and members of minorities to the faculty. One of the fifteen, Elizabeth Bartholet, said unequivocally that the matter reflected "the white male nature of this institution" and the "arrogance and elitism" that the school fosters. Others saw the parody as simply tasteless and stupid and of no greater significance than that.[8]

I see the crudeness of the parody as attributable to the moral vacuity of the people who wrote and published it. But I also see the incident, as I have placed it here, as part of a long history of tension between traditional conceptions of law as emanating from reason alone, and challenges charging that whoever holds power in a society defines what reason is and what reason sees. It is a long history of tension between insiders and outsiders, between men and women, and the stakes are high. I see the ugly parody as reflective of fear on the part of traditional elites that new claims to power are gaining hold. It reflects uneasiness about new voices being heard, speakers not completely silenced by the standards that have in the past successfully defined them as not serious, as subjective and emotional. When the outsider voices invade the *Harvard Law Review*, it is clear that the old standards alone are not enough to invalidate the challenge. And those who claim priority in the prevailing system, the new generation of privileged men about to enter it and claim their rightful places, are moved to panicky shouting to put down the challengers.

And yet the challengers keep coming. Consider, for example, the story of the Asian-American student I mentioned earlier in connection with the nontraditional teaching of the black female visiting professor at Harvard. The student's story is one that demonstrates both the persuasive power of the prevailing norms and their silencing effect on someone who sees necessarily from a different angle of vision. But it demonstrates also

8. Boston *Globe*, April 21, 1992, pp. 1, 22.

the young woman's eventual questioning of the norms and her claiming of a different place from which to speak. She described her experience movingly in a paper she wrote for a law school course and in the group interview I did with the women students in 1990.

The woman in question had entered law school with some sophistication in issues of power and disadvantage, having worked in both government and public interest agencies concerned with race and sex discrimination. Warned by civil rights lawyers in these agencies, she had expected to find at Harvard a corporate-oriented environment impervious or even hostile to her political concerns. Finding instead a number of professors advocating various progressive causes, she assumed that Harvard was above the narrow interests she had anticipated, "that the warnings of my lawyer friends must have applied only to 'lesser' law schools." Thus reassured, she was wholly unprepared to understand the reaction she did have in her first year of "self-doubt . . . extreme alienation . . . and a deep sense of resignation." That is, she found that she was not responding to classroom discussions with the insight and excitement that seemed to move other students, and she assumed that the reason was her own intellectual inadequacy.

Because of her shaken confidence, she says, she didn't think of noting and analyzing the points at which she felt distressed or at a loss in the classroom, a procedure that she eventually learned would reveal patterns of difference between her assumptions and those of her professors—and most other students. Not seeing any pattern, she did not see that her difference in perspective came largely from her race and sex. Without that degree of self-knowledge, she could not articulate her differing viewpoints or even decide calmly *not* to articulate them if the moment seemed wrong. She was hurt when she received humiliating criticism from her criminal-law professor for objecting to his comparison between a battered wife who killed her abusive husband and the "preppy murderer" Robert Chambers, who strangled his date in New York City's Central Park. The cases were similar in that the accused people both claimed self-defense. But the young woman argued that the professor had not given attention to the differences in the cases and, particularly, to the physical and psychological circumstances of battered women. She was then taken aback when her professor's response was not to examine those particularities, but to criticize her "emotional, biased, and stereotypical 'female' stance."

In her contracts course, she felt a "recurring sense of discomfort and intellectual chaos" during discussions of contracts affected by duress, undue influence, and fraud, and only later realized that she was reacting out of her own knowledge of power imbalances that shape such contracts but that were no part of the class discussion. So great was her distress that she could not talk about it with others. "I didn't even talk about my feelings with my friends for fear of being seen, since I am a woman of color, as inherently less capable of 'cutting the mustard' than my white, male peers," she later wrote.

What she did for most of her first year was to try to think and perform in the approved fashion. "Much like a pigeon in a B. F. Skinner experiment, during the few times that I was able to muster a typical, mainstream legal argument based on 'due process' or 'institutional competence,' I received positive reinforcement"—acknowledgment by the professor that her idea was, indeed, in accord with a respected analysis by a certain expert or was one of the relevant factors in his own view of the issue. She notes that both the expert and the professor would almost always be white and male.

An incident near the end of the second semester of her first year broke through the confusion in which she had been working and allowed her to grasp the significance of her difference. In one class, her section had been shown a film portraying the dispute-resolution practices of an African tribe, and many students had laughed at what seemed like ridiculous tribal customs, a reaction that angered other students, who found it racist. Strong feeling spilled out of the classroom but was not addressed in class by any of the professors involved. Disturbed by the situation, the young woman herself initiated a series of meetings to discuss issues of racism in the law and helped to compile materials for them—thereby, for the first time, coming across legal scholarship on issues of difference.

"I cannot fully capture the full extent of my reaction to this discovery; it was akin to how most people have described a religious experience, or how a person born blind, through some miraculous medical procedure, becomes capable of seeing the world for the first time in her life." She then went on to examine in depth the literature of different voices—from feminists and from racial minorities. She discovered that a leading contributor on racial difference was Derrick Bell, whereupon she enrolled in Bell's courses and became a convinced advocate of the need for racial and sexual diversity on law faculties to convey and legitimize the fact of different perspectives.

Somewhere on her intellectual/emotional journey through Harvard, the young Asian-American formed the ambition to become a professor herself. "In spite of my criticism of the law school," she said when I talked with the students, "I have felt really alive and challenged here.

My dissatisfactions have filled me with the fire to do something about them. More so than ever, I want to be a law professor."

At this, another woman in the group, a *Law Review* editor already disenchanted with the legal mainstream, rolled her eyes and remarked, "That sounds like hell on earth!"

THESE ARE YOUNG WOMEN seeking voices that will give them equal standing with their male peers in the shaping of the law for their generation and for the future. The forces they are up against in the old tradition that discounts their differing points of view—forces including their own attachment to traditional ideals—are strong, if not hellish. To combat them at their strongest, in the crucible of law school debate, takes great courage. But the courage appears to be there.

3

FATHERS

THE SILENCING OF WOMEN in law school brakes their movement toward equal authority in the profession, in part, and subtly, by undermining the intensity of their connection to the law—the sense that it belongs to them and they to it. Another experience that can produce a certain inner turbulence that disrupts women's reach for authority is one so common that its importance is easy to overlook. It is the profound cultural and psychic drama played out over and over again between fathers and daughters—literal fathers and daughters, and the fathers of a powerful profession and the daughters, the young women, entering it.

The issue, the turbulence, has to do with the passing of power and authority from one generation to the next. The cultural model that has, classically, shaped this passage is the Oedipal struggle, the contest for power between fathers and sons. In literature and in life, this drama plays out continually—in the halls of Congress, the groves of academe, the law firm, the boardroom, the ballpark, and the average American home. The plot, as outlined by Sigmund Freud in *Moses and Monotheism*, requires that the son vie for supremacy with the father in a conflict inevitably marked by eruptions of anger, remorse, guilt, or even violence. But in spite of the anguish this struggle generates, power does pass, and fathers—like it or not—accept the legitimacy, the rightness, of their sons' claims.

But what of the daughter? Ancient cultures defined her not as the father's rightful successor but as his possession—in some societies virtually an article of exchange, a commodity to be bartered in marriage transactions. And well into modern times, her drama consisted of being won away from the father by another man, then to become *his* possession—her passage from one to the other marked by the father's "giving her away" in the marriage ceremony. In this century, daughters have created more public room for themselves, leaving home on their own, becoming educated, agitating for equal rights, and supporting themselves, possessing themselves. But nowhere in the myths, dramas, traditions, and histories feeding American culture has room been opened up, *as a matter of course*, for a daughter to claim and take over her father's authority. In the father's world of public power, there is no clear space for her.

One exception to this general rule, at least in recent times, has been the tradition of the surrogate son. The exception occurs when there are no sons to take a father's place, or when a son dies, or a living son is somehow unsuitable as a power holder. In such circumstances a daughter may move into the son's position and prepare herself for public life, often with the father's approbation. Famous examples include the suffragists Elizabeth Cady Stanton and the Grimké sisters, the psychiatrists Anna Freud and Helene Deutsch, and the politicians Indira Gandhi and Benazir Bhutto.

To fulfill her role in the fathers' world, however, the surrogate, like a biological son, must at some point become equal in authority to her father and ultimately displace him. This means that she is liable to engage in the traditional father/son contest for power and to suffer the anguish it usually brings. But that contest may also face her with nontraditional forms of trouble. In the case of the biological son, the father, backed by deep-rooted social sanction, must finally accept his son's ascendancy. In the case of a daughter/son, the father may not be able fully to relinquish his authority, fully to recognize hers. He may feel justified in retaining the upper hand, and she, unsupported by tradition, may feel unable to challenge him and to claim full and equal power.

And a surrogate son must deal also with the implications of her woman's body and the cultural systems that surround it. Will she marry and introduce a husband, the traditional father-displacing figure, into the picture? Will she have children and introduce conflicting claims to her mind and responsibility?

Finally, how does a surrogate son relate to other women? Does she, as a woman, identify with women as outsiders in the fathers' world or, as a son, identify with male insiders? If she claims power, can she use it on her own terms, on the basis of values and goals derived from her own experience, perhaps her experience as a mother as well as a professional? Or does her surrogacy require that she adopt her father's terms, his values, his worldview?

The problem implicit here is that the fathers' worldview has always held constraints for daughters. How could a daughter adopt a father's norms without, in some significant way, constraining herself? The early work of Freud and Josef Breuer proposed that symptoms of hysteria in women, notably an inability to speak, a loss of language—as in the famous cases of "Anna O." and "Dora"—had their source in patriarchal prohibitions against a woman's full use of her intellectual and creative powers. That is, a woman seeking independent space for herself could not find it without renouncing her father's world, which her love for him, along with a barrage of social sanctions, made virtually impossible. She could not speak without speaking against, verbally destroying, the world she knew.

At present, with the old extreme limits on women's freedom removed, the issues of constraint are not so blatant. But as the law school stories show, power to make the society's rules is still vested in men. And in many matters, differences persist between male and female views of what the rules should be. So the tension between women and the rule of the fathers is still there, and as the stories from both law school and the big firms reveal, the reaction of many women is still silence.

But when metaphorical father/daughter conflicts are tied into a daughter's personal relation to her own father, the issues they present become even more complicated, and even more significant as barriers to a woman's authority. It is these stories that are collected here. In some, the issue of silence remains important. Others tell of more acute symptoms of psychological distress, such as depression or the inability to eat. These are symptoms that feminist psychologists see as modern forms of what Freud and Breuer called hysteria—self-punishing, self-denying responses by women trying to enlarge their roles and entitlements in a society still following old rules and constraints.[1]

Several different patterns of father/daughter conflict emerge within the overall drama the stories outline. One is the pattern of the rebellious daughter, the young woman who is not confused about the differences between her father's power and her own, or between his values and hers. This is a daughter who opposes the prevailing social and political system

1. The contemporary literature on the psychology of women is large. To cite just a few sources: in general, Elaine Showalter, *The Female Malady: Women, Madness, and English Culture, 1830–1980* (New York: Penguin, 1987); on depression, Maggie Scarf, *Unfinished Business: Pressure Points in the Lives of Women* (Garden City, N.Y.: Doubleday, 1980); on eating disorders, Kim Chernin, *The Hungry Self: Women, Eating and Identity* (New York: Times Books, 1985). The nineteenth-century references are from Sigmund Freud and Josef Breuer, *Studies on Hysteria* (New York: Avon Books, 1966). A useful collection of essays is Lynda E. Boose and Betty S. Flowers, eds., *Daughters and Fathers* (Baltimore: Johns Hopkins University Press, 1989).

and seeks to change it precisely by rewriting patriarchal rules. And yet when her course places her in opposition to her own father, she may, in spite of her convictions, suffer internal division and confusion out of love for him and a desire to please.

In one such story, the daughter of a professional father describes a painful moment of decision that crystalized for her the conflict between her political rejection of her father's world and the place she necessarily occupies in it. The woman in question was in college in the late 1960s and early 1970s, and she spent nearly a decade afterward engaged in various forms of community organizing for social change before entering the Harvard Law School. And when she did, it was with great misgiving. She had, in fact, thought of going to a less prestigious school where the students were not headed, as at Harvard, for the nation's centers of corporate power. But she thought that a Harvard degree would lend weight to the political activities she intended to continue and, further, that at Harvard she would be able to see close up the corporate establishment she was fighting.

This inner division about attending Harvard was compounded when she was faced with a major decision while working on an antipoverty project during the summer after her first year in law school. She had already become deeply involved in the summer project when she learned that her first-year grades had put her near the top of her class and thus qualified her, without further competition, to join the *Harvard Law Review* as an editor.

The young woman was staggered by the news. An editorship on the *Harvard Law Review*. What should she do? If she joined the *Review*, she would have to leave her activist work and return to Cambridge. Even worse, the move would put her right at the heart of the legal establishment, inside the system her strongest political convictions opposed. But on the other hand, the professional credibility she would gain as a *Harvard Law Review* editor would help in the continuing political fight she sought to wage. Then, as she wrestled with this dilemma, she learned that her father was dying.

"The whole significance of the *Law Review* thing was really tied up with the relationship with my father," she recalls, the pain still evident in her eyes. "He had this perception that I had been sort of the prodigal daughter for years because I wasn't doing things that he could identify as bona fide achievement, and I think that the *Law Review* was sort of the first thing—I mean going back to law school I think was one thing that made him feel that I was back on track—but the *Law Review* was sort of the crowning thing in his mind. And this phone conversation that I had with him before he died, this conversation trying to figure out whether to join the *Law Review* or not . . . That whole thing became very charged and very mixed-up with my relationship with my father and the sort of ambivalence that I really did feel . . . which is really the same ambivalence about going to Harvard Law School, to sort of say what I had to say through their channels, being in communities that I felt uncomfortable with. . . . The whole *Law Review* thing became a very painful sort of playing out of that."

She did join the *Review*. But because the law codifies and protects the values of a social system this woman seeks passionately to change, she could not escape—and has not escaped in her later career—the question whether she can use the credibility of the law, and its promise of fairness, as a launching ground for radical challenges to the system. Can she stay within the fathers' institutions and challenge their very premises? Or must she go outside, in exile from the fathers' world, in order to work for change? She continues to struggle with the question whether it is possible to be a radical lawyer, a feminist lawyer, or whether these terms are hopelessly contradictory.

In contrast to this story of conflicted rebellion against the fathers, many women appear to enter the law in search of a father to embrace. In some cases, they seem to be seeking a father they never had; in others, a replacement for one who failed them, who did not provide the strength, rationality, clarity, or probity that the law promises. These women are likely to give their loyalty eagerly to the "good" patriarch represented by the law and to accept his terms as their own, only to suffer particular pain and confusion when the terms do not connect well to their own lives.

Recall the story of the woman who entered law school after her family was saved by the law from financial devastation that might have resulted from her father's culpability in an automobile accident. This woman also revered the law for protecting her mother during subsequent divorce proceedings. Once *in* the law, however, the daughter found it an intellectually and temperamentally alien place, and she left after only several years of practice in a big firm. "I had thought the law was prestigious, exciting, and dynamic," she says. "Well, it is prestigious, but exciting and dynamic it ain't. It is a grind. And I just thought, 'Well, what the hell am I doing here? I don't want to make partner, and I'm not enjoying myself. Why am I an associate?' " Still, she adds, she astonished herself as well as her friends by actually leaving a place she had trained hard for and that conferred automatic respect as well as a high salary. She left finally because, she says, "My heart wasn't in it anymore." It didn't mean what she thought it would mean.

Other daughters of unsatisfactory fathers have fared worse, finding in the law, not the solid fairness they expected, but betrayal by the gendered rules, the double standards discussed in Chapter 1, that push women to the professional margins. Sadder yet, some women, unwilling to give up their belief in the good father, end up blaming themselves for their own marginalization while remaining loyal to their vision of good law.

Then there are the daughters of lawyers or men of comparable professional standing who are happy to have their intelligent daughters follow the paternal example. These women are the classic surrogate sons, with all the advantages and disadvantages of that conflicted figure. Many, with powerful parental backing, travel along a path of considerable professional success. But while they are headed toward the top, they find themselves afflicted with a certain nervousness in relation to their fathers, perhaps a fear of losing paternal love by stepping outside its bounds combined with uncertainty about where the bounds are. Most of them are also afflicted with traumas produced by childbearing and other family issues for which the father's model provides no guide. And they are also ill-prepared by their father's love and backing for discriminatory treatment by other men who see them not as sons but as women.

Such is the story of a woman who is the daughter, granddaughter, and great-granddaughter of prominent lawyers, and who was herself "promoted to the status of son" when her older brother died as a child. She was the second oldest and highly verbal, and her father, she says, transferred his attention to her, applauding her success all the way through her schooling. However, she had also received all along the classic double message for women of her mid-sixties college generation: "Do well academically" and "Marry and raise a family." Her recollection is that she went to law school because she was not engaged to marry right out of college and she had to do something, and because a strong-minded woman friend whose lead she had followed throughout college was going to law school.

She was not sure what her father thought about her decision. He had not directed her toward the law, probably assuming that she would marry early, as most of her college classmates were doing. But early in her first law school year, he signaled his approval. "I received a package in the mail. My father is the kind of person who not only had never given me a physical gift in my life—always 'Take a check, take a check, buy yourself something'—but he had almost never sent me a handwritten letter, either. I mean, he communicated by Xeroxing pages from magazines with notes at the top saying 'Send to children.' . . . He wasn't into hands-on gift giving or communication of any kind. And in comes this bulky package from my father's office, and I open it up and it is a nicely framed thing with four pictures in it— my great-grandfather who was a federal judge, my grandfather who was a lawyer, my father, who was a lawyer, and then my high school picture. It was the most adorable thing I ever saw. I still have it. I just couldn't believe he'd gone to all that trouble. He had to go get all those photographs, he had to take them to the framer. . . . That said as loudly as anything could to me that he was pleased."

But her path into the profession was not going to be so straight as that of her forebears. In her first year at law school she was caught up in a round of feminist revelation and activity. "It's 1970," she explains. "*Ms.* magazine is coming out. I remember reading over the winter of 1970 *Sisterhood Is Powerful*, and [the friend who had led her to law school] got very interested in all these things and started taking me off to meetings of the Boston Women's Health Collective, and it was just an instant. The minute I heard about feminism I went, 'Oh boy, this explains a lot of things about my life! Here I'd been encouraged to be a high-achieving woman and I'd been encouraged to think of myself as just a spouse and of course there's been tension there and that doesn't make any sense!' And, you know, it all just kind of began to clarify."

With her friend and some like-minded law school rebels, men and women, she joined in establishing a small commune and set about challenging the system. She was part of the group that organized the first student-taught course at Harvard on women and the law.

But total transformation of consciousness and identity rarely occur all at once, and even this almost-instantly-radicalized young woman had her limits, which turned up first in a matter of style. "This was a period in my life when I wanted to come across as very tough," she says. "I had a shag hairdo, no makeup, no bra, and I wore great hiking boots and bell-bottoms. And I had ceased shaving my legs." But of the nonshaving she adds, "I wasn't able to go quite the distance with it. I bleached the hair that grew in. I think that was typical of how I handled things at this point. And I bleached it with a mixture of ammonia and peroxide and Ivory soap which I would apply in the bathroom of the commune, you know, so I'd be in there, bleaching my hairy legs."

At this point it would seem that in spite of some aesthetic ambivalence, she was on a collision course with her father's world. And, in fact, in the following year conflict erupted between the claims of long family tradition on the one hand and mounting feminist criticism of that tradition on the other. What happened was that the friend who had been leading the way ideologically had developed increasingly radical views on the disparity of power and interest between men and women—views implying serious conflict between the sexes—and she was pushing the storyteller here to adopt these views.

But this was further than the lawyer's daughter was willing to go. She had opted for a milder feminist critique that pictured both men and women as sadly and foolishly victimized by social rules that set them at odds. She talks about her grandparents, her grandmother hungering for love and support while her "salty, crotchety" grandfather went out to shoot ducks with other men or fished solitarily at dawn. Her grandmother suffered in her isolation, but her grandfather, she thought, was also unhappy, "shut away from women in his grumpy loneliness." And, she says emphatically, while young women were degraded by media messages teaching them that their value lay in sexual appeal to men, men were degraded by the same messages that targeted them as meal tickets.

The political significance of this position is that it does not call for united action on the part of women challenging male-dominated institutions throughout the society. It does not range the daughters against the fathers. Rather it calls for consciousness-raising that alerts both women and men to the social messages oppressing them and allows them as individuals to reject those messages and escape from the limits of sexist conventions in their own lives. It's an approach that—like the law—relies on reason, not raw power, to resolve conflict.

The political disputes between the two young women rasped at their friendship, and ultimately the more radical of the two, the leader—the older sister, in effect—insisted that her erstwhile follower leave both the Health Collective and the commune. This was a terrible blow to the lawyer's daughter, and in ideological and psychological turmoil she dropped out of law school, only to encounter her father's intense displeasure. He stopped supporting her. She went into psychotherapy, for the first and only time in her life, for help in dealing with this double rejection.

But while leaving the scene of political turbulence at law school, the young woman did not leave the precincts of the law. She took a job as a paralegal in New York, observed the daily, practical workings of the profession, and liked what she saw. She then returned to Harvard to finish her degree, although she remained acutely discomforted there by her suspension between the rampant sexism of the law school culture and the radicalism of her feminist friends. She could not locate herself happily in either space.

Once in law practice, however, she returned definitively to her father's world, counting on it to respond rationally to the disclosure that it had been preaching equality while treating its daughters unequally. Her own father's response to women's new claims to equal rights confirmed her sense that reason was the key to change.

"When I got home, right after law school, I remember having lunch with Daddy. They wouldn't let women go in the front door of [his club,] let alone be members. . . . I had to go in the side door, eat in the ladies' dining room, and I said, 'Daddy, this is absurd. How long is this going to go on?' And he said, 'Well, I'd give it ten years.' . . . Well, it was fifteen. And the fact that he actually underestimated that, he had actually swung around to being in the more liberal group . . . Now, he wasn't going to be the first one to propose a woman member . . . before he thought the club was ready. It wasn't a subject he was going to get out in front of. He was still a traditional male and wasn't going to do that, but he did at least see that it was absurd and knew that it wasn't going to last. . . . Still, he would have found women getting together to raise issues about change quite disconcerting. Like most of his generation, he was more of the type: 'Well, merit will out!' I remember he told me that if I got up every day and did the best I could, I would rise like cream. [She assumes her father's voice:] 'Sweetie, if you just get up every day and do the best you can every day of your life, you'll rise like cream!' "

While she now affectionately mocks her father's certainty that good work pays off every time, for everyone, male or female, she had adopted essentially this position herself, modified by the recognition that those who encounter discriminatory practices must identify them and call for their removal. But like her father, she finds women's political organization for change disconcerting, and she has not engaged in radical feminist protest in the twenty years or so she has been in law practice. And this in spite of the fact that she herself has had to struggle professionally, even with a considerable degree of family support behind her.

She was bumped off the partnership track in her first law firm by an antinepotism rule when she married another member of the firm. She then spent some years as a government prosecutor, tried out another law firm, then formed a small firm with other women, before becoming a partner in a major firm fifteen years out of law school. She acknowledges that in a profession that is tough for everyone, women have it harder than men.

"I've seen all these women that I know who quit. . . . We were the early classes, and so many of us don't practice anymore. . . . You have to work awfully hard in this career to be as good at it as you have to be in order to be satisfied. In order to get that level of quality, you just have to kill yourself. And in order to put those kinds of . . . not just hours, but the intensity of the hours, so it's not only just time you're putting in, you're just bleeding yourself into your work every day and therefore coming home depleted. In order to do that, you have to have an awful lot of things work for you at home, with your marriage, with your children, with your family, with your financial situation, with your health, with your energy level. You have to have a lot of things happen right for you . . . because it isn't set up so it's an easy, normal thing to do. . . . I know I don't maybe work very well as an example because I've had ungodly good fortune in so many areas."

But she has not altered her political stance. Her nonactivist feminism remains unchanged. Her main feminist activity, she says, is "just doing, just having the children, raising the children, working full-time, trying to be successful." She adds, "Trying to be successful is some kind of a statement at this point."

She also specifically affirms her faith in the legal system that the fathers, including her own male forebears, created. "Just being in the American justice system, playing a part in that system, whatever part, is very valuable," she declares, "because I think it's a marvelous system. I just think it works . . . and I think all of us who are in it are lucky to be in it."

So she has no quarrel with the law of the fathers. And yet, in spite of her approbation of the system, and in spite of her own "ungodly good fortune," there is dark language in her account of her life in the law: "You just have to kill yourself . . . you're just bleeding yourself into your work every day." Reason has not gone far enough. Perhaps she suspects that by itself, it cannot.

ANOTHER DAUGHTER of a successful lawyer/father speaks graphically about the unforeseen issues she encountered, and the pain she endured, trying to pattern her career directly on that of her father. A Harvard Law School graduate of the mid-seventies, now a partner in a large and renowned law firm, she speaks of identification with her father, feelings of guilt about her mother, the difficulty she has had expressing her femaleness in the midst of these pressures, and a certain ambivalence in her father's acceptance of her success. And the conflicts spill over into her relations with older male partners. She feels in herself as well as in them undefined barriers against her asserting a status equal to theirs. She sees her own reactions as stemming from a personal dread of competition with men, especially with older men.

As it was for Anna O. a century before, the battlefield for this woman's conflict seems to have been her body—she has suffered bouts of depression, severe weight loss, fertility problems. She is amazingly open and direct about these issues, while not seeming to be a person given to self-dramatization or display.

"I was always Daddy's girl," she says. She was the oldest of three, with a younger brother and sister. Her father always put achievement first, for himself and his children. He went to Harvard College and majored in classics, and so did she. He was Phi Beta Kappa. So was she. He went to the Harvard Law School, and so did she.

Her mother had started out on a political career track and followed it until she had her first child after marrying in her thirties. She was active in various citizens' organizations and also in electoral politics as a campaign manager. After her children were born, she switched to volunteer work in the city where her husband practiced.

Perhaps regretting her own loss of profession, the mother encouraged her children, her two daughters as well as her son, to plan for professional careers. She would tell her daughters particularly about women friends who were divorced and had been left helpless, with no training for work, and she made it clear that she didn't want her daughters to suffer that plight. She also told her children about the blight of anti-Semitism that might affect them. Her husband, who was Jewish, had been excluded, despite his brilliant academic record, from the most prestigious "white shoe" law firms, the old Ivy League, Protestant firms that formed the heart of the legal establishment. She, however, was not Jewish, and she hoped that her children might escape the prejudice that burdened their father.

With backing from both her parents, the elder daughter ended up in law school—which she hated. She got involved with Legal Aid, as her father had done as a law student, but she didn't like that, either. Then she took a step unprecedented in her father's career—apparently the first such move out of his pattern. She did something her mother might have

done in her political days: she joined—and soon ran—the Law School
Forum, an organization that brought outside speakers—usually renowned, usually engaged in public affairs—to the school.

During an election campaign, the Forum sponsored a candidates'
night, which was held in Sanders Theater, in Memorial Hall. The prep-
arations included a security check of the building to safeguard the candidates against assassins, and the woman recalls standing in the Memorial
Hall ladies' room with a security agent who showed her the window an
assassin's accomplice was most likely to use to enter the building—and
then made a pass at her. Later, she sat on the stage with the candidates
and stared through the lights into the audience, imagining an assassin out
there with a gun. (This is almost too neat, I remember thinking during
our interview. The first time she switches her identification from her father
to her mother, she is sexually harassed and imagines somebody is gunning
for her.)

She was back in line, though, when it came to applying for jobs.
She aimed for the top eastern firms and got the one she most wanted.
Thrilled, she called her father with the news, only to be met with a wholly
unexpected response. "He said, 'Well, you're relatively intelligent. You
went to the right schools. You're relatively attractive. You're not Jewish.
It's not so odd.' " He had always pushed her. She had done what he
wanted. And now he seemed ambivalent about her success. "His reaction
just flattened me," she says. She did not understand it. Perhaps he re-
sented momentarily her access to places denied to him. Or perhaps he
feared that although she had been admitted, she wouldn't be able to stay.

Two years later, her mother became seriously ill, and for a year the
firm allowed her a lot of time off to help out with the crises that arose.
Then, after her mother died, she went into a major depression. Her
feelings about her mother were unresolved. She was in a rut at work,
having fallen into odds and ends of uninteresting projects because she
was taking so much time off. She wanted to quit. She wanted to change
jobs. Instead, she got married, and her firm provided her with the change
she wanted by sending her to its Paris office—the first time it had sent a
woman to Europe. (During our conversation, she notes that women lawyers are now sent everywhere in the world, and she tells me of a woman
at her firm, just coming off maternity leave, who was reassigned to Tokyo,
and whose lawyer husband was then, obligingly, transferred to Tokyo by
his own firm on account of *her* need to move.)

Speaking again of her mother's death, she says that it can't be a
coincidence that within weeks of the death, both she and her father met

the people they would later marry—out of fear, she thinks, of being drawn too closely together by the strong emotional pull between them.

Once settled into work again, she had to face the issue of moving to partnership, or, rather, to deal with not having faced it. She had never said to herself that she wanted to be a partner, she tells me. She found that she had great trouble admitting to herself that she was actually competing with men. "If you're brought up to look up to men, it's hard to be equal or to aspire to be equal, and it's hard to supervise them." She found the role of associate fairly comfortable because looking up to the male partners was natural—for her and for them. "They like working with bright women," she says, "especially if you're presentable." In other words, the proto-daughter in a law firm occupies a familiar and comfortable role as long as she is a subordinate, but when she reaches the point where she must claim the authority of the fathers, she feels herself to be on shaky ground.

Nonetheless, she did become a partner, and this time her father was unambiguously delighted. "He was beaming," she says. But she was in for another bout of trouble. During her first year as a partner, she was tense the entire time and after a while went into another severe depression, this time centered on trying and repeatedly failing to have a child. At the worst of it, she couldn't eat and became dangerously thin. It was a bad time professionally, too, because her firm was not so supportive as it had been at the time of her mother's illness and death. She notes during our interview that people are not so tolerant of emotional problems as they are of physical illness. (But, I find myself wanting to respond, much of her trouble at this point *was* physical. It had to do with fertility. It may be that the firm was more naturally inclined to be sympathetic about disease than infertility.)

She had postponed the issue of pregnancy until after she made partner. Then, not becoming pregnant, she went through a long process of fertility testing and some corrective surgery, her biological clock ticking ominously all the while. Finally, she and her husband settled successfully on adoption. At the time of the interview, I met their lively daughter, then three years old.

But throughout it all, she had to face the terrible self-accusation that she would not have been so frantic, so pressed to come up with solutions to her fertility problems, had she tried to get pregnant earlier, had she not waited until she got her partnership. She also blamed herself for starting fertility testing at various times and then not following through because she was afraid of what she might learn. At times she blamed the delay on her mother's illness, at times on her firm and its expectations. But finally she blamed her ambition. She had put achievement first and had not faced the complications of living in a woman's body. Her father's script provided no directions for that. Nor did her mother's, not as long as she was tracking her father.

To complicate matters, in the early years of her partnership, she was not working well. With so much medical trouble, she couldn't work on an equal footing with her colleagues. So while her womanhood was not being expressed and satisfied in maternity, she was also not a fully functioning partner, and this failure weighed heavily on her spirit. Having come through this thoroughly bad time, she now urges young associates not to postpone children, and tries to convince them that putting career security before children is wrong.

With a child in the house and her work back on track—she is doing corporate finance now, taking phone calls concerning the acquisition of a Canadian company by a French corporation even as I interview her— the worst conflicts seem resolved. Yet some tensions with her father remain. She remarks that she now earns more money than he, a high earner, ever did. And although he is now retired and certainly pleased at her success, the money issue rankles. She tells me that she tries to convince him that it's all a matter of inflation, that in spite of her income she could not afford the kind of house he had provided for his family. In other words, she is assuring him that she has not exceeded his power. He is still father to a daughter, not to a son who has rightfully displaced him.

The other problem in a profession that routinely demands sixty-hour weeks is that she is constantly pinched for time. She has bought a portable fax machine, she says, so that she can stay away from the office nights and weekends and still be within reach. I ask whether it really helps, and she says, "It eases my guilt, if nothing else." She adds that her daughter is fascinated by the machine and that one day she let the child load paper into it. "There she was," she recalls, "lying on the floor of the living room feeding the machine, and she looked up and said, 'I'm faxing with you!' " The lawyer/mother looks as if she does not know whether to laugh or cry. She certainly knows that her own father was never in such a bind.

A WOMAN WHO GRADUATED from the Harvard Law School in the late seventies and became a partner in a large East Coast firm had not followed the footsteps of a lawyer/father but, rather, the insistence of an educator/father, a "God-fearing man," that his children obey the rules and do the right and respected thing. This meant, when they were students, getting good grades, going on to higher and higher levels of education, and taking the values and directions of revered educational institutions as their own. And the dutiful daughter followed this script. Graduating from college in the mid-seventies, she applied to law school, a step that bright women with high grades were then taking increasingly, and in due course she found herself at Harvard. "I thought that my worthiness was marked by what I could do that men typically did," she says now. "I couldn't do it in sports, but I could in school."

Once in law school, however, just following the beaten path began to give her trouble. Not so much in the first year. "The first-year courses have to do with people," she says. "Torts, criminal law. You start out with 'feminine' courses [she gestures the quotation marks]. People actions, flesh-and-blood morality questions like 'What is reasonable behavior?' " But things changed in the second year. "Then you proceed to securities regulation." She laughs—this is her present field of practice. "I liked the people courses. The others, the ones that taught you the rules of the game, were somewhat lost on me." She was enjoying a wonderful social life, getting to know Boston, dating law students, and making friends, and she also tried to study, but the courses presented issues remote from her interests. Then one day, in her second year, while trying to read a tax case, she couldn't get beyond a certain page. Her eyes kept moving over and over the same words, taking nothing in. She started to cry and just sat, sobbing uncontrollably.

This looked like the end of her venture into the law, an inner rebellion against assimilating and becoming the agent of "the rules of the game." But an intervention from another side of the fathers' world, the caring, healing side, kept her on course. She met and fell in love with a psychiatrist, and for the rest of her time in law school, she more or less lived at his house and socialized with his friends from the medical community. She now sees the affair as a means of having someone take care of her, and of escaping the full brunt of law school. I would say that she found a loving and nurturant father-substitute to protect her against the harsh patriarch of the law. In any case, she was able to stop crying and continue school with grades that put her in the respectable middle of her class.

She did not, however, resolve her massive confusion about why she was in law school at all. She simply plodded on, following the rules, which prescribed that she seek jobs at distinguished big firms. And she got one. "My first job was horrific. It was a worse shock than law school. The professors were relatively informal, some very informal, but [the firm] was extremely formal. . . . I felt I was encountering a new sort of male, a very overtly aggressive lawyer type. The men I knew [the psychiatrists] were sensitive, attuned to feminism. They respected me. They were good men. And the professors, they didn't prepare me for this type of lawyer, as most of them haven't been out of the academic world themselves. Negotiating an acquisition is different from the kind of legal thinking professors teach. . . . That was the first job I'd had in my life, and it hit me between the eyes. I had no clue how to function. I got no help from the women above me. There were a few. I'm not sure what I expected them to do. . . . The men there [the young lawyers, her peers] had the code down. They knew what to wear. The women entering the firm would come in in print dresses. Some carried backpacks. Not to thumb their noses, they just didn't know. But the males understood that you need a Cross pen and a London Harness briefcase. The men entering conducted themselves better. They wouldn't be emotive. They wouldn't express fear, ramble on when they didn't understand something, expose their ignorance. Instead, they stonewalled. I think they get through a lot of tense situations just by—it's an area in which men often have a lot of problems in their personal lives. They can't express themselves. But I felt the women I saw try and cope with [the firm] were much too expressive, causing their superiors to lose confidence. You're supposed to close your door and do a lot of quick reading to find out what in the hell you're talking about. You don't expose what you don't know. Or even if you know it, you don't show your tensions about it. You keep it all under wraps."

She chose to work in real estate law because she thought it was tangible. "You can see a building," she says. But, in fact, she did not see buildings, or even clients. As the firm represented huge developers, the work consisted mainly of organizing financial transactions that were as abstracted from the final product as any other form of finance, and the young associate was acutely miserable. "I went on a very severe diet," she recalls. "I didn't need to lose weight. I think that was a response of wanting to get away. I would shrink my body so I don't have to walk into the hall." (Here is another eating disorder appearing as a response to conflict with the fathers.) She quit in less than a year, without having lined up another job. She adds that all but one of the women who entered the firm when she did quit within a few years.

For a short while, the plot of this story shifts direction. The young woman who tried to shrink herself into invisibility and then, sensibly, quit her plum of a job tried next to enter the art world, not as a lawyer but in more creative production positions. She believed—as many people do, however mistakenly—that a law degree is a badge of general competence and that a Harvard Law degree makes you welcome anywhere. "I thought I was bestowing a gift on the art world by sacrificing income to go into it, and I was surprised that they weren't interested," she says, a bit wistfully.

So she returned to law, this time finding work in a small but growing firm where she devoted herself to learning the nuts and bolts of corporate law under the tutelage of a mentor. "I've always done this, found a male mentor," she says. "My cello teacher, the psychiatrist, my father. I've usually gone out with men ten years older than I am, or more. I idolized my mentor and romanticized him. It wasn't sexual. In fact, while I was working so hard on becoming a better lawyer, I wasn't dating at all."

It was here, she says, that she "developed toughness." But not at first. She was criticized for being too easy on subordinates. She tolerated a secretary she shared who gave priority to the male lawyers' work. She stayed late to clean up the mistakes of young lawyers who left at a normal hour to go home to families. "My [annual] reviews [by supervising partners] said I'd better learn to kick ass. It so horrified me." But she learned, and she did it.

But then she was betrayed, or so she thought, by the men she had been learning from and serving with devotion. She had been told in a review that she would be made partner the following year, but when the time came, she was told that the partnership would be deferred one more year. Outwardly accepting—she thanked the partner who told her the news—she was raging inside. "You bastards, you fucking bastards, you lied!" she screamed silently. Then she quit.

Next, she joined a big firm on the understanding that a partnership decision would be made in two years, which it was. She was made an income partner (the lower level of a two-tier partnership system), essentially a high-salaried permanent associate. Before the partnership, she had once again attached herself to a surrogate father, not romantically, but personally as well as professionally. He and his wife and daughters more or less made her a member of their family. She says that the relationship worked better, however, when she was an associate, taking a great deal of responsibility but still acting as second in command. Once she was a partner, she and her senior colleague were in some way competitors, and they both felt a subtle strain. For example, she says, "Last spring, on the phone with a male friend, I was talking about the celebration of a closing my mentor and I had worked on, and it seemed that he [the mentor] was the star, the head of the team, although he had been away through most of the critical work, and I had really done it. I cried on the phone for about an hour telling my friend about it."

Here, I think, is another father/daughter issue. She may have been crying about lack of recognition, lack of equality, but she may also have been crying out of the confusion of unresolved daughterhood. That is, if she does gain full equality with her mentor/father, she will no longer *have* a mentor/father. She will no longer be a daughter. And this issue takes literal form when she has to decide whether to try to move from income partnership to equity partnership—to a share in the ownership and management of the firm. On this point, she is full of ambivalence. Does she want to join the fathers as an equal, as one of them, or not?

But the question of partnership is not the only issue that troubles her. On many levels, she seems uneasy about the extent to which the fathers' rules and mores have taken over her life. "I think even now I don't look enough at what I'm doing professionally. I want to stuff that all under the couch. I want to think of my job as what I do during the day, and my after-work life—friends, books, activities—as what I really do, what really counts."

But one issue that apparently will not stay under the couch—it keeps recurring throughout the interview—is the issue of toughness. After talking about her first job in the big, formal firm where she tried to achieve invisibility through dieting, she announces wryly, "I'm now a partner in a big firm, and I have altered my behavior greatly. I'm now a dragon lady. Isn't that great!"

What is a dragon lady? "I hold people below me accountable," she explains. "I make them meet deadlines. I think I laugh freely on the job. But I also chew them out. I act like I mean it. I had a falling-out with a woman senior to me in the firm because of what she calls my sharp tongue. . . . It worries me. I wonder if I've crossed some line of what is appropriate. I think about it. I'd like to be a bit softer. I think I'm still trying to find my stride, and I'm not comfortable."

She is also uncertain about what, if anything, she as a woman owes to younger women trying to make their way in the still male-dominated profession. "I got no help from women above me. . . . I never looked for help from my mother, nor from female professors, and now I'm not particularly helpful to young women. I'm not proud of that. I don't know what I feel should happen just because you're the same gender." She adds that she faced a dilemma recently when two men in the firm asked her to speak to a young woman associate about the inappropriateness of wearing long hair falling to her waist. She refused, although she, too, thought the young woman should cut her hair. "You get attention in the wrong ways if you come into a corporate law environment with hair swinging below your waist," she says. But still, she snapped at the men, "You chickens. If it bugs you, deal with it." Then she had second thoughts—whatever inadequacies the men have, she figured, the young woman is going to suffer for them, so perhaps she *should* pass on the message, although she also thought the young woman would probably resent her for doing so. In any case, she did nothing—except recognize her own uncertainty.

What should she have done? She herself has conformed in order to succeed in an environment that demands conformity. Why not act, in effect, as a mother and let the young woman know what the rules are? Does she keep silent because she does not like the rules and does not want to be their enforcer? Does she inwardly cheer the young woman, whose extravagant hair proclaims that its wearer is most definitely not a man? Or is she, more simply, resisting the role of mother? From the beginning, and in spite of considerable doubts, she has been running along a track defined by the fathers, and when she stumbles on questions that are outside the scope of the fathers' rules, she is perplexed. She has no guide.

Not surprisingly, the perplexity reaches truly serious proportions on the issue of lawyer/mothers. "I'm not particularly proud of saying this, but I've been very disappointed at how the women in my firm who have had children have conducted themselves afterward. Most of them have ended up quitting or been fired. And I don't know. I don't have children. My best friend has two children. She was a lawyer with me at [the small firm]. I know her very, very well, and I think there's something I can't appreciate. There must be this bond, an incredible bond. I just find the personalities who used to function, do good work, they're not into it anymore. No. They may go half-time, but even the half they're there, they're not there. So I feel—it makes me wince—Why would a male institution take chances on women? A lot's been invested in training lawyers. Maybe it's all envy on my part. I'm personally confused whether I want children. I'm certain that a lot of my personal turmoil is connected to my reaction to this, but I don't know what they expect. I mean, how do they want to be treated? It's not motherhood and apple pie—suddenly you've had a child, we should drop our requirements because you've had a child. I think the woman should leave and find something that fits better. It's harsh. But I haven't gone through it."

This is deep ambivalence. She has said she wants marriage. Here she says she may want children, she's not sure. But when talking about women with children, she uses the second and third persons—"you," "they." The first person, "we," refers to those who run what she calls "a male institution." She identifies herself with the male institution, not with the women with children, though she acknowledges that she might see things differently if she had children, if she experienced the "incredible bond" she imagines mothers feel for a child. Her choices and allegiances are clear: Stay in the fathers' world and follow its rules, the rules that define, as she said earlier, a worthy person. But still, at every turn she describes a lack of fit between the rules and the person that she is, or may be, or would like to be.

Looking at this whole picture from the point of view of her father, whose rules defined the direction she would take in the first place, the woman says, "He probably would be happier today if I were the best secretary in the world or taught high school band. I think he's horrified at what he created, because it's caused me to eclipse his own life and he doesn't understand what I do." As for her own summing up, she says, "So here I am, a partner. I guess I feel like the old Peggy Lee song 'Is That All There Is?' I don't know what I expected."

ANOTHER LATE-1970S GRADUATE sped along the fast track as a classic surrogate son, never questioning the terms on which she was operating until they virtually blew up in her face. And although this woman was married and had children, it was not the conflict between work and family that caused the break. It was the unwillingness of the fathers to relinquish authority to a woman.

For a fast-track runner, this woman started slowly, unsure of her direction. She loved the exactitude of math and physics and thought of engineering as a career, but in college she felt out of her league in those subjects. She was drawn to history by a charismatic professor and wavered between graduate school in history and the practicality of law school. Twice she applied to the Harvard Law School and was accepted but did not go, pursuing instead various graduate school options in Europe. Then she applied a third time, was accepted, and decided to give it a try, much to the relief of her father, a businessman pushing for practicality. "I always say he wanted to hand out cigars when I finally went," she says. Her remark is casual, but the reference to cigars nonetheless suggests a moment of birth—her rebirth as a son.

Throughout childhood, she was apparently in competition with her brother for her parents' interest and approval, and she notes that they never reacted so strongly to her consistent high grades in school as to her brother's occasional A's. Being admitted to the Harvard Law School and finally deciding to go was clearly a winning move in that competition.

She does not, however, picture herself as setting off into the law in a state of internal conflict about her role as a daughter/son. Not many young women do, but this woman in particular has always been profoundly apolitical. In college during the American invasion of Cambodia during the Vietnam War, when other students were staging vehement protest strikes she stayed in the library and wrote her papers. In law school, she had no consciousness of sexism, no interest in women's issues. And she had no interest whatever in the philosophical side of law. She liked the rigorous system of legal analysis and subjects, like tax, that allowed her to work with numbers, but the subject matter of most law was unsatisfying. "The rules make no sense," she says now. "I mean, you can't derive them just from your mind, like math. They come from historical things, or what some court said. It's not logical, in my opinion, the way that finance is, or math is, or physics is."

In a big firm after law school, she gravitated to corporate law because of its financial component, but she quickly became bored and impatient with the passivity of her role. "The business lawyer is just a guy who papers the deal after the businesspeople have done all the interesting things. They've cut the deal, figured it out, done the numbers, then the corporate lawyers, they show up at the printers and write the papers." So, four years out of law school, and by then married to a young lawyer, she left the law to get into the deal-making herself, in an investment banking company.

Here she was in her element, although it was, even more than big-firm law practice, a male element. She had begun by this point to recognize some forms of sexism. She had seen, in several situations, women subordinates doing the basic work of an office while the men in authority got the credit. But—apolitical as always—she did not imagine that such a dynamic need apply to her. And, for a while, it did not.

In the financial heyday of the eighties, she and two older men in her company formed a team that sought and organized investment opportunities in the start-ups, mergers, and acquisitions of companies throughout their region. She was the "computer queen," adept at "doing the numbers," and was greatly prized by her associates. "These two guys, maybe they represented father figures. I loved working with them. The three of us traveled around. We did deals together. It was very exciting. We made a lot of money for the company. We had a great time. We had a fun time. I liked the work. And it stayed that way for a number of years."

But getting up at 4:00 a.m. for a 6:30 flight to another city for a day's financial adventure became difficult after the birth of her first child and impossible after the birth of the second, and she was happy to accept a promotion to become the administrative head of the regional division at which she worked. In this position she described herself as "the mother of the office," keeping tabs on everyone, applauding good work, and supplying emotional support as well as business guidance to the staff.

What happened then, she says, is that her two buddies were promoted to the company's national headquarters, one as the chief financial officer. This was a move she couldn't have made because of her family. But that wasn't the worst of it. A new chief of the regional office had to be appointed, and she was a likely candidate. But before they left, the two rising stars orchestrated the appointment of another longtime associate of theirs—a man. This, she thinks, was their consolation prize to an old friend who was not rising with them, someone whose ego would be bruised in a way they did not imagine hers would be. "I was supposed to help him do it, see. I was supposed to do all the work, and he was going to, you know, have the name." What she had observed in offices elsewhere had finally happened to her.

She was deeply shocked and hurt. She had been with the company for eight years and had seen herself as a member of the club. If her two associates were "father figures," she was a surrogate son, moving up behind them, ready to step into their shoes. But they saw her not as a son but, she tells me, as a mother, a woman, a natural subordinate and a supporter of others. She was smart, a key player, but not one of them. She did not, however, accept subordination. To everyone's astonishment, she quit. "As soon as my bonus check cleared, I was out of there."

These events occurred less than a year before my interview with her, and she was still angry when we talked. But continuing to leave politics out, she stopped short of casting the story as a betrayal by her friends, let alone by a male power structure generally. She says she would not have enjoyed the top administrative job for long anyway, with her two valued associates gone. And she focuses her anger and hurt on a minor grievance: when she left, no one gave her a party. "A secretary leaves that place, a big party. They did not do jack squat for me when I left. Because I was their mother. People don't celebrate when their mother

abandons them. That's the way I've come up with it." That is, she has
focused on problems inherent in her role as mother, not in her far more
conflicted role as surrogate son.

But she does go on to talk about the reaction to all this by her real
father, and all the classic conflicts between fathers and surrogate sons are
present in the recounting. "This is a telling story," she begins. "I made
a lot of money as an investment banker, and I was proud of that and I
wanted to tell my parents. I think, in fact, for the last few years I made
more money than my father did, which was a benchmark in a way."
(Earlier she had remarked, "If I were to get divorced tomorrow, for
example, I'd have plenty on my own to go and do whatever I wanted,
with or without alimony and child support, so I would be an independent
person.") She felt uncomfortable, however, announcing to her father
directly that she had exceeded his earning power. "I worked it into the
conversation. I didn't come right out and say, 'I'm real proud of how
much money I've made, here's how much I made.' I sort of worked it
around, but they knew I was telling them that." And her father had
trouble acknowledging her superior prowess. "I discussed this with my
mother since. I got, to my way of thinking, like no reaction. It was like
when I was a kid and came home with straight A's and they'd go, 'Oh,
nice report card.' And my brother, who was a C student, would get one
A and they'd go, 'Oh, Joey got an A in English!' But I told them how
much money I made, a lot of money, and I got no reaction. And I said
this to my mother a few weeks ago. I said, 'You know, you didn't have
a reaction. Dad, he didn't pat me on the back or do anything.' And she
said, 'That's incredible that you would say that, because in fact what he
did was go around to every single person we know in this town and tell
them how much money you made.' And I said, 'Well, he may be tellin'
all them, but I didn't hear it. He didn't tell *me*.' "

Apparently, her father can take pride in her accomplishment when
he can present it as an extension of himself—"My daughter earned *x*
number of dollars last year!" But to acknowledge this to her would be to
affirm between the two of them her greater power, a reversal of the proper
hierarchy, and this is difficult. In fact, she says, he seems happy that she
quit. "I mean, I always thought my father would love it if I became a
lawyer, and the thing he is really happiest about, apparently—I never
really discussed it with him, which I need to do and I know I do—is
since I've quit and become, in his point of view, a full-time mom. He
thinks that's just dandy. An interesting twist on the whole deal. Here I
try to please him for all these years makin' a lot of money and bein' an

investment banker and this, that, and the other, and in fact, he was happiest when I quit."

That is, she thought that if she acted like a son and did well at it, her father would be pleased—and he was, for a while—but he, like her father/colleagues, saw her most basically as a woman/mother and approved of her most strongly in that role. And she is baffled because she felt she was all these things in one, and is astonished that the men she has trusted do not share that vision, astonished that their world has little space for such a combination.

So what is she doing off the fast track? Not being a full-time mom. When we spoke, she had kept her baby-sitter who ferried the children back and forth to school. She was spending some time on financial consulting, but more on tennis, yoga, piano playing, reading, re-knitting old friendships with women—and running. She was training to run marathons. She was not up to speed yet, but she had her eye on Boston. Beyond that, she had no idea. She had run right off the beaten track and would have to invent a new course for herself.

THE CAREER OF A BLACK WOMAN GRADUATE of the early seventies followed a very different course from those of the women in the preceding stories. This woman was the first in her family to go to college, let alone on to postgraduate study, so she was on her own in entering the territory of the law. And her initial welcome from the fathers of the profession was anything but protective. As a new associate in a big law firm, she was called a nigger by a client during a softball game, and when she yelled back angrily, she was reprimanded by a partner. The clients pay the bills, he told her, and can call young lawyers anything they want.

Disenchanted with big-firm practice, she left and went into government, where she prospered under the guardianship of two unlikely protectors. Both were older white men in institutions whose white male power structures were staunchly resistant to the pressures of affirmative action. Both men, however, recognized the young woman's capabilities and gave her room to grow.

The first of her protectors was the chief counsel of the regulatory agency she joined after leaving the law firm. "The chief counsel was this gruff Irishman," she recalls, "who underneath it all was this little teddy bear, but everybody was scared to death of him. I wasn't. He came into my office out of nowhere. The agency at that time was under pressure to expand and offer more opportunities to women and to minorities because, being the regulator of Wall Street, it was a reflection of Wall Street, and it was—yes! you've got it!—another white boys' club! [This is what she had previously called the Harvard Law School of her student days, and her law firm.] Anyway, it was reported back through the grapevine that the chief counsel, who always resisted being told what to do about anything, had been irate about being forced into affirmative action, and he reportedly said that he wasn't going to cooperate. Then he shows up at my doorway with no warning, saying, there's an opening in his office, did I want it? Well, I was suspicious! That office had historically been all male and also predominantly Irish. There had never been any women or minority lawyers. The person who left, whose job was open, was the only Jewish male in the office—his position was known as "the Jewish chair"—and everybody assumed that his successor would likewise be a Jewish male who had 'paid his dues' within the division. I did not fit the ethnic or gender profile for the job, and had only been with the agency four months, and I thought maybe I was being set up! So I listened and asked questions and said, 'I'll think about it.' And the chief counsel was floored because everybody and his mother had been in his office lobbying for the job and he showed up in my office and I said, 'I'll think about it and I'll let you know.' And all the other lawyers in the division came down and beat up on me—'What's wrong with you! Are you crazy?' Well anyway, I thought about it and decided to gamble on it and try it."

At first she was subject to a certain amount of hostility and resistance, both from lawyers within the agency and from people in the business community receiving regulatory opinions from her office. But the chief counsel repeatedly backed her up. "He would stand up for you if you were right on the law . . . and it was the first time in my professional life that anybody had ever stood up for me. And I was amazed! I really loved that job."

After four years, the chief counsel recommended her for a job on the staff of a congressional committee that oversees business regulation, and urged her to take it on the grounds that she had outgrown her job with him. She was reluctant to leave, but he insisted. He said that she was sticking around because it was comfortable, a nice little nest, but that it was time to leave the nest, especially as he was himself retiring the next year. (This is a reversal of the usual scenario of the surrogate son. Far from feeling reluctance to pass power on to a daughter, this surrogate father wanted to be sure that his protégée took the next step up while he still had power to help her.)

So she moved, only to find that her new boss, the congressman who chaired the committee, was another older, gruff, white "man's man," a hunter whose office was filled with stuffed animal heads—a man who had never been known to work with professional women, let alone black women. And, at first, her relations with him were a bit stiff. Then, at one point, he remarked, teasingly, that she sometimes seemed terrified of him, apparently expecting her to deny it. But she replied sternly, "Of course I am. You have a horrible reputation. And look at all those dead things on the wall! What do you expect?" That remark, she says, broke the ice between them, and after that they had no trouble talking to each other. "I wasn't afraid of him anymore," she adds.

What the young woman seems to have done here is to invoke the frightening old traditions of the father's complete ownership of the daughter, his control of her that justified all manner of punishment and even death. She has acknowledged the fact of the father's power, but also, by insulting her boss humorously, she has asserted her own power to resist it. And the result is that she opened up space for herself in the father's world. She will work within his rules but not completely under his control. That is, she has asserted a degree of self-possession that permits the adult working relation that ensued. And she tells me that the congressman, for his part, has taken the same line as her previous boss in making it clear to the people she deals with that her authority is to be respected.

But after ten years on the job, she has found that the professional space she occupies, while wide and full of challenge, owing to the congressman's trust in her, contains certain discomforts. For one thing, the pace of work is relentless and grueling. "People have no idea the hours that the members put in," she says, "especially at the end of the term when everything has to come to closure, and in addition we have meetings with constituents, meetings with lobbyists, hearings, markups, House-Senate conferences, late-night sessions. . . . It's horrible. I don't know how these guys do it."

Then, she must always keep in mind that she is working for an elected official accountable to a constituency and that she must be careful to reflect his positions accurately and not to jeopardize his standing with the electorate. As she says, "Everything I do, I don't just have to worry about how it will reflect on me as a person, I have to worry about how it will reflect on [the chairman] and how it will reflect on the committee, so that my personal and professional life have to be scrubbed through that process."

Under these pressures, and in spite of a solid political and personal rapport with her boss, she came to feel an increasing need to find a space of her own, to act completely on her own, expressing her own ideas without the need to fit them into another agenda. Her solution was to run, in the mid-eighties, as a petition candidate for the Harvard University Board of Overseers on a slate opposing the university-approved candidates. The purpose of the opposition was to change Harvard's policy on several controversial issues, notably its retention of investments in South Africa. And, most unusually, a number of the nonapproved candidates won— including the woman in question here.

On the day that she won, her boss was momentarily thrown off-balance when she missed a major committee hearing by going off to Cambridge for the announcement of the new board members at the Harvard commencement. She knew he was somewhat irked, she says, because "the next day, in his office, he teased me before a reporter about working for the committee 'part-time.' " But actually, she adds, he was deeply pleased. He has taken to calling her "Madam Overseer" at all times, and bragging about her to others, "like this really proud father."

And what did she do on her own when she stepped out of the shadow of the father? She engaged in fights on the Board of Overseers on issues of sex and race and class. In each case, she joined the protests of outsiders excluded from the privileges of "the white boys' club." The race issue was the demand for divestment of Harvard's South African holdings. The sex issue was the denial of tenure at the law school to Professor Claire Dalton, a "femcrit" whose work was criticized as lacking scholarly weight. The class issue was the unionization of Harvard's clerical and technical staff.

And how did it feel to step out from behind the chairman to become a political actor in her own right? She says it wasn't easy, especially at first, when the conflicts between the board members elected by petition and the Harvard administration were frequent and sharp. In fact, she wrote me in a letter sometime after our interview, several personal attacks from faculty members over the Dalton case, and a "vicious verbal attack" by the outgoing board president, were so upsetting that she almost resigned. "But then," she added, "I got angry—very, very angry—and I stayed."

Still later she informed me that the initial conflicts and divisions among the members of the Board of Overseers had largely subsided, and that in an "ultimate irony" she had been chosen to chair the board's standing committee on financial policy, whose investment practices she had challenged in her election five years before.

This was a remarkable achievement. An outsider on all three counts

of race, sex, and class, she had successfully claimed a place in one of the
fathers' innermost sanctums. And further, in that place she did not have
to worry about speaking for her congressman. Having been elected in her
own right, she could say whatever she wanted, in her own voice.

THE WOMEN in these stories are very different from each other. They
have different relations with their fathers, different attitudes toward the
law, different conceptions of the issues women face as claimants to authority in the law. The stories do not provide a neat model—negative or
positive—of father/daughter relations in the legal profession. We cannot
draw clear lessons from them about what fathers and daughters should
do to avoid the problems the daughters in these stories have encountered.
Rather, the difficult moral of the stories is that daughters entering the
fathers' world cannot avoid trouble with its structures and systems.

Fathers and daughters in the law are deeply entangled in their love,
in their decency, in old social rules that give fathers primacy and that
urge good daughters to become mothers, and in new rules that declare
daughters equal to sons. And entangled in the relations of daughters with
both literal and figurative fathers is the trust of daughters in the law as a
good father, the guarantor of fairness. To imagine that the law, as we
have inherited it, cannot make good on that promise, cannot accord equal
space to daughters and sons, is extraordinarily difficult. What the stories
above record is simply the fact of these psychic and cultural tangles operating in places where they often go unrecognized.

4

BODIES

FOR WOMEN LAWYERS to share equally in the country's rule-making, they must talk, negotiate, argue, plead, savor wins, suffer losses, and endure boredom on equal terms with male colleagues. They must engage with men in the particular intimacy, the emotional intensity, of high-pressured work, which can place its participants in close physical proximity for hours, even days, at a time. But they must do this within a cultural context that heavily sexualizes male-female contact and that imposes on it rules that severely undercut the equal standing of women.

One obvious complication for women working in conditions of professional intimacy is the likelihood of sexual involvements ranging from office flirtations to full-blown love affairs. Such liaisons may be happy and harmless, or they may be confusing, disturbing, and ultimately debilitating. The problem for women, in any case, is that they generally have less professional power than their male colleagues and are therefore less able to protect themselves if romances end badly. And with that danger always present, women tend to assume the responsibility for monitoring relationships, managing them, keeping them restrained if that seems wise, discouraging advances without hurting feelings if that seems politic. This is the stuff of endless drama, in life, in novels, in films, in sitcoms, in soaps.

But professional intimacy also generates, between men and women, forms of sexual tension and conflict that have little to do with love—and a lot to do with inequality. Among the most important is a deep resistance on the part of men to accepting women as powerful, rational thinkers, because the culture identifies women not with minds but with bodies. And the more beautiful the woman, the more sensuous her body, the less likely she is to be credited with a mind. Hence the "blonde" jokes emphasizing the stupidity of women who, like Marilyn Monroe, conform to

the highest popular standards of beauty. But this is just to state the
extreme. The culture teaches men to look at women generally and see
bodies first.

One of the first women to enter the Harvard Law School in the early
fifties provides a remarkable description, forty years later, of what it felt
like to appear in male eyes as someone other than herself. She remembers
the hush that would fall when a woman reached the top of the wide ramp
that, instead of stairs, brought hordes of students up to the main dining
hall in the newly completed concrete-and-glass Harkness Commons. "You
were aware of all eyes on you, and my response was to walk a little
straighter, with more dignity, like an actress on the stage. It was a performance, rather than being natural. You were almost a little divided.
Because a part of you was reacting so that you would show them that you
were even better than you felt inside possibly, and the other part was
standing there staring and saying, 'I don't believe this. I can't believe it.
I know who I am. I'm not some kind of crazy, unique, eccentric, figure,'
and you were being made into this person that you really weren't. . . .
They made it into a stage for you, because suddenly it would be like the
theater, where the people were talking and then the curtain went up and
there was the total silence and then I was an actor on the stage. And I
really had a sense of bewilderment that I, this little kid from the Bronx,
could cause that response."

The person being described here was an intelligent, well-educated,
energetic, idealistic, ambitious young woman. This is how she understood
herself, a whole, integrated person, a student, like the hundreds of other
law school students in all their variety. But at the top of the ramp in the
law school dining hall, she became "almost a little divided." She became
two people—the person she thought she was and the person her male
peers saw. And this sudden perception bewildered her, threw her off
balance, then forced her to pull herself together, to put on a performance,
to be "this person that you really weren't."

But what was the effect of her performance? And what would be
the measure of success—to convince her fellow students that she was
someone she really wasn't, given the fact that they would not accept the
person she really was? The point is that the power to determine who this
woman was, as a law student, and later as a lawyer, was with the men.
It was their view of her that would control, or at least powerfully influence,
her identity as a lawyer. And this male power to impose identities on
women professionals remains in force—not totally controlling, but still
there—a generation later.

At issue here, as in the earlier discussion of law school training, is the conception of reason and its centrality in the law. We have seen that the explicit purpose of law school professors as they reveal the mysteries of "thinking like a lawyer" is to enthrone reason as the basis for legal judgment—to vanquish emotion with discipline, intuition with logic, assumptions with facts, and personal preferences with objectivity. We have also seen that women are under chronic suspicion as dealers in emotion, intuition, unfounded assumptions, and subjective preferences. What does not generally become explicit in Socratic dialogues is the connection of this suspicion to women's bodies, to the identification of women with their bodies.

This is not to say that the long history of Western thought that produced the tradition of Anglo-American law did not raise the issue of the relation of body to mind. Aristotle worked out in great detail the theory that separated *polis* and *oikos*, public and private, virtue and necessity, mind and body—and the capacities and functions of men and women. The necessity of caring for the physical needs of bodies—raising and preparing food, building shelters, disposing of waste, making and cleaning clothes, giving birth, tending children, nursing the sick, burying the dead—were lower functions carried out in the *oikos*, the household, by slaves and women. Contemplation of what is right and good and the making of rules for the community were higher functions carried out in the *polis*, the public space, by men. And the separation of the two, the functions of the body and the functions of the mind, was necessary to liberate the capacity for reason from the dulling effect, the distractions and confusions, of physical work and needs.

This concept of the body as a threat to the mind, and in Judeo-Christian thought as a threat to purity of spirit, rooted itself deeply in Western culture and lived on into modern times.[1] Throughout the ages, men charged with the functions of highest reason have undergone special disciplines to curb the unruly body, to keep its appetites and desires from undermining the careful operations of reason. One mark of this effort is the ritual clothing adopted by the thinking professions in past centuries and continued, at least ceremonially, today. Its main feature is some form of body-enveloping, desexualizing fullness or asceticism. Think of aca-

---

1. This is a necessarily quick sketch of a complicated tradition. For depth and varied interpretations, see Susan Moller Okin, *Women in Western Political Thought* (Princeton: Princeton University Press, 1979); Jean Bethke Elshtain, *Public Man, Private Woman* (Princeton: Princeton University Press, 1981); and Wendy Brown, *Manhood and Politics* (Totowa, N.J.: Rowman and Littlefield, 1988).

demics' robes, priests' robes, judges' robes, and scientists' long white coats. The standard business suit, with its straight lines and sober colors, covering a shirt buttoned to the neck and held firmly closed with a tie, performs the same function. The body of the wearer is negated or under control. The mind is free to follow the dictates of reason alone.

But the body-subduing, mind-releasing traditions of the reasoning professions do not apply to women in the same way they do to men. The problem—again, going back to Aristotle—is the ancient association of women with bodies. The social assignment of women to the realm of necessity, the physical care of bodily needs, reflected strongly held assumptions about the nature of women themselves. Women *are* their bodies. Women cannot separate mind and body to achieve the same heights of reason that men can—or that elite men can. Women are buffeted by hormones, by their menstrual cycles, by pregnancy, by menopause. They are sensual by nature, animal-like, unpredictable.

In the face of this tradition, women entering the reasoning professions have tended to do so under the claim that they *can* accomplish the same detachment that men can, that they *can* subdue their bodies and release their minds to purely rational functions. And they, too, sought— and were taught—to signal their detachment through clothing.

As one woman says of her entry into a major law firm, "When I started, in the early eighties, it was still, you know, the man's suit with the little bow tie and the white shirt. . . . The secretaries wore dresses, or skirts and blouses, or even slacks—more colorful, more comfortable, clothes. Some would wear sexier clothes. One of the partners was talking with me once about a fairly senior woman associate who dressed somewhat unconventionally—like a leftover sixties person would dress if she had sort of cleaned up her act but not a hundred percent, more flowing things, and rougher, natural weaves, tribal-looking jewelry. So the partner said something like it was better not to dress that way, or you couldn't go wrong if you dressed less like this person and more like a lawyer. This partner liked the woman but thought other partners may not. The sense I got was that you were sort of suspect by being a woman, and to the extent that you dressed wildly, you just raised more questions, but to the extent that you kind of blended in, in all kinds of ways, that was not so upsetting to them or less of a red flag."

But where the sober dress code was taken for granted as right for men, it raised perpetual questions for women. If they departed from the code and revealed the shape of their bodies, they were suspect as non-serious. If they did not, if they successfully hid their breasts and hips and legs, if they subdued their hair and fingernails, they were also suspect as nonfeminine, not themselves. This was an issue in *Price Waterhouse v. Hopkins*, the case of a woman who sued the accounting firm Price Waterhouse for sex discrimination when she was denied a partnership. One of the reasons given for her rejection, in spite of her highly successful practice, was that her clothing and general personal style were unfeminine and off-putting. After years of litigation, she won her suit in 1991 on the grounds that the firm had used discriminatory sex stereotypes in the partnership decision.

From observing women of the 1990s in all kinds of legal work around the country, I've sensed that the prim uniform that prevailed into the eighties is no longer strictly required. It is still in evidence, but so are a variety of other styles. I've seen a pink linen suit with matching pink heels in Atlanta, a bright red dress with a deep flounce at the knee in Boston, corduroy jeans on an associate in a big firm in Los Angeles, a purple-and-green silk suit in New York, many silk dresses, and a lot of fairly ordinary skirts and blouses as well. There seems to be some leeway for color and exuberance of style.

But the insignia of sexuality still give rise to tension. Hair, for example. Recall the woman (in Chapter 3) whose male partners asked her to warn a younger female associate about the inappropriateness of her waist-length hair. Not only was the hair itself too powerful a symbol of carnality to be contained within an ethic of rationality, but the very subject of hair was too hot for the men to handle, and the tension surrounding mind/body issues too confusing for the older woman to sort out with clarity. She ended up doing nothing and feeling guilty about it.

African-American women have particular problems desexualizing their hair because tight curly black hair has an extravagance to it that cannot be concealed unless it is clipped short, close to the head—and then it appears to be tough, defiant. One black woman who joined a big firm right out of law school says that the partner she worked for always criticized her short hair. "It signified rebellion to him. It was unfeminine. It was black, it was stark, instead of being demure and feminine, as he perceived it." And she startled clients, too. "I would walk in and I'd be the only woman, the only young person, black, with short hair. All of these older, silver-haired men. They'd look, and you could see the look of surprise and shock on their faces when I'd walk into the room." And yet long hair, in a bushy Afro, would no doubt have startled them even more. She did not stay long at the firm and eventually left the law entirely for the business side of the entertainment industry—an environment, if anything, tougher and more competitive than the law, but culturally freer.

More recently, an issue for black women in professional roles has been whether or not to wear their hair in beaded braids—a style that is neat and controlled but still bespeaks a lushness, a lavishness, an exoticism, that celebrates both blackness and female sexuality rather than underplaying them. Paulette Caldwell, professor of law at New York University, has said that it took her several years after being tenured before she felt free enough to braid her hair—and that on the way to tenure she so tortured her hair to keep it subdued that she ended up with bald spots.[2]

I heard another hair story from a young white associate who had just received her annual review and been told that she played with her hair too much. When I met her, her hair was shoulder-length, hanging unrestrained from a side part so that it fell forward across her face as she moved her head. And as it fell, she twiddled and twisted it back, continually. She had also been told that some people thought that her clothing was too feminine, that it gave the impression to colleagues and clients who did not know her personally that she was not serious. The dress I saw was enveloping—it was high-necked, long-sleeved, and full-skirted —but the silhouette was soft and loose. Its contours did not contain the body in the straight lines that suits impose. Like her soft, slipping hair, her body's curves, draped in pliable fabric, were not under control. Therefore, the signal being sent was, Body, not mind; sensual, not serious.

The issues raised by the female body in traditionally male spaces have a particular pointedness for women judges. Women engaged in any kind of lawyering must operate through the strictures of reasoned analysis, but judges are under an especially demanding charge. They are supposed to subdue in themselves any personal attitudes toward the parties before them, any biases or preferences, which is one reason that they cloak their individuality, symbolically, in voluminous robes. But again, the identity of a woman, and the suspicion that attaches to that identity, is hard to obliterate. One interviewee, a federal district court judge, muses on the issue, not reaching clear conclusions, just trying to locate what she feels is an oddity in her role:

"I think there's a whole sexuality issue that nobody ever talks about.

2. Remarks on a panel called "Boss/Threads—Appearance on the Job," at the Critical Legal Studies Conference on Policy in the Nineties, April 10–12, 1992, Boston and Cambridge, Massachusetts. More extensive remarks can be found in Paulette Caldwell, "A Hair Piece: Perspectives in the Intersection of Race and Gender," *Duke Law Journal*, Vol. 1991, No. 2 (April 1991), p. 365.

I think that when you become a judge—and I don't think this is true of men—that you just get neutered, and it takes a long time to even figure out that that's what's happening and then a longer time to come to terms with it. And I don't know what answer there is for it. I'm not sure there is one. You have to become a sexless figure because I think the judges who retain a strong sense of their own sexuality, at least one or two on my bench, women, are subject to a great deal of criticism, none of which, of course, is in those terms, none of it. It's about 'Oh, her hair is too'— I don't know, whatever—'and her earrings are too long, and her skirts are too tight,' but I think it is a very complex, difficult issue how you wear your sexuality when you become a judge."

But the issue of appropriate covering for the female body in court extends beyond judges, as a minor incident recalled by one interviewee suggests. A partner in a small civil rights firm, where casual dress was more the rule than in the corporate world, she got an unexpected call one morning to go to court right away. "I happened to be dressed appropriately," she recalls, "not in jeans, as I sometimes am when I expect to spend the day in the library. And I was all set to go when a young associate—male—said to me, 'Hadn't you better button your blouse?' It was out of the blue! My blouse wasn't unbuttoned unusually low. And this was not a conservative guy. But he thought one more button was necessary for court. I started wondering if my authority was being undermined by one button."

Other evidence suggests that the courthouse is a site of particular tension over female sexuality. Many state court systems, in the late eighties, published extensive self-studies of gender bias operating in the courts, including the subjection of women lawyers to sexually charged attention from male judges, lawyers, and court officials. The 1989 Massachusetts Gender Bias Study, for example, reported that 64 percent of the women lawyers surveyed had observed male lawyers, in court, making remarks or jokes that demean women, 43 percent had heard inappropriate comments of a sexual or suggestive nature, and virtually everyone had heard remarks about the clothing or physical appearance of women lawyers, and the use of endearments such as "sweetheart" or "honey" directed at them.

Sexual remarks of any kind made by an opposing (male) counsel may well be consciously intended to undercut the authority and effectiveness of a woman lawyer. But it is clear from the gender-bias reports that much of the sexist behavior noted in them is unconscious, as very low percentages of men report observing what 40 or 50 or 60 percent of women say they have seen or experienced. The unconscious behavior—in part, at least—is the culture speaking, and saying that women's identity is sexual, not intellectual. And such behavior is particularly intense in courthouses because it is there, in the place of solemn judgment, that the strong tradition of supposedly disembodied reason in the law is especially concentrated, especially sensitive to the alarms set off by a woman's body.

Always under suspicion, their intellectual authority perenially threatened by ancient beliefs about their sexuality, professional women live with constant pressure to deny the significance of their bodies. But at the same time, they are subject to a second powerful cultural force that insists on their primary identification with their bodies, not their minds. And that is the ancient imperative that women's bodies be available to men.

Under the old order of sexual rules—marriage rules privileging a husband's will, social rules prescribing a double standard for nonmarital sex, rape laws favoring the accused, prostitution laws targeting prostitutes but not their customers—the operating principle was the rightness, the naturalness, of the availability to men of women's bodies. Different rules applied to the different relations—marriage, prostitution, and so forth—but the common denominator was availability.

I remember, for example, sitting in the state district court in Lowell, Massachusetts, as a reporter for the Lowell *Sun* in the summer of 1957, listening to a wife's charges of assault and battery against her husband. The charges included pushing and punching, but also forced sexual intercourse as a result of which the woman had become pregnant with the couple's sixth or seventh child. "She should have brought him in years ago," one of my fellow reporters muttered. I had been listening fairly idly to the assault charges, as the *Sun* did not report domestic cases, but forced sex was something different. The woman plaintiff was tall and thin, her face drained of color, her voice barely audible. Her body bowed forward slightly, like a parenthesis, when she stood. She seemed deeply exhausted. I was a college student on a summer job, a history major heading toward law school. I knew nothing about marriage to a violent man or about unwanted pregnancies, but I could see that this woman was suffering and thought that she should be granted whatever relief she was asking. But her husband's attorney argued that forced intercourse in marriage is not battery, it is simply part of marriage. I was puzzled. I had never thought about this question before. And, it soon appeared, neither had the judge. He seemed genuinely taken aback. He asked the lawyers some questions in an exploratory kind of way, then said he would reserve judgment about that issue.

I don't know what happened next. I was assigned to another beat and then went off to law school, where I don't recall ever hearing spousal rape discussed, or even named as such. Maybe it was mentioned, but not so that I noticed. In any case, it was the furthest thing from my mind that that woman's experience of forced sex in marriage could have any relation at all to the experience of women working in the legal profession. And it was a very long time before I grasped that it did.

The connection is the endemic practice, in law offices as in other workplaces, of sexual harassment—meaning unwelcome, as opposed to mutually desired, sexual attention and activity. Like sexual demands on an unwilling wife, sexual harassment of women by male co-workers expresses the ancient rule that women *should* be sexually available to men. And at the same time, it reminds the professional woman especially that while she appears in the workplace as the supposed equal of her male colleagues, she is not really an equal. It tells her that although she is gaining some economic independence, or even some rule-making authority, she is still subject to an old order in which she is ultimately subordinate to men, ultimately and naturally defined by her body as a male possession.

In recent years, as women have claimed greater and greater authority for themselves, sexual harassment and other, more violent assertions of male control of women have become more common. And yet, until October 1991, when Anita Hill told the Senate Judiciary Committee and the entire country her story of harassment as a young government lawyer by Clarence Thomas—whose nomination to the Supreme Court the committee was reviewing—harassment was, at once, the most common and least discussed difficulty women faced in dealings with men at work. In a 1989 survey of nine hundred women lawyers, 60 percent reported being sexually harassed in some way by colleagues, but few of them had raised the issue in the form of a complaint.[3] Few firms or legal departments had policies, formal or informal, on sexual harassment. It was an issue that was common and ignored, common and denied. Anita Hill herself, after all, had maintained a ten-year silence about the harassment she described in the Senate hearings. And then, when she made her charges public,

---

3. "Curbing Sexual Harassment in the Legal World," *New York Times*, November 9, 1990, p. B5. The survey was conducted by *The National Law Journal* and the West Publishing Company.

they hit the country like a bombshell, as if the issue, the idea, the very concept of harassment, had come from nowhere. How was it pronounced—*har*assment or ha*rass*ment? And what was it? The media scrambled widely to find explanations, as they do when an astronomer announces the discovery of ancient light waves or a president has an exotic illness.

In fact, when Hill's experience of harassment began in the early 1980s, the law of sexual harassment was already quite specifically defined. But outside the circle of feminist activists and lawyers who had contributed to its development in the preceding decade, it was an area of law that was virtually unknown. And this negative fact—that the law of sexual harassment, like the act of harassment, was a kind of open secret—signals deep conflicts surrounding the subject. Under the new rules of equality between men and women, sexual harassment in the workplace must be prohibited because it undermines women's equal place. And federal law, by 1981, did prohibit it. But under the old cultural rules by which women are subordinate, sexual beings, sexual advances to women workers by male colleagues simply express the natural relation between the sexes and should be condoned unless they involve physical force. And as a matter of informal social practice, such behavior has generally been condoned. That is, the formal law of sexual harassment protecting equality remained unknown because older, deeper social law protecting inequality took precedence.

The very genesis of the federal law against sexual harassment reflected the ambivalence behind it. Its foundation is the Civil Rights Act of 1964, which, in its Title VII, makes it unlawful for an employer to discriminate with respect to hiring, firing, compensation, or other terms of employment on the grounds of "race, color, religion, sex, or national origin." The point of the law was to protect and promote equality in the society by ensuring equality of opportunity in the workplace. But the overwhelming purpose of the law was to protect against race discrimination. Sex got into it at all only as a kind of joke. The original bill, focused on race, was amended to include sex at the initiative of a southern opponent of the legislation who hoped, thereby, to trivialize and thus defeat it.[4]

Then, when the Civil Rights Act was passed, that part of the law

4. For more on this quirk of political fate, see Carl M. Brauer, "Women Activists, Southern Conservatives, and the Prohibition of Sex Discrimination in Title VII of the 1964 Civil Rights Act," *Journal of Southern History*, Vol. 49, No. 1 (February 1983), pp. 37–56.

applying to sex discrimination was simply not taken seriously, even by the agency responsible for administering it: the Equal Employment Opportunity Commission (EEOC)—the agency that Clarence Thomas would later head in the Reagan administration. In part, the EEOC focused its first efforts on race discrimination because that was the clear purpose of the 1964 law and the clear purpose of the civil rights movement that had put the issue of employment discrimination on the national agenda in the first place. But to some extent, the lack of official response to sex discrimination reflected the lack of interest in the issue, or resistance to it, on the part of reformers at the time.

This split sensibility is perfectly captured in the story of a young white woman who graduated from the Harvard Law School in 1967 and went straight into a legal-aid training program sponsored by the Office of Economic Opportunity (OEO), one of Lyndon Johnson's "Great Society" agencies aimed at fostering social change at the community level. The legal-aid program was a magnet for activist and radical lawyers, and the young woman found herself caught up in intense discussions on the cutting edge of social thinking in that turbulent period.

Everything was being challenged, she recalls, including marriage and all the conventional roles for women, but there were limits to the questioning. "I had been emboldened by a lot of the women that I had met there," she reflects twenty-odd years later, "although they frightened me at the same time, because all this was very new. But I remember asking a black male speaker from a government agency—he was talking about Title VII and his basic thrust was racial discrimination—but I said, 'But what about a woman who has been discriminated against?' And there was laughter from many of the men. But he responded to me that discrimination against women should be treated the same way as racial discrimination, and they stopped laughing because this was coming from a black man. But I was kind of shocked. Because here I had thought everyone was probably more radical than I was, and yet there was this laughter when it came to sex discrimination."

In fact, it was the scoffing and laughter of male reformers over precisely this issue—the prohibition of sex as well as race discrimination under Title VII—that ushered in the first organizational phase of the present feminist movement. The National Organization for Women (NOW) was formed in 1966 by a group of women's-rights proponents who had hoped that women's equality could be advanced by getting new laws, such as Title VII, on the books, but who began to see that laws without active enforcement changed nothing. They also saw that active enforcement was going to require political pressure. And so they organized, and turned their attention immediately to the EEOC. What they wanted the EEOC to do was to write regulations or guidelines specifying the actions the agency would regard as sex discrimination, and then to bring proceedings against employers violating the guidelines.

By the late sixties, pressures from women's groups had moved the EEOC in this direction and against resistance that came not just from uncomprehending or unsympathetic men but also from black women who saw white women pressing claims that threatened to displace crucially needed attention to racial inequities. If black women were discriminated against by black men, to complain about it would breach the solidarity of a community under racial siege—a predicament, as I noted earlier, that was to surface painfully for Anita Hill.

Nonetheless, by the early seventies federal agencies dealing with discrimination—in addition to the EEOC, the Department of Labor, and the Office of Civil Rights, which had responsibility for discrimination in education (and which Clarence Thomas headed before moving to the EEOC)—had unequivocally included sex as well as race on their agendas. The connection between equality in employment opportunity and equality for women had been firmly made. And it was on this base that the laws against sexual harassment were constructed.

I will trace the development of sexual-harassment law in some detail in Chapter 8, where I examine the strategies of activist lawyers seeking social change. I would note here only that it was a saga of feminist advocacy working brilliantly to identify sexual harassment as a serious social problem for women, to translate the problem into available legal principles, and to advance the principles in the courts and in government agencies to the point that new law providing remedies for the problem was defined.

The upshot of this effort, the new law on sexual harassment, consisted of two main points. The first, developed in court cases in the mid-seventies, was the basic definition of sexual harassment as a form of sex discrimination prohibited by Title VII. This was a crucial first step—to give a name to unwanted sexual advances and demands in the workplace and to declare such behavior an illegal denial of equality. The second point, established in EEOC regulations promulgated in 1980, was an elaborated definition of harassment. Highly specific guidelines defined harassment first as sexual demands that carried expressed or implied threats of retaliation—such as demotion or firing—if the demands were refused. But they extended also to any "unwelcome" sexual conduct that has "the purpose or effect of unreasonably interfering with an individual's work performance or creating an intimidating, hostile, or offensive working environment."[5]

The EEOC regulations followed a survey that had produced hard data on the extent of sexual harassment within the federal government itself. Conducted by the United States Merit Systems Protection Board, the survey had found harassing behavior, especially in the form of demands on women by a boss or other superior, to be widespread and frequently repeated but also rarely reported. Most victims said that they had not talked about the experience with anyone, in part because they did not think that anything effective could be done about it, especially when the perpetrator was someone in authority. As a response to these findings, the regulations were designed to bring the issue into the open, and to provide clear procedures for lodging complaints with the EEOC or other designated agencies. And most important, they clearly defined *any* unwelcome sexual conduct, whether or not it carried threats of retaliation, to be harassment and thus illegal. Finally and clearly, the regulations recognized that women could not achieve equality in the workplace if they were subject to the old sexual rules.

But governmental enforcement of its own regulations depends on political will, and the political will of the federal government concerning the regulation of the workplace changed abruptly with the presidential election of 1980. The regulations on sexual harassment were the last gasp on the subject by the Carter administration, renowned for its concern about race and sex discrimination. The Reagan administration, coming to power in 1981, had a different agenda. The government was not to be the agent of social change, not the primary promoter and protector of equality. The social and economic configuration of the country was to be a matter of private negotiation, of markets, and of personal efforts and decisions.

To carry out this deregulatory mission in the arena of civil and economic rights, the new administration tapped a young black lawyer who had made a reputation promoting the philosophy of private routes to equality—Clarence Thomas. As head of the Office of Civil Rights in the Department of Education, Thomas was responsible for the enforcement of Title IX of the Civil Rights Act, which prohibited race and sex discrimination in educational institutions. Then, as head of the EEOC, he was the enforcer of Title VII, which by the time he took office included

---

5. 29 Code of Federal Regulations 1604.11(a) 1980.

the highly specific guidelines on sexual harassment. Or rather, he was charged with carrying out a policy of de-emphasizing governmental remedies to inequality in education and employment. So, before the country had a chance to hear about the new guidelines on sexual harassment and to grasp their challenge to old habits, the guidelines effectively disappeared from view. And they remained virtually invisible to the public in spite of a 1986 Supreme Court decision (*Meritor Savings Bank v. Vinson*) specifically approving them, unanimously, as a correct interpretation of sex discrimination under Title VII.

But if the law against sexual harassment was kept under wraps by the Reagan administration, the issue of harassment did not disappear. Rather, it remained in the state of tension that had been reached by 1980. Increasing numbers of women claimed equality in the workplace, their claims backed by antidiscrimination law, while many men continued to engage in equality-denying harassment, their behavior backed by ancient cultural permission. Conflict between old and new rules was constant, if usually undiscussed. And an eruption of trouble out of this tension was inevitable.

But who could have imagined that the trouble would arise out of harassing conduct by the head of the very office that had written the law against it—and that the issue would confront him just as he was about to become one of the supreme law-keepers of the land? Anita Hill, in bringing her charges of sexual harassment against Clarence Thomas in this context, seems to have enacted an almost mythic accusatory role.

Hill was a young black woman who had moved swiftly from a poor farming background in rural Oklahoma to the Yale Law School, and from there, in fairly short order, to Thomas's staff in the Office of Civil Rights and, subsequently, with him, to the EEOC. In both offices, Hill later testified—graphically and repeatedly, for hours at a time, as each Judiciary Committee member combed through her story—Thomas subjected her to explicit and unwelcome sexual talk and requests for dates, which she refused. He recounted scenes from pornographic films he had watched, described his own sexual performance and prowess, and, at one point, picked up a Coke can as they worked in his office and asked, "Who has put pubic hair on my Coke?" Nothing in Hill's testimony suggested that Thomas had touched her sexually, let alone used physical force in his pursuit. He simply conveyed verbally, through crude sexual imagery, his desire for her. And he did so repeatedly, against her protestations. Thomas's behavior upset her deeply, Hill told the senators, but she was so embarrassed by it, and also so concerned about keeping jobs that meant a great deal to her, that she did not report the incidents to any official and did not talk about them, except to a few close friends.

Thomas vehemently denied the story from beginning to end. Not a scrap of it was true, he maintained in the hearings, and the only reason Hill could be bringing it forward was to prevent him, as a black man, from achieving high office. It was "a high-tech lynching," he said, conjuring up images of black men hanged from tree branches in the Old South if they defied the rules and the power of whites. But as the prototypical lyncher was a white male, not a black female like Hill, Thomas's use of the image was confused, or implied that Hill was being manipulated by others.

The drama hit the nation like a meteor from out of the blue. It riveted public attention for days. Television networks turned over hours of time to it. The running testimonies of Hill and Thomas and the witnesses who corroborated their respective stories filled the newspapers, along with side stories analyzing sexual harassment and gathering public opinion about it. And the topic dominated conversations everywhere. On a trip to New York in the midst of the hearings, I shared a cab uptown from Pennsylvania Station with a stranger, only to become embroiled within several blocks in an argument about the issues. We agreed that Hill was telling the truth but disagreed about whether the issue of harassment was important enough to cause such trouble for a public figure and such divisiveness in the country. My cabmate worried that respect for the Supreme Court would be undermined. I argued that it should be undermined if it wasn't deserved. The only person I recall speaking with at the time who did not talk about the hearings had, just at that point, landed in the hospital with a broken hip. She had more immediate trouble to worry about. But the women gathered around the bed of her hospital roommate covered the issues at length. Hill was lying, they concluded. My dentist, it turned out, agreed with them, vociferously. An argument that began civilly enough when I arrived at his office picked up steam by the end of the appointment, and he was exasperated. "If I wanted to romance a woman, I wouldn't tell her dirty stories!" he exclaimed as we faced off by the receptionist's desk. "It wasn't about romance. It was about power," I snapped. "I agree," the receptionist said quietly.

But the public reaction differed markedly from the responses to Hill and Thomas from the senators on the Judiciary Committee. The citizenry was intensely caught up in the need to form an opinion about *who* was right and wrong, and *what* was right and wrong, while the senators were frantically preoccupied with ensuring or blocking Thomas's appointment to the Supreme Court. Lost in the confusion was the law against sexual harassment and its significance, its relation to women's equality, to women's real power and authority in the society.

As the Judiciary Committee structured the debate, it focused almost wholly on Hill's veracity. The Republican senators, in defense of Clarence Thomas, poured out all manner of accusations against her. She was lying. She was crazy. She was delusional. She had been in love with Thomas and provoked his advances. She had been in love with Thomas and spurned by him and was taking belated revenge. She was the willing tool of Thomas's political enemies. She was the dupe of Thomas's political enemies. She was a publicity seeker who wanted to cash in on the notoriety she was causing by selling her story to the media. And they hinted at worse. Republican senator Alan Simpson of Wyoming gestured toward his jacket pockets and said he had piles of information coming in about the true character of Anita Hill, although he revealed nothing specific.

The attacks were a perfect practical demonstration of everything that had ever been said about the fate of harassment victims who speak out. But the Democrats who opposed Thomas's appointment and therefore sought to defend Hill's credibility clearly had no idea how to do it. They flailed about as helplessly as the public, trying to find firm ground to stand on. They tried, feebly, to counter the specific Republican charges by allowing Hill to deny them. Was she a woman scorned? No. Did she intend to write a book about the scandal? No. They elicited the full details of stories from the friends in whom Hill had confided when the harassment occurred. They laid down minutely worked-out lawyerly grounds for doubting the plausibility of witnesses for Thomas.

But they did not use the Merit Systems Protection Board's report that demonstrated with great specificity how common sexual harassment was and how typical and therefore plausible Hill's story was. She was harassed by a superior. The incidents were repeated. She tried to ignore them. She told no one about them except friends. She was gravely distressed by them. The authors of the report could have testified to the complete plausibility of this account, but the Democrats did not dwell on the endemic nature of harassment. Thus they allowed the impression to stand that Hill was describing a freakish event and left her vulnerable to the Republican charges that she was the freak.

Even more serious and inexcusable on the part of Hill's supposed defenders, lawyers all, was their failure to make clear what the law against sexual harassment was. They simply did not emphasize, as the basis of their inquiry, the court decisions establishing that sexual harassment *is* sex discrimination. And they ignored completely the affirmation by the Supreme Court that the EEOC had correctly defined harassment to include precisely what Hill was talking about—unwelcome verbal conduct of a sexual nature that creates an offensive working environment. And because they did not place the weight of the Supreme Court behind the gravity of Hill's charges, they left her with a greater burden of doubt than she might otherwise have had to carry. That is, Hill faced doubt not only about her credibility—was she telling the truth?—but about the seriousness of her charges, even if they were true.

In bringing her charges to the committee, Hill was, in effect, arguing that sexual harassment is a highly serious matter, that it causes serious harm, and that anyone who has engaged in it should be considered unsuitable for positions requiring careful, balanced judgment about women's issues in the law. She was, in other words, asking the country to bury the ancient conventions that made harassment seem nonserious, a peccadillo at worst.

And this, finally, even in the public mind, was the basic question. As fascinating as the personal confrontation between Hill and Thomas was, the real grip this drama had on the public imagination was its subterranean connection to the lives of men and women everywhere. What is sexual harassment? What is the matter with it? Is it serious? Can you do it without knowing it? Isn't it something dreamed up by man-hating feminists? Aren't men supposed to take the initiative in sexual relations? Aren't they supposed to be in charge generally? Aren't women supposed to like sexual attention, be flattered by it? Do men really not understand the difference between sexual attention and sexual aggression? Aren't men sometimes harassed by women? What about lesbians and gays—don't they harass one another? What are the rules? Where is the rule book?

Of course, the Senate Judiciary Committee was not responsible for answering all these questions, but they were responsible for assessing and conveying to the general public the seriousness of the matter before them. The Republicans, by focusing on the question of truth-telling, and by demeaning Hill, succeeded in diminishing by implication the seriousness of the harm she described. If Clarence Thomas did what Hill said he did, they kept saying, and if she didn't like it, why didn't she complain at the time? Or leave? And their repeated conclusion was that since she didn't do either, Thomas could not have engaged in the heinous behavior she was describing. Or if he did, she didn't mind.

Implied here are the old rules pure and simple. A male employer's aggressive assertion of sexual interest in a female employee was something to be expected. If the woman involved did not want these attentions, it was up to her to discourage them, or put up with them, or report them —or leave. Nowhere in this scenario is there any serious condemnation of harassment as a phenomenon or any authentic examination of its effects on women subjected to it. And nowhere is there any real concern expressed for one possible result of the imagined sequence—the driving of a woman out of her job.

But the Democrats, while mouthing platitudes condemning harassment, did no better than Hill's attackers in defining its actual harm— how it works and how it connects to the larger issue of equality. They did make a feeble effort to seek reasons, in testimony from Hill's friends, for her failure to bring a complaint against Thomas at the time the harassment took place. As a young lawyer just starting out, the committee learned, Anita Hill wanted to keep her job. She did not want to be labeled a troublemaker. She wanted to stay on the right side of an influential public figure. However, the practical reasons for Hill's reactions do not explain the full extent of the injuries caused by harassment, and it is this deeper harm that the committee did not explore and thus take seriously.

Hill testified to the acute emotional distress she suffered at the times Thomas made his advances, distress that she believes contributed to a stomach ailment that put her, eventually, in the hospital. The significance of Hill's testimony on this point is that it describes a common reaction to the experience of harassment and that it relates directly to the common reluctance of women to speak about the experience. I have heard similar stories of emotional anguish and silence from a number of interviewees. Women who would talk to an interviewer with incredible openness about a wide range of intensely private and painful matters would freeze on the subject of sexual harassment. Typically, they would speak about the issue hurriedly, in a low voice, and then rush on to something else. Or they would speak haltingly, beginning a sentence, then cutting off the thought halfway through, choking back the words that would describe painful events. One highly successful woman who spoke of an experience that had occurred more than twenty years in the past said that she had never before even mentioned it to anyone. A young woman associate in a large law firm described continuing harassment by a male partner for whom she worked, then insisted that it didn't mean anything, that she could handle it, and ended up berating the other women in her office for gossiping about the situation. In both these cases, and in others as well, the woman involved dealt with harassment by practicing a form of denial, a mental maneuver that allowed her to function *as if* nothing, or nothing serious, had happened.

And this is precisely what Anita Hill described—internal distress of painful proportions, and external nonchalance, or at least civility and continued professional contact. And the committee could easily have taken testimony from psychologists verifying the typicality of this reaction. Without such information, neither the senators nor the public could learn that a verbal assault such as Hill described hurts its victim by seriously demeaning her, by undermining her sense of self.

To take the specific situation of the young professional woman, harassment conveys to her that a respected superior does not regard her primarily as a professional colleague, defined by training and knowledge and skill, but as a generic woman, a sexual object. He is disregarding the complex, whole person she is—her integration of mind, feelings, spirit, and body—and reducing her to body alone. And women just starting out in a profession are especially vulnerable to deep hurt by this kind of attack precisely because they are in the process of building a professional identity against the impediments that society still puts in their way.

Women are still ridiculed as unfeminine if they are too smart, too educated, too clever, too tough, too successful. They have to work hard against social risks to assert their full intelligence and talent. And if this is true for white women, it is immeasurably more so for women of color. Kimberle Crenshaw, discussing the racial dynamic at work in the Hill/Thomas drama, points out that black women, regarded as the sexual property of white men during slavery, are still vulnerable to the assumption that they are always sexually available.[6]

In the case of Anita Hill, a young black woman had transformed herself through the hard work of higher education from a poor farm girl into a Yale lawyer. She had built up a professional self that should have armored her against the assumption that her sexuality was her foremost characteristic. Then, as a twenty-five-year-old, in one of her first jobs as a lawyer, she had the dignity, the authority, the self-possession of that construct repeatedly battered by her boss. It was her sense of herself as a whole person, body and mind together, that was under attack, as it is for all women who are harassed. Their very identities are at stake.

And so is their power. Anita Hill, in becoming a lawyer, in seeking

6. Kimberle Crenshaw, "Whose Story Is It Anyway? Feminist and Antiracist Appropriations of Anita Hill," in Toni Morrison, ed., *Race-ing Justice, En-gendering Power* (New York: Pantheon, 1992), pp. 402–40.

a policy-making position in the federal government, was claiming power in the society. Clarence Thomas, by harassing her, by treating her not as a lawyer but as a naturally accessible woman, challenged that claim. Symbolically, his action challenged the claim of all women who reject subordinate status and insist on becoming rule makers in some capacity. In the person of Anita Hill, it was they who were also being attacked.

And this, finally, is the significance of the issue that Anita Hill raised, and the Senate Judiciary Committee came nowhere near finding it. Sexual harassment perpetuates inequality. It is an act that is wrong on a level of personal morality because it causes misery. But it is also wrong on a level of political morality because it denies equality.

In the months following the Senate hearings, Anita Hill herself, who had seemed in her testimony to have thought about her harassment in personal terms only, began to study and talk about its broader meaning. She told students at the Harvard Law School in May 1992 that the women who were the most likely to be harassed were the "trendsetters," women engaged in work traditionally assigned to men, and especially those in work requiring a high degree of education. She called harassment a tool of the powerful, and declared, "I believe it is purposeful and I believe it is meant to exclude."[7] Her conclusion was supported by a June 1992 article in *Working Woman* magazine, which reported widespread harassment of women corporate executives. Of nine thousand such women earning fifty thousand dollars or more, 63 percent said they had been subjected to harassment, and the article concluded that the higher a woman's position, the *more* likely it is that she would be harassed.

The ferocity of the attacks against Anita Hill reflected the fact that she was implicitly asserting a new set of rules that would disrupt old normalities and the security and power that they protected. Under these new rules, which define harassment as clearly wrong, women are not naturally the prey or possessions of men. Men have no natural claim of access to women's bodies. They have no natural entitlement to press their sexual interest against a woman's protests. Men and women are equal sexual agents. Her will and desire carry weight in sexual negotiations equal to his. These are rules that underwrite a shift in power that affects dealings between the sexes from the most personal to the most political, upsetting the personal and economic and political relations of men and women throughout the entire society.

No change so revolutionary could be accomplished by legal regu-

7. Boston *Globe*, May 6, 1992, p. 34.

lations alone, even if wholly endorsed by the Supreme Court. Old rules
and habits deeply imprinted in millions of psyches drag heavily behind
new standards. But nonetheless, images from the Hill/Thomas hearings
had, at least initially, a powerful political effect.

For many women, something they knew but had not clearly "seen"
hit home, and that was the simple fact that American government, federal
and state, was controlled by men. Suddenly, as they stared at the all-
white, all-male Judiciary Committee, thousands of women "saw" that
men who either did not understand women's issues, did not take them
seriously, or were actively hostile to changes that shifted power from men
to women were in control of women's lives. As a result, hundreds of
women entered races for political office and thousands pulled out check-
books to contribute to women's campaigns. Emily's List, an organization
that raises money for women candidates across the country, collected three
times as much for the 1992 elections as it had in 1990. And in November
1992, more women were elected to legislative office than ever before.

Four were elected to the United States Senate, bringing the total of
women senators from two to six, and in several of these races, the issue
of sexual harassment played an important role. In one, Carol Moseley-
Braun, who is black, had defeated an incumbent senator, Alan Dixon, in
the Illinois Democratic primary, making criticism of his Senate vote in
favor of Clarence Thomas central to her campaign. In Washington State,
Patty Murray won the seat vacated by Senator Brock Adams after he
called off his campaign for a second term in the midst of sexual-harassment
charges brought against him by eight women. Barbara Boxer, one of the
two women elected to the Senate from California (the other was Dianne
Feinstein), had, during the Hill/Thomas hearings, led a delegation of
congresswomen into the Senate chambers to resist attempts to dispose of
Hill's charges summarily. The races for seats in the House of Representatives were less dramatic, but the results were no less remarkable. The
number of congresswomen went up from 29 to 48, and the number of
states with women representatives from 19 to 27.

And there were other repercussions. Just a month after the hearings,
President George Bush gave up a two-year fight and signed a new civil
rights bill, making it easier for women and minorities to sue and collect
damages for discrimination, including sexual harassment. In the spring
of 1992, two women members of the Massachusetts legislature filed a bill
that would require employers with six or more employees to provide
training on the issue of sexual harassment, and other states followed suit.
Then, in early summer of that year, the pressure of public attention to

the issue forced a major sexual-harassment scandal in the United States Navy out into public view.

Trouble in that service was signaled by a positive-sounding announcement in June 1992 that all active-duty members of the Navy, about 576,000 men and women, would be required to go through a training program on sexual harassment. "Our position," said the Navy's chief of staff, Admiral Frank B. Kelso 2d, "is to make fundamental changes in our behavior, in our way of dealing with women and some of our long-held traditions."[8]

Officially, the Navy had already proclaimed—in 1989—its "zero tolerance" for sexual harassment. But in practice, Navy officials had continued to tolerate a great deal, including a notably bawdy annual convention of the "Tailhook Association," an organization of naval aviators. One of the convention festivities each year was the enticing or forcing of women to run a gauntlet of drunken male officers who variously slapped, grabbed, and fondled the women, ripping off the clothes of some of them.

After the 1991 convention, however, a female Navy officer who had been forced into the gauntlet complained to superiors. And with the Hill/Thomas hearings raising alarms about harassment, the Navy went through the motions of an investigation. By the spring of 1992, it had produced several muddled, conflicting, and inconclusive reports, as well as the new commitment to sensitivity training. But emboldened by the continued public concern about the issue, several dozen other women reported their experience of the gauntlet, and photographs of it surfaced, as did a story that Navy Secretary H. Lawrence Garrett 3d had been in or near the area of the gauntlet when it was going on.

By the end of June 1992, Garrett had resigned, the Department of Defense had taken over the Tailhook investigation, the Senate was holding up the promotions of forty-five hundred Navy officers until it had a confirmed list of names of those responsible for the gauntlet, and Representative Patricia Schroeder, on the House Armed Services Committee, was keeping steady pressure on the Navy for full disclosure by raising budgetary questions and by calling for congressional hearings on harassment in the military.

In July, the Navy relieved two officers of their command for not preventing or stopping a lewd skit about Representative Schroeder at a naval aviators' banquet, and two admirals lost promotions due to their involvement in separate harassment incidents. Then, in September, the

8. *New York Times*, June 6, 1992, p. A7.

Defense Department issued its findings on the Tailhook affair, thoroughly blasting the Navy's handling of it and announcing the forced retirement of two admirals and the reassignment of another for undermining the original investigation.

None of this—the harassment, the acceptance of it, or the cover-up—was news within the military, or even to an attentive public. Two years before the Pentagon issued its Tailhook report, it had conducted its first major survey of sexual harassment in the military and found that more than a third of the women in all the services reported being harassed, and many also cited the failure of superiors to whom they had reported such incidents to take any effective action. Yet the 1990 report had little practical impact. No admirals or generals lost their commands at that time. The difference between 1990 and 1992 was the shock to the political system administered in 1991, when Anita Hill forced the public to confront an issue it had preferred to ignore. She had forced to the surface the deep contradictions between the old cultural rules that protect a system of male domination and the new laws designed to promote and protect sexual equality.

But the resistance to moving from the old system to the new is so strong that the issues remain confused. Attention still focuses excessively on sexual wrongdoing. Moreover, I suspect that much of the public backing for a crackdown on harassment stems from puritanical attitudes toward sex rather than political commitment to equality.

To reach the issues of equality clearly in the phenomenon of sexual harassment, we have to come to terms with Aristotle. I mean that we have to recognize and explore the connections of harassment to the continued vitality of the mind/body split. Harassment expresses the conviction that women's basic identity is in their bodies. And this conviction connects to the belief that thinkers, reasoners, must curb the body's riots through discipline in order to allow their minds to function well. And the final connecting thought is that women, profoundly identified with their bodies, cannot manage this discipline as well as men can. As a consequence, their proper realm is in affairs that do not require high reason, which means that they cannot hold equal authority with men in public rule-making. They cannot hold equal power. They cannot be equal.

As the earlier discussion about clothing and hair styles demonstrated, women seeking legitimacy in public affairs have generally accepted the Aristotelian premise. They have generally insisted that they can detach mind from body as well as men can. And this is a dangerous move, a serious mistake, because it reinforces the premises of the mind/body split and, in doing so, reinforces the very division of labor—men in charge, women in support—that women are trying to overturn.

On the other hand, to challenge the traditional divisions—as Anita Hill implicitly did—is to invite the kind of ferocious attack that was turned on her. And the reason is that to challenge the ancient division of labor is to challenge male power in all spheres of life. It is to challenge male control of Congress, of the military, of corporate management, of education, and of all the professions. It is to challenge male control of women's bodies. It is to challenge male control of the law.

A prominent sign of a challenge laid down is the unprecedented number of women who assumed high governmental office in 1993 as appointees of President Bill Clinton's. But if women throughout the society are willing to take on this challenge—and, obviously, many are—they have to deal with issues of the body. They cannot pretend it is not there, or not important. In fact, the most dangerous feature of the acquiescence by professional women to the mind/body split is that having identified themselves with mind, they become so shocked when they are treated by others as body that they fall silent. And their silence helps to perpetuate the oppressive behavior that perpetuates inequality.

Instead of falling silent or denying more strenuously the influence of their bodies on their minds, women must contest the belief that *men* are not influenced in their thinking by their bodies. They must contest the mind/body split and insist on recognition that bodies and minds work together in both sexes. They must identify the claim that men can transcend their bodies to speak from a plane of detached reason as actually an insupportable grant of power to the supposed detached reasoners. They must claim equality in the capacities for reason *and* unreason in women *and* men.

But where we would be if we succeeded in discrediting the division of body and mind I do not know. If we admit the influence of bodies on minds, and if we admit women on equal terms to the places where minds are used, then we have accepted sexual differences in the processes of reason. And this is new and troubling territory. We have always feared the specter of intellectual and social chaos that could result from the abandonment of belief in a form of reason that leads everyone who uses it properly to common conclusions—at least about general principles of right and wrong. And among lawyers, women and men, the fear of admitting multiple perspectives into legal thinking is acute because the very concept seems to undermine the necessary universality of law, the promise of fairness that depends on the same law being applicable in the same way to everyone.

But chaos in the law is not the necessary result of the admission of sexual differences and their operation even in legal thought. Many kinds of response to the acknowledgment and naming of differences are possible. They might include finding commonalities that coexist with difference; incorporating difference explicitly into the law; recognizing different viewpoints and deliberately choosing one that will prevail; compromising difference; and, probably, others. The point is that the embodiment of thinking does not—or does not have to—detract from its quality.

The danger to fairness in a legal system dedicated to equality lies not in the fact of different bodies and different bodily experience but in the power to define what those differences mean. They cannot mean the continued, if furtively held, belief in the intellectual inferiority of most women, and therefore the exclusion of women from the society's rule-making. The new question must be, How can we acknowledge difference between the sexes and still achieve equality between them? Answering that question is an immense new project, and the design must be undertaken by men and women together, the voices of both contributing to the new arrangements. (I will review some of the current thinking on the subject by feminist legal scholars in Chapter 9.) My own belief is that the key to that radically different future is the prior recognition that bodies are not extraneous to minds, that thinking is diminished, not enhanced, by attempts to liberate it from bodies, and that the differences in male and female bodies, as confusing and mysterious as they may be, must be integrated, respectfully, into the law.

5

CULTURE

AMONG THE MOST POWERFUL of shadow forces that resist the full authority of women in the law, along with father/daughter confusions and mind/body rules, is the culture that defines the highest reaches of the legal profession—the big-city big firms. It is, obviously, a culture that was formed by men who assumed that the profession was naturally a place of men and would always be so. And the maleness of the culture positions women as strangers—as Simone de Beauvoir's "Other"—in some ways that seem not to matter very much, and in some that cause serious dissonance.

Few would argue with these observations, and yet it is difficult to define what maleness or male culture means and how it operates to affect women. These are subjects that quickly raise all the old bedeviling issues of nature and nurture. Are men and women marked genetically to behave in certain ways mysterious to the other? Are they doomed to a perpetual inability to understand the other or to function well in spheres formed by the other? Will women always be strangers in the law, and men always strangers in places of domesticity? Or does the society teach people what maleness and femaleness mean in lessons that can be analyzed, learned, and used by the opposite sex, or challenged and changed if they are not usable?

Women maneuvering daily in the cultural construct of the nation's big law firms answer these questions differently, but for most the answer is something like this: Women *can* break the cultural codes of big-firm law and adapt to them, but a great many decide at some point that they do not like the cultural system they find themselves in, and so they leave. Quite a few are quick to say that the big-firm culture is uncongenial to many men as well, but that the same social rules that allow women to withdraw from high-status positions, or even applaud their withdrawal, operate to keep the men securely in place. In other words, many women suggest that the big-firm culture is not just male, but male in a certain style that is off-putting to nonconforming men as well as women.

What, then, is this culture that is male but also unappealing to many men? The physical sites of the law firms, their visual appearance, signal a domain of importance, of high seriousness, of power the more impressive because it is withheld, not brandished. Most big firms moved in the eighties from long-settled quarters of whatever elegance earlier financial booms had created to the high towers that mushroomed across the country in the Reagan years. Some firms, in the process, adopted sleek modern décor; others carried over the mahogany, the hunting prints, the beaded paneling, the grandfather clocks, and the dark, imposing desks of their former incarnations. But whether their fittings are modern or traditional, the atmosphere of the big firms is strikingly the same. Most noticeable is the hush. Whisked up forty or sixty floors in a soundless elevator, a visitor enters a softly lit space that seems, at first glance, to be filled entirely with large flowers. A carefully groomed receptionist at an imposing desk asks gravely, and barely audibly, how she can help. An appointment confirmed, the visitor is seated, perhaps on a leather couch facing a huge abstract painting, or on a peach-and-white brocade chair nestled among prints of English country life. Large windows command—in fact, seem to own—views of the city or, sometimes, the sea. Young men and women move lightly up and down the wide interior staircase that connects the many floors the firm occupies. People nod or speak in low voices. The receptionist murmurs on the phone, repeating the firm's multiple names over and over, like an incantation, like a prayer. A few minutes of this, and the visitor has no trouble assuming that she is in a sacred precinct, that down the quiet corridors, behind the closed doors, the high priests are communing with their gods and conducting their murmurous, mysterious rituals.

The hush in the big-firm atmosphere conveys a sense of seriousness, of work conducted intellectually by reasoners tapping deep-rooted sources of legal authority. But the quiet also signals a system that works according to unspoken rules, a system in which the initiates know who they are, what they are doing, and how they relate to one another. It is a system that developed in the earlier years of the century, when members of the most esteemed law firms were highly homogeneous, not only by sex and race but by class, ethnicity, and religion as well (recall the woman whose brilliant lawyer father, a graduate of Harvard College and the Harvard Law School, could not aspire to a position in the top law firms because they excluded Jews). Succeeding generations of the legal elite did not need to engage in a constant process of questioning and definition. Dressing in much the same way, speaking in much the same way, carrying common values out of a common upbringing and education, they understood much of what was expected of them personally and professionally without being told. And even as the firms slowly broadened their membership, the old forms persisted, requiring fast feats of assimilation on the part of outsiders.

But for some, assimilation can go only so far. White males of any ethnicity can, with effort, approximate the appearance of elite white male Protestants, but women and blacks cannot. Furthermore, women in particular do not sound "right." In part this is due to their voices, which are generally (although certainly not always) higher and softer than men's. But more significantly it is due to male codes of communication that include stereotyped assumptions about women, attitudes at odds with the perception of women as fellow lawyers enjoying equal status in the firms. That is, professional male speech patterns portray women as different and unequal, and women cannot adopt them without ratifying the assumption of their own inequality. But not adopting them, they sound different.

In short, no matter what they do, women cannot present themselves completely in the established mode of the big-firm lawyer, and one apparent consequence is their effective invisibility and inaudibility in many settings. They are present in the big firms in ever-increasing numbers, and, more than in the past, they are becoming partners, but still, in some sense, they are not seen or heard.

The comment of a woman who is a partner in a prosperous middle-sized firm is typical. "What I find very frustrating is, now I've paid my dues, I've climbed up the ladder, I've made partner, but I find there is still resistance to giving women a real voice of authority and really listening to what they say. . . . Even women who bring in business, who are very bright, women with very strong personalities, they're just not members of the club. . . . It's very hard to pin down. . . . The wall that you beat your head against is getting the respect, having people listen to you on an administrative matter, on promotion things, just sort of the running of the firm, and that I think women still have to a much lesser degree than men. . . . And the younger men I see coming up in the firm are no different. They're still very macho, male-oriented, into male, hierarchical games. You would expect that generation to be different, but they aren't. They're still into that masculine, tough-it-out, we're-going-to-beat-the-shit-out-of-you-so-you-can-prove-to-us-that-you're-a-real-man kind of thing. It's very frustrating."

But the problems of not being seen or heard or recognized as potential equals are the most severe for black attorneys, and particularly for black women. Of those with whom I spoke who had spent some time in big firms, all but one had been acutely unhappy in them, several had become seriously ill with stress-related problems, and all had left.

One young black woman, an early-eighties graduate whose parents were both lawyers, went into a major New York firm straight from law school and stayed through her fifth year as an associate, but left not long after she landed in the hospital with an illness exacerbated by tension and stress. She says that no matter how hard she worked, or what successes she had on major deals for which she was the senior associate, she never felt the personal acknowledgment, the sense of inclusion, the signals of particular approval, that tell an associate she is being brought along to partnership. "The difference between those who are smart and work hard and make partner, and those who are smart and work hard and don't make partner, is someone in the upper echelons who has guided you along. Someone who says, 'I like this person. They remind me of me when I was twenty-five years old, and I'm going to bring them up.'" And it rarely happens that a white man—or a white woman—reacts that way to a black woman.

Rather, this young woman thinks, blacks tend to be seen stereotypically. "All the black professionals I know—lawyers, bankers, everyone—get the same review. My brother, who works in another law firm, got the black review. My husband, who works in advertising, got it. Everyone gets it. 'You're very smart. You're very personable. But you need to work on your writing.' I've won awards for my writing. I've published. I have no trouble writing. My husband has a Ph.D. and has no problems writing. My brother has published. But that's the black review."

She describes an incident in which she was the senior associate on a major deal for which she did most of the actual work because the partner in charge was involved in other things. She negotiated and drafted all the documents. The partner reviewed all the work and did not change anything, which meant, she says, that her work must have been okay, because the deal was extremely important. At any rate, the deal closed. It was a success. And the partner was so grateful that he and his wife took the woman and her husband to the ballet and dinner, which was very unusual. "Then, when I got my review from him, it said I was very smart, very personable, I had good negotiating skills, but I needed to work on my drafting. I had just finished drafting two ninety-page documents he made no changes on, and he says I have to work on my drafting. That's the black review."

It was after this that she fell ill. Other small incidents—for instance, a cab ride during which a partner with whom she had worked prodigious hours during a hot summer ignored her completely, chatting instead with a young white male associate—discouraged her. "You would have to be deaf, dumb, and blind not to see that you do not have a future at this place," she told herself. "Leave. Now." And she did, joining the in-house counsel staff at a TV network.

This woman, for a while at least, had wanted to remain in her firm, wanted to be accepted and to belong, but her nonconforming skin, she believes, made it hard for other people to recognize her merits, her intellectual and professional kinship to them. And to a less acute degree, the same might be said of many white women as well.

But other women encountering pressure to fit themselves into the cultural norms of the big firms choose to leave because they do not like the squeeze. That is, their difference from the prevailing male look and style and sound and manner is so great that they have to reshape themselves drastically even to approximate these standards. And many, feeling themselves forced to abandon parts of their own identity that they value, refuse to conform.

"Being in a big firm is not just a job, but your social life as well," an early-seventies graduate says. "You have to fit into the structure, and I resisted that. I'll abide by the big rules of an institution, but the little rules, trying to make my personality fit in a cookie cutter, was not doable. I am blunt, not to the point of being tactless but I tend to say what I mean and mean what I say and pull no punches. . . . I have a very large personality, sort of with gestures and laughter. I'm not a Brooks Brothers suit. It's not me. I'm dresses and dangly earrings and nail polish. I'm not a WASP. I laugh. I cry. When people I've known a long time come here for meetings, I don't shake their hands, I hug them. . . . I'm sort of— within the confines of appropriate behavior and propriety—I'm me." She had gone into a big firm straight out of law school but left within several years for the public sector, where she was when we talked.

An early-eighties graduate speaks of recognizing how stifled she felt in the big firm she had joined after law school when she subsequently worked in a district attorney's office. On this job, she says, "I felt for the first time that my professional, my working self, and my nonworking self were sort of one and the same, that I could be myself, really, in terms of not having to watch what you say or how you looked or who you were talking to or who you weren't talking to. . . . In the firm, if you were just standing around and chatting about what you did on the weekend or arguing or talking about a movie, you would hate to have a partner walk by. And I felt that the things I thought were funny, most of the people there wouldn't. At the D.A.'s office, four lawyers and one secretary worked in one small room. It looked like a real estate office. You couldn't help getting to know the other people. And some days were so crazy, with nutty people, or a judge in an odd mood, you had to let off steam and tell stories about what happened; where in the firm, either they really were more pompous and more serious or they were trying to be that way because it was expected. You felt that in the firm, you were under scrutiny because not everyone would be kept. Your work was one thing, but it was also important how well you fit in. That was less articulated. You got reviewed on your work, not your personality, but you felt that someone who had gone to the right prep school and was a good squash player would go a long way with some partners."

She speaks too about the characteristic quiet in the halls of the big firms, and notes that what this meant for her was isolation, a process of individualized, not collaborative, work. "We did work on teams in the firm," she says, "senior partner, junior partner, senior associate, junior associate, paralegal—but I didn't feel I was working together with people. There was no sense of joy or camaraderie, or pulling together for a common purpose. I felt more common purpose in the D.A.'s office, where people had separate caseloads but more similar outlooks on the importance of particular work. At the firm, partners didn't have time to explain things to you or take you along on the fun part of a case. And among associates, there was a certain competitiveness. People are not going to be really open with ideas. So it's not just quiet, but you have a lot of cubicles and people working in their own little isolation units." Now in a small firm established to allow its partners the cultural freedom the big firms squelch, she adds, laughing, "Sometimes here in my office I'll be yelling to a colleague across the hall, and I still feel like maybe I shouldn't be doing this!"

Another woman, trained in psychology as well as law, maintains strongly that full maturity, full adulthood, is incompatible with the institutional definition of behavior that big firms impose. She says that it is important to do something else first before going to law school to prevent the school experience from defining you. This is particularly important at Harvard, she thinks, because the law school is "so large, so self-important and self-satisfied," that students are easily cowed by it and infantilized. "And if you get infantilized in law school and go directly to a large firm where you get infantilized again, you may never grow up. You will only grow up in the image of the large law firm. They really will be able to mold you into this person who defines herself in terms of how many emergencies she's had to handle, how many sleepless nights she's had to deal with, how many times she's had to leave her children when she *really* didn't want to, how many times she's had to not pay attention to her parents, whatever, and that's because the system has molded her before she's had a chance to find out who she was and that there are other things in life that are a lot more fun and can also make you feel very valuable and very important and very good about yourself." She, too, is now in a small firm that allows its members wide latitude in setting their own rules.

These remarks deepen the issue from problems produced by the fact that women do not look the part of the big-firm lawyer to questions about the value of the part that women, as well as male lawyers, are asked to play. To some extent, that is, the culture of the big firms positions women as outsiders and rejects them as members of the club. But to some extent, women reject the culture. The psychologist/lawyer rejects the high value placed by big-firm culture on intense, fast-paced work. Like Virginia Woolf, she found that approach not heroic, but dehumanizing.

For many women who enter big law firms and find that they dislike the prevailing ambience, the overriding issue is the ethic of competition that shapes much of their experience. They find that they do not like the institutional structure that places lawyers chronically in antagonistic relations to each other. Yet the precise reasons for their disquiet are not easy to pin down.

The law, in its Anglo-American format, is necessarily a site of conflict. It provides a means of settling disputes, but the means are combative. By design, lawyers work as adversaries, as embattled pairs. The courtroom is perhaps the best-known adversarial setting but by no means the only one. Lawyers for buyers and sellers of anything argue the terms of the sales contract down to the last comma. Anyone who has been through a divorce knows about constant contests between "my lawyer" and "your lawyer." Anyone at all aware of politics in the mid-1980s recalls images of Oliver North in the Iran-*contra* hearings, persistently questioned by government lawyers, fiercely defended by his lawyer, Brendan Sullivan, who at one point declared indignantly, when reprimanded for constant interruptions, "I am not a potted plant!" Sullivan was reminding the investigators that lawyers are not supposed to sit quietly. They are not supposed to cooperate with their opponent's efforts to glean information from a witness. They are supposed to engage vociferously in the advancement of their own client's interests.

The premise behind this contentious system is that ardent, strident representation of both sides to a dispute is the best mechanism for unearthing all the relevant facts and defining all the relevant law while still respecting the rights of the individuals involved. And the further premise is that with the best case for both sides out on the table, whether in a congressional hearing room, or in a court before a judge, or in direct negotiations between opposing lawyers, the side with the greatest merit prevails. Therefore, in the interest of ultimate fairness, lawyers compete with all the skill, energy, and creativity at their command. Like football players or armed warriors, they are licensed to compete with the serious aim of defeating the opposing side.

But many women, drawn to the law by its promise of fairness, shun chronic engagement in battle. Bearing out the stereotyped image of woman as peacemaker, not warrior, they tend to shy away from the most adversarial arenas in the law and to gravitate toward those forms of practice that are most consultative and conciliatory, or those that are bound by harmonizing rules. This last includes fields such as securities, antitrust, bankruptcy, and tax, in which doing the work is like solving a puzzle. As one woman attorney says, the subject matter itself is not earth-shattering, but the analytical process is satisfying because "it allows you to straighten out masses of confusion." Another finds working with the Internal Revenue Code satisfying, "like studying Latin," because if you took the time to understand its purposes and processes, it provided a manageable frame of reference that was fun to use. "Within this defined universe, if you sort it all out, it all makes sense, and there's a kind of wonderful harmony in the symphony that it's playing out."

Many women in big firms opt for a corporate law practice because it allows them to work cooperatively with groups of people who have conflicting interests but also a common interest in putting together a particular deal or solving a common problem. These women express satisfaction in working out sound arrangements between borrowers and lenders, or between investors and companies seeking growth.

But the more aggressively hard-edged the practice, with trial work at the extreme, the fewer women are involved. This is a fact, but the question is, Why. Has nature programmed men hormonally to do battle and women to avoid it? Or do women shun competition because the larger culture socializes them to dislike it, teaches them that their virtue lies in sympathy, understanding, patience, cooperation, and peacemaking rather than in combat? Or is it mainly a lack of practice? Would women feel more comfortable as competitors if their families and schools and communities placed girls in the same gladiatorial roles that boys assume from early childhood onward? Or is it that women, entering the legal profession with more social training than men in quiet dispute-settling, see the lawyer's reliance on adversarial procedures as excessive? Are women rejecting, as a matter of consciously formed critical judgment, the degree of competition they find in the law?

These are hard questions to answer because the women themselves cannot know, with certainty, whether they are moved by unconsciously held social teachings or consciously formed mature values. Yet the answers are important if women are to gain equal authority in the law. Because a competitive ethos defines legal culture at present, either women must become more competitive to establish their authority or the culture must become less so. And the large question is, Which *should* it be?

Most women lawyers struggling with these issues are skeptical of the claim that women, by nature, lack some necessary capacity for competition. They point to abundant examples of fiercely and successfully competitive women colleagues. Rather, they say, those who have themselves avoided the most extreme adversarial roles have done so out of choice. And many explain their choice as based on the conclusion that adversarial processes are often unsatisfying, inefficient means for solving legal problems. That is, many women feel that the adversarial system too often fosters game-playing as opposed to problem-solving or truth-finding or justice-dealing, that, too often, the system operates more for the pleasure of warrior/lawyers than for the benefit of problem-besieged clients.

This is an issue that kept recurring in the story told by an early-eighties graduate who had left a big law firm just short of a virtually promised partnership because her civil-litigation practice, while successful, was not meaningful enough to be satisfying. The battles waged by opposing lawyers often seemed pointless to her. Seeking social service, she joined a government unit investigating public corruption and was pleased with the substantive work she was doing except, again, battling in court—this time, in criminal prosecutions of various public officials.

"Other forms of confrontation don't bother me. I'm not a shy person," she began. "But there's something about the legal adversarial process that I find extremely distasteful. Maybe it's because I'm not convinced that it's a truth-finding system. . . . I'm really interested in the right answer. I'm not interested in all the games that people play. I find that very distasteful. That's a large part of what I didn't like, jockeying for position, trying to conceal your hand. I like to be open with people."

Bringing court proceedings for the investigative unit, she told me, she would win and her opponent would keep coming back with "some silly motion," dragging the matter on endlessly. And she thought, "I hate this. I mean, it's *Bleak House*. I don't want to be part of a system that's *Bleak House*. I want to work so that I can use my energies in a way that they're productive and don't just dribble into the sand. I could spend two years pursuing this guy, and he's going to continue to elude us, and it was two years of time down the drain. Finally I said to my boss, 'I'm sorry. Find somebody else to do it. I'm not going to do it anymore.' There's really that sense . . . of 'What do you have to show for it?' Maybe if I were involved in a case I really, really believed in, I'd feel differently, like the woman who brought *Roe v. Wade* all the way up from Texas. I went to law school with the idea that I would be doing that kind of litigation, but I found myself in a world where that wasn't what I was doing. . . . I think, to some measure, the bill of goods that you get sold in law school about how the adversary system is a great engine for producing the truth . . . I'm not convinced."

At another point, she said that government prosecutors, on the one hand, and private defense attorneys, on the other, both see the world in black and white, but from opposite sides, and that she rarely does. Also, she added, once again, "I'm not a big fan of confrontation. I like looking for common ground between the parties."

Another woman, an assistant U.S. attorney, spoke disapprovingly of the "macho" ethic of her office, the emphasis among the male attorneys on winning as the ultimate value, their habit of bragging about their victories as personal triumphs, and also the prevailing assumption that success as a prosecutor requires tactics of forceful aggression. "In handling a case, the style was, you have to be able to go to the person's house, and *frighten* them into agreeing to plead guilty, before they're indicted. . . . The idea was, you have to have . . . some kind of ability to scare people . . . to be able to get admissions out of your witnesses or potential witnesses." This young woman enjoyed her work in court and did not think that success depends on the aggressive adversarial style she described to me, but she did not like working in an atmosphere dominated by macho premises and practices, and was, in fact, packing up to leave for work in an entertainment law firm when I arrived for our interview. She did not frame her objections as criticisms of the adversary system as such, but rather of the kind of behavior that a systemic emphasis on competition and winning seems to produce—not truth-finding but, very possibly, truth-intimidation.

A related criticism voiced by women who dislike courtroom competition is that of the structuring of trials so that the outcome can only be a win or a loss. As a state court judge who had graduated from law school in the 1950s remarked, "I think doing trials isn't comfortable for women, as a trial draws on a playing-field mentality. Women prefer to settle. They don't like the winner-take-all philosophy—and, I think, rightly so. Women like to roundtable it and come out with everybody feeling a little bit the winner and a little bit the loser."

A former law-review editor, several years out of law school and doing civil litigation in a large, well-known firm, sat in her office amid papers piled on every surface, including the couch and several chairs, and questioned the good sense of settling business disputes through adversarial procedures. "Litigation is strange," she said. "It's a strange way to settle problems. It's war. It's a game. I mean, there're these little battlefields and this is the way you're supposed to shoot the other person. It's just absurd. . . . I'm good at it. Probably it's what I'm best at in the world, but it is sort of silly . . . because the outcome doesn't matter much to me or to society . . . and it's incredibly wasteful."

A law school graduate of the early sixties, now a federal magistrate, reflected at length on the differences between men and women on the issue of competition and the reliance on competition as an approach to solving problems. She suggested, although elliptically, that the adoption by women of male mores may be not only undesirable but, perhaps, unnecessary. "I have observed at different times in the practice of law," she said, "that men do, in an all-male group, have a certain kind of metaphor that they use. . . . I believe that language not only expresses values but influences them. . . . Men who grew up in the fifties and weren't accustomed to having women in decision-making positions use these metaphors that have a lot to do with sports and teamwork and with the kind of competition that men engage in—physical games, physical competition, and that sort of thing. . . . Now, I believe this language and metaphor, and the physical-competition/virility culture that it comes out of, really influence the values of the business. To the extent that women don't share that, to the extent that women bring different views, there can be new and different and creative approaches. You really don't have to do something this way because it has always been done this way. But what I have seen more often is the women learning the male metaphor, not applying the female view but learning the male metaphors—or pretending to—whether they're comfortable with it or not. I would urge women to think for themselves. . . . Of course, you have to use some common sense about what you can influence and what you can't. But saying that does not mean you have to buy into the male culture. . . . Women ought to be able to think for themselves enough to identify what their values are and be true to them in situations where they have a choice, where they have an opportunity to be creative. I hate to see a person, male or female, conforming to an institutional structure. . . . If we could do that our institutions would be more humane and flexible."

The strongest endorsement I will hear of the competitive ethic in litigation comes from a public interest lawyer who, in effect, through large class-action suits, is a prosecutor of the government. Not only does she accept the combativeness of the courtroom, but, as she describes vividly, she has overcome a distaste for techniques of aggression and intimidation to the point of actively enjoying them. She is an early-seventies graduate who has been a public interest litigator for most of her nearly twenty-year career.

"It's my own feeling that it took me much more time than a male with a comparable academic background to get into feeling comfortable in court. I think it has to do with the whole way that women tend not to have experiences in being under that sort of public pressure. . . . And these are precisely the sorts of experiences [she mentions high school debating] women need to have in order to get rid of the psychological barriers to full participation in litigation. I don't ever recall men talking about the sort of psychological pressure involved in feeling comfortable in court. And I now, in practice, have a couple of times been in court and watched women with A.G.'s [attorney general's] offices, who are pretty young, just make a hash of oral argument and just be terrible in ways that I thought were related to so much panic over the experience of being involved in litigation that they weren't being able to call upon the skills that they did have. . . . Other than giving women the chance to be under public pressure in earlier stages, I don't know what the solution is."

She goes on to talk about specific, bold courtroom techniques. "One of the things you learn in litigation is that sometimes you just have to bullshit, and I think women are just far less socially prepared for the times when they just have to wing it and there's no other way to go. And so much of what happens in courtrooms depends on looking comfortable. I realize since I've come to be comfortable with myself as a litigator that

I've watched myself get away with all sorts of stuff in court that the judge won't allow a younger lawyer or a lawyer that he or she doesn't trust as much, and opponents won't challenge things because they get intimidated. I guess the first time I really realized how important this was, was there had always been a lawyer in the A.G.'s office in Wisconsin that I was petrified of because he was a very aggressive person. But once, I had a significant trial with him, and I realized at the end of it that I was just laughing at him because there was nothing behind the bombast, and once I was ready to go toe-to-toe with that sort of bombast and not react defensively to it, everything had disappeared. It wasn't just that I could stand up to him, but that he was an easy mark; and getting that sort of level of comfort and being able to use the intimidation factor as something I do to other people is just so important and seems to come much easier in men. I don't know whether that's sports. . . . I just think that's a really important factor in decreasing the performance of women in court."

She then turns to the moral issues involved in the behavior she has described and endorsed. She speaks first about her daughter, who, with the encouragement of her lawyer mother, does participate in high school debate. Says the mother, "I watch her debate and see the obvious pleasure she gets out of creaming some poor little kid, and I suppose that's good, because she isn't going to go through the trouble I had with litigation at first." But the other side of the question of being a good trial lawyer, she adds, is trying to figure out how to be a good person. "A lot of things that are encouraged as personality traits in litigation are really not very attractive among human beings. I try to continue to be sensitive, but it's hard because I get tremendous pleasure out of being successful in this sort of thing, but it's just like the Socratic class. There's an undercurrent of really unpleasant things going on in that sort of exchange. Even intimidation stuff—I mean, that's not a very attractive way to be as a human being. And yet I love it!" She laughs. "I would be less than honest if I didn't say it."

Is her pleasure in battle a matter of individual temperament? Is it as likely to be found—although I have not found it—in women who prosecute for the government? Or is there a connection between the underdog role of the public interest lawyer and her willingness to exult in the defeat of an enemy? Is this an attitude that a woman who is herself an outsider, however privileged, would be unlikely to hold when she wields the immense power of the state? Perhaps some level of outsider identification with an accused person—along with a socialized shrinking from combat—may block an impetus in women prosecutors to mounting all-out assaults in the courtroom—or if not to doing it, to taking pleasure in it.

Beyond a generalized distaste for competition or criticisms of its effectiveness, some women have found the intense competitive engagement in trial work to be specifically incompatible with the responsibilities of caring for small children. That is, the courtroom as a battle scene where the only outcome is a win or a loss, and where the smallest slip can give the opposing lawyer a decisive advantage, sets up mental pressures that are all-enveloping. And as the needs of small children are also constant and pressing, the conflict between the two sets of demands is more than many women are willing to sustain.

The clearest conflicts in the stories I'm told arise for women who have children and, also, a litigation practice that puts them in court, conducting trials, with some frequency. To some extent, the conflicts these women describe are logistical: problems of time, unpredictable crises, out-of-town depositions, or wearying negotiations with opposing counsel. But beyond logistics, many speak of the mental invasiveness of a trial practice that makes simple daily thinking about their children, and responding to them, difficult.

The problem is that the demands of court trials are multifaceted, changeable, and intensive. As one woman whose work is in civil litigation puts it, conducting a trial requires "getting the information from a client, getting that client to be able to testify as a witness, dealing with somebody who's a hostile witness, getting information that you want, dealing with opposing counsel, dealing with the court and the court rules, and having to cope with it all." Another woman, doing criminal trials as an assistant district attorney, says that when a case is on, she is totally wrapped up in it and can think of nothing else. She dreams about it. Typically, she will get up at 5:00 a.m. to prepare, and often gives witnesses an early call to be sure they are up. I'm told repeatedly, by women without children, that during a trial, their private lives are on hold, nonexistent. They don't do laundry. They don't pay bills. They don't read newspapers.

Adding children to this picture, many women find, is simply impossible. In Boston, a former litigator affirms the pleasures and the pressures of courtroom work but says she gave it up as incompatible with family life because preparation for litigation is so intense. "I couldn't balance it . . . the mental preoccupation, even when you come home. If I'm going into court for any kind of proceeding, I'm going to be mentally rehearsing those arguments in my head, and if you were talking to me I might not hear you because I'm practicing, doing an internal practicing of how to say this, how to explain that."

The public interest lawyer who spoke of her pleasure in courtroom combat says she manages to combine her trial practice with family life because her trials, given the particular function of her agency, are all out of town. "I think that's a major advantage," she says, "because you are so enveloped by a trial, so wrapped up in detail, that it would probably cause tension if I were at home and yet not doing any work for the family or not really available." In other words, she resolves the conflict by periodic removal from her family—on the average, she says, about one week a month.

Another woman found the conflict so overwhelming after the birth of a child that she not only left her trial practice, she fled the city to take up a long-distance lawyering life in a remote rural town. Her daughter had been born at a time in her practice when she was getting into big trials of her own, and, she says, the baby seemed to know when a trial was on, waking frequently and fussing. "She was probably picking up my tension," the mother explains. "I was a wreck. I was losing sleep. I was tied up in knots and feeling ineffective everywhere. I wasn't doing anything good for anybody." So she quit and the family headed for the country. Her husband, also a lawyer, got a job in a small city nearby, and she did part-time work at home, preparing briefs referred to her by her old firm. She says that the concept was idyllic but after a while she began to find small-town life terribly lonely. Then came the week in which the neighbor's cows trampled and ate new shoots coming up in the first perennial garden she had ever created, and she skidded off the road in a freak ice storm and then fell while walking to a nearby house for help, cutting her knee and bleeding all over her clothes. Nature, she discovered, could be an even tougher adversary than the ones she had confronted in court.

So the family moved back to the city and the lawyer/mother returned to her firm, but not as a trial lawyer. Rather, she has specialized in appellate work, which means presenting arguments to a judge on disputed points of law after disputed points of fact have all been settled at the trial level. The procedure is still adversarial, but the arguments are about principle. They are based on research, and organized ahead of time in written briefs. Presenting appeals is a far more knowable, predictable, and easily scheduled process than conducting trials, more a scholarly argument than a shoot-out, and therefore less totally consuming.

But the new form of work has not wholly resolved the work/family problems for this woman, because there is always the problem of time. She and her husband share child care fifty-fifty, but, she says, "There is something about Mommy that's just different. I'm the one my daughter calls when she's sick. My husband can go away for a weekend or a week and . . . it doesn't faze her a bit. When I'm away, or when I'm even busy—I remember one time last winter going through papers she brought home from school and it's all wonderful and then I got to this paper where she's gotten a sixty-something. And I said, 'What happened here?' And she looks at me and she says"—the mother assumes a pitiful voice— " 'That's when you were in Virginia.' "

The approach this woman takes to her daughter's desire for more time with her is to clear her schedule after a busy period, to pick up her daughter after school and spend afternoons at home. More fundamentally, however, she lets her child know, forthrightly, that she is a working mother by choice. "That's what I do. That's what I am. That's what I want. It would be easier to pretend that I do it to earn money for the household, but the basic reason is that I want to work—and that's what I say." And, she says, the child basically accepts this, as a fact. But it would not be an acceptable fact to either of them if the work continued to cause the mother the emotional anguish that her trial practice did.

Another woman litigator went through a similar, yearlong period of intense reflection on the question of integrating competitive adversarial work and the care of children, but came to somewhat different conclusions. In the process, she identified a wide range of issues involved with unusual clarity.

Are women in general, or most women, ill-suited to highly competitive work? Does maternity soften a woman's competitive edge? Is a mother's bond with her child naturally more intense and urgent than a father's? Beyond nursing, does a child need a mother's direct care more than a father's? Is high-quality nanny care or day care just as good as parent care for a small child? Is it possible, in a marriage of high-powered professionals, to sustain a fifty-fifty division of child care? Can marriage partners sustain a commitment to equality with each other if their earnings are vastly different, or if one is earning nothing at all? Can women (or men) function at the same time as aggressive adversaries at work and loving nurturers at home? Is the adversarial persona required of civil and criminal litigators, and others in the world of big-firm law, in some way dehumanizing—emotionally damaging to those who assume it? The final question, of course, is, Can women with small children remain in competitive, big-firm practices without risking emotional harm to their children or themselves?

A member of a late-seventies law school class, the woman who posed these questions was, when I first interviewed her, about ten years out of law school, a new-made partner in a large, respected East Coast firm, married to another big-firm lawyer, and about eight months pregnant with her first child. We talked again, by phone, about a year later, and then again—in a second face-to-face interview—some months afterward, by which time she was expecting a second child.

I would say at the outset that this woman does not speak for all professional women in the conclusions she has reached on these questions. She certainly does not speak for women who do not share the privileges that allow her to explore her difficult issues carefully and make choices according to her own values, knowing that she can count on considerable emotional and financial support for whatever she decides. For many women, especially those who are the sole support of their families, the range of choice is much narrower. On the other hand, it is *because* this woman enjoys wide freedom of choice that she confronts the issues as fully as she does.

When we first spoke, it was at her law firm, high in a cluster of urban office towers. The subject that was uppermost in her mind, and that she wanted to be sure that I understood, was the necessity for women lawyers to plunge wholeheartedly and fearlessly into the competitive culture of big-firm law if they were to gain meaningful influence in the profession. She described herself as having traveled a long way intellectually and psychologically to arrive at this unambivalent commitment to the mainstream. "I used to wake up at law school and think it's a joke that I was there, like Curious George ending up in an odd place," she remarked. As the daughter of a lawyer and much influenced by him, she was in some ways a natural candidate for law school. But she was also young, straight from college, and looked even younger than she actually was because she was small and classically cute. And suddenly she was in a highly competitive environment run by men.

She found herself off-balance in law school because for the first time in her life she had trouble performing in class. A big talker in college, she was intimidated by the large law school classes and couldn't respond well to "getting hammered at, not in an exploratory way, but in a hostile, adversarial, justificatory mode." This, she's come to believe, is a male style of communication, a matter of sparring as opposed to seeking understanding or agreement, and many women do not like the competitive and adversarial elements of it. And not liking it, she suggested, they turn off. She recalled that the women in her section got together for lunch one day, early in the first year, and went around the table, each talking about why she was there. And every woman said that she didn't intend to try for law review. "Everyone felt it necessary to say they weren't competing!" This, she is certain, is the heart of the problem of women in the law—the shunning of an ethic of competition. And she thinks women must, and should, overcome their distaste, as she feels she herself has finally done—although it took some time.

Her goal on entering law school was to practice some form of public interest law, and this direction was confirmed by a stint as a summer associate in a big firm. There she found herself part of a hierarchical system that required its participants to fit into "a pin-striped, unemotional, conservative male mode" that felt completely alien to her. Furthermore, she had developed health problems that seemed to militate against a mainstream career. During first-year exams, she had fallen seriously ill, and she was ill again in her third year. Then, after passing the bar, she had a third episode of the same illness and nearly died. She had never experienced anything like these attacks before. They were attributed to stress, and their recurrence made her ask why she was driving herself so hard. Then she came to think that she was stressed not by the work she was doing but by the uncertainty she felt about committing herself to a serious career. She thinks this decision is peculiarly difficult for women because social rules that prescribe such a choice for men leave it open to women to drop out at any point along the way—and to drop into other, more approved roles.

Nonetheless, like many other young graduates she entered a big firm for the experience and stayed—in her case, as a litigator—because of the challenges and the stimulation. "I like being around smart people," she told me. "I like the prestige of a high-paying firm. I have a tremendous sense of satisfaction with the finished product of my work, even if a case has no particular social significance." She said that what she found valuable about being a litigator was helping to make the judicial process work. She liked to think of herself as "participating in an honorable way, with skill, judgment and ability," in a legal system that at its best provides a fair means for straightening the tangled affairs of business. Also, her lawyer husband, a member of another big firm, encouraged her to stay in that world.

Perhaps most important to her role as an advocate of competition for women, she has trained herself to care more about money. She sees this as a kind of growing up. "Not caring about what you make is like not caring whether you make law review—it's a form of refusal to compete," she stated firmly. In fact, her preoccupation when we initially spoke was the continued second-class status of women in her firm—their lesser prestige and lesser compensation—even after becoming partners. And she had her sights set on getting women onto the committee that decided on the firm's division of profits.

She told me that she overcame her own anxieties about competition through therapy, which put her own conflicts in the context of social norms devaluing women generally. She saw herself—and most women —as having internalized a high level of sexism growing up, thinking that being a boy is better than being a girl, seeing feminine characteristics as weak. She had felt driven into a man's world because that was what would make her valuable. She had gladly embraced the role of the surrogate son. But she wanted social approval as a woman too, so she carried into the male domain, as most women do, the rules that tell women to be not competitive but cooperative, not aggressive but modest, not self-interested but concerned about others. She came to see the sense of virtue that attaches to approved female behavior as masking an acceptance by women of their own social devaluation. And, she concluded, the only way to change the value system that consigns women to secondary status is to relinquish stereotypical female behavior. She doesn't accept the assumption that women naturally do or need to act nonaggressively or nonpretentiously. This, she thinks, is learned behavior and is professionally dangerous for women, because the legal system is innately adversarial and men are more used to functioning that way than women.

But accepting the need to play by men's rules does not resolve the great and often traumatic issue of childbearing. For this woman, the prospect of starting a family while still an associate was terrifying. "You have no control over your time as an associate, and I thought if I had children I would be completely out of control. But for a while, if I saw a baby in a restaurant or if male colleagues showed pictures of their babies, I would burst into tears." Still, she put off starting a family for fear of compromising her career. Then, after being made a partner, she conceived twice and had miscarriages both times. "At this point the issue wasn't wanting to be like a man, but wanting to be like a woman. I felt I wasn't fully a woman if I couldn't have children. All I cared about was being pregnant. I wasn't even thinking of a baby after a while, I simply wanted to be pregnant. Then I got pregnant and was nauseated all the time!" With this pregnancy nearing its term at the time of the first interview, she said she planned a maternity leave and then a return to work full-time.

Her commitment to a fast-track professional life was clear and firm. "It's about being a really full participant in the process of competition, not about changing or humanizing the environment. If women don't engage in competition, they will not gain power in society or over their own lives. The people controlling firms are men. If women don't compete for control, they will remain disenfranchised. Avoiding competition by claiming sensitivity is a cop-out. You ought to be honest about what you're doing. That's what motivates me to hang in there. I think it benefits other women for women like me to grapple with these issues, at not inconsiderable personal sacrifice. I think it's important to continue to struggle at this level. Women are always in the front lines of charities and volunteer activities and public interest groups, but that's not really where control over the allocation of resources in society takes place. Women have to enter the big-business arena to gain access to control over resources. The society is organized so that the sources of power are money or politics, and a law firm is a microcosm of the whole society. You can be on the sidelines arguing for maternity leave and so forth, but you will have no influence unless you get on the executive committee, and you get on the executive committee by being recognized as a person with a considerable client base, bringing in income."

This, I thought, listening, is the authentic voice of the seventies, a feminist argument for women to enter the places of highest power in the society and to operate in them as men do in order to gain what men have—power and money. In no uncertain terms she is holding on to the principles of equal rights and doing it straight through the eighties in spite of the constant attrition of women in the big firms, and the continuing inequality of the women who remain.

But then, a year after she made her bold and determined declaration of professional intent, she called me to say that she had recanted. It was her last day at work before going on leave, she said, perhaps for a year, perhaps forever. The baby had changed everything.

But her convictions had not changed simply and easily overnight. Rather, she said, she had gone through a protracted period of emotional confusion and pain before coming to the conclusions she had announced. She asked whether we could talk again so that she could explain the new shape of her thinking, and about six months later we met at her home, with her eighteen-month-old daughter running about and the litigator-turned-mother imminently expecting the birth of her second child.

Her daughter, she told me, was born in March 1990, and she followed the plan she had described earlier, taking three months' maternity leave and returning to work in June. She solved her child-care problem with a live-in nanny. "I had no trouble going back full-time at that point," she said. "The nanny was good. The baby was eating and sleeping normally. It was nice to come home to the baby. Although right away I had a week of late hours and nights, I didn't feel stressed out, even though I had a mild recurrence of the health problems I had had before."

But over the summer she began to feel a troubling conflict between home and work. She didn't have a huge backlog of cases waiting for her attention, but building up new work would have put her back on her old heavy schedule, with late hours and unpredictable late nights. And she was reluctant to make that commitment because, as the weeks went by, the baby was becoming more responsive, more active, and the mother at work missed her. She began to see that the baby's life had an ebb and flow of its own, a certain rhythm that had nothing to do with the schedule of a mother trying to hold, feed, bathe, and sing to the baby between 6:00 and 8:00 p.m.

By the time the child was nine months old, the mother's state of anxiety was acute. "I had a hard time feeling an involvement and interest at work, which was a complete turnaround," she declared, "because until the baby was born, marriage and work were everything in my life." Her husband kept assuring her that she was simply in a difficult transition and when her work picked up again and got more interesting, after the three-month hiatus, she would feel differently. But she saw it the other way around. She was coming to think that as a child grew, its need for the mother grew, and so did the bond between them. "I would sit in my office, and I felt something like physical pain, wanting to be with her," she said.

On the other hand, she had always felt that women were wrong to throw away their careers when their children were born, and she thought her husband might be right, that she just needed time and some support getting back into the competition. The baby did not seem to be suffering. She didn't cry when the mother left for work, and seemed happy with the nanny, who had been with her since she was two weeks old. But for the mother to get back into work wholeheartedly she would have to, she told me, "shut down feelings of attachment to the baby, repress them." And this she did not want to do, because "they were the best feelings I'd had in my life." She also worried that the baby, in order to accept her mother's leaving every day, would necessarily be closing off her own growing feelings of attachment.

Further, the mother said, she began to feel that having a child allied her with other women for the first time in her life. Until then, she had always been, and wanted to be, associated with men. But with the baby, she said, laughing, "I became a member of the female race."

Finally, as the child approached her first birthday, the mother reached a point where she no longer felt conflicted. She knew she did not *want* to stay at work, but her husband still resisted the idea of her quitting, and they struggled to find a common understanding of what was happening and what they should do. They had always been equals. They were the same age, both lawyers, and they had traveled the path to partnership at the same time, although in different firms. In the dynamic of their relationship, it had always been important to her to be earning equally. And now she proposed to change their relation drastically. In effect, she was breaking their partnership agreement.

Although both were high earners, her husband was uneasy about the prospect of assuming sole financial responsibility for the family. He was also anxious about the baby's becoming more attached to her than to him. And he feared that she would be unhappy at home, because he knew her to be driven and intense at work and thought that her intensity would not be channeled productively if she resigned. He worried that she would become overinvolved with the child and make her neurotic.

What he did not understand, his wife came to believe, was that for the first time in their life together, her position and feelings differed sharply from his. Though he said that he, too, would love to stay home with the baby rather than go to work, her view was that this was not true for him in the same way it was for her. She told me that he had stayed at home for two weeks after the baby was born, but that he did not suffer when he returned to work. Actually, she said, at the end of the two weeks her husband was itching to get out. He seemed to have an urge not to let an attachment to the child draw either himself or his wife away from the world he thought they really belonged in. The difference between husband and wife at work as the baby grew, the wife thought, was the difference between his missing the child and feeling pangs of sadness and her being in a state of near breakdown when she was separated from the baby all day. She also thinks these differences are true of most men and women.

As the marriage partners argued this fundamental issue, the wife realized that she was trying to gain her husband's agreement to her decision to leave work, to gain his permission to do it, and that he was not going to agree. She saw that if she was to change the basic pattern of their lives, she would have to do it on her own. She then made her choice, which by that time, she said, "was almost not a choice: I *had* to be with this baby, I *had* to be at home." And she announced that decision to her husband. She told him he could either help her to figure out how to make the transition positively or continue to resist and make both of them miserable. It took him about a month, she said, but he finally accepted what she was doing and helped considerably to figure out how to do it.

The crux of the matter, this determined young woman concluded, was that she found it difficult to function in a competitive world *and* be at home, where she wanted to create a calm, supportive, nonstressful atmosphere. She said that a peaceful homelife was wholly at odds with "the behavior and personality traits you have to encourage in the work world, and in litigation especially." In that world, she declared, "Everything is adversarial. You have to deal with conflicts in the substance of your work *and* in the politics of the firm. You have to compete with your colleagues, argue with your clients, and even become adversarial with the associates working for you when they think you are overdemanding and critical." She paused, then added, "I didn't want to spend the day fighting with people. I couldn't split myself like that. There was no question about it."

Then she found that staying home with the baby was "new and different and delicious." And despite her husband's concern that her drive to achieve and succeed would be dangerously frustrated at home, relief from the stress of work, she said, "has made me a content, happy person for the first time in my life." Also, she finds that she is much more involved with her extended family—her parents and her husband's parents—than she used to be. She has found that a woman at home, by being in touch with everyone, can tend to the fabric of the family in an ongoing way. "I can visit the sick," she said. "My mother can call me and I can give her time. This is a whole part of life that is very important, and I had never been inclined to devote time to it." Musing on the new shape her days had taken, she added, "I go to sleep thinking of happy things that happened. When I was working, you had to forget what you had been doing to get to sleep."

When we last spoke, she was still trying to think through the new relations within the family that her decision had set in motion. She said that while she was at her law firm, she relied heavily on her husband for the emotional support she needed to deal with the jolts, fights, and daily demands of her pressured work. Now that she had left all that, she said, she was in the role of the person who could give support, for a change, which gave her pleasure. She was also thinking about the nature of a family and how it functions. "You can't have children and think you can pursue your former individual lives as if there were nothing there," she began. "There's a unit now. You have to think how *it* functions. If both parents are working all the time, they have little energy to give to the family as a whole, and their lives are imbalanced." She had also concluded that children necessarily suffer when both parents have high-powered careers that leave the children little of the constant, daily connection that builds intimacy.

The future, she said, she was leaving open, unplanned, for the first time in her life. Her second child's birth not far off, she intended to stay at home for a while. Perhaps when both children are in school five days a week, she suggested, she would try to reenter the work world—but not on the same track she had left. She wanted to fit work into family life, rather than family life into work. She might find some unpressured area of law, she thought, or take on public interest projects, or she might look outside the law completely. She told me that she felt released from any ambition to move back into high-status legal work, because she had left already successful at one of the toughest games in town. She had made partner at a highly regarded, highly competitive law firm, and she had done it in litigation, not in a traditional woman's field.

She added that she didn't feel insecure at parties when she couldn't say that she worked at some specific thing, and had, in fact, come to find work talk boring. She preferred to talk with women, especially women with children. "All my life," she said, "I felt I had to go to the best schools and get the best jobs, but now I think that work, in the future, is not going to be the sole or major source of my self-worth."

And what does all this mean for other women, and other men, and for the practice of law in general? I asked. It sounded as if this young woman had wholly rejected the equal-rights convictions of the seventies and come to accept the old rules that put men at the top of powerful professions and women at home or on the professional margins. And she seemed to think that the reason for those rules was that women with children were not just culturally but naturally inclined to put children first in a way that men were not. Is that what she meant, I wondered?

Not exactly, she said. She believed that a lot of men had accepted the competitive atmosphere of the big firms and the toll it took on their family life because they thought they had to, and they felt lucky if they had a good homelife that could bolster them. Others may not have liked the nature of the work but thought that engaging in battle every day is what it is to be a man. But she also believed that the majority of men putting in long hours and driving the law firms and the major companies were people who liked competition and did not miss a homelife. And those who couldn't stand this pattern of life dropped out—as she thought an increasing number of new associates, male as well as female, were doing.

Does this mean, I then asked, that there is something fundamentally wrong, emotionally constricting and unhealthy, about the professional environment she herself had been happy to leave? That was a judgment she would not make. "That's the real world," she said firmly. "That's human nature. It's the nature of the process. The legal process is an adversarial, competitive process. The business world is a competitive environment. That's fundamentally the way the world works. 'Like it or leave it' is my view. I don't think you can change the way people conduct business. It's naïve to think so. Law firms sometimes try to work on morale problems, but if morale is bad for associates, it's because they have to work hard for eight years with no assurance of a future at the firm. Tension is built into the system. And it's worse in bad economic times."

In any case, she added, the core work of the legal system was an exciting, stimulating process to have been involved in. "The system is flawed," she admitted, "but there is something honorable about struggling within a flawed system. I don't have the expectation that things will work the right way. You have to see life as it is and find your own way to happiness."

That was essentially the same credo of realism that she had espoused when we first talked, before the birth of her first child, when she still assumed she would continue to practice as a litigation partner in a major, powerful law firm. At that time, as in these last remarks, she insisted that women must take the big firms as they find them if they are to gain professional authority. They must recognize that the practice of law is structured by a relentlessly adversarial system and that women who want to be taken seriously cannot shy away from it. In this third conversation, the new element in her thinking was her hard-won recognition that she could not be an adversary and a mother at the same time. She could not be aggressive and competitive for eight or nine or ten hours a day and then, on her return home, become loving, sympathetic, patient, and generous. But she had not concluded that there is something radically wrong with a system that breeds in adults a style of behavior that is harmful to children. She had come to believe only that *she* could not stay in that system. She is not a radical reformer.

A careful lawyer, this woman did not venture philosophically beyond the issues she needed to answer for herself, but the experience she described is full of large questions, both for women generally and for the society. What appears in her story is a portrait of a competitive ethic so extreme that it sets up painful psychological conflicts for someone engaged in the normal activity of caring for a child. The woman declared that this extremity is the way of the world and must be accepted as such—take it or leave it. But is extreme competitiveness so necessary, so valuable to the practice of law, as to be beyond question?

Certainly, at present, the culture of the big firms praises and rewards practitioners who demonstrate the masculine qualities of toughness and aggressiveness that make them successful competitors. And it also praises, if it does not reward, the women who drop out to give time to families. Within the terms of the prevailing culture, these women have appropriately chosen to express the feminine virtues of nurturing, caring, and giving to others. That is, the culture and its rewards harden the dichotomy between masculine and feminine, the man's world and the woman's world. And in so doing, the system both pushes women out of big-firm practice and validates the competitive ethic of the men (and women) who stay.

While this might be the way of the world, it is a way that is pushing the world it organizes into patterns of more and more serious social inequity—not just with respect to women in the law but, more generally, with respect to the society the law serves. And the two forms of inequity are connected. The woman in the story above correctly links the competitive ethic in law firms to the competitive ethic of the business world, and it is this basic pattern of competition that needs to be examined for its part in the conflicts many women feel in big-firm practice.

Americans, more than any other people in the industrialized world, have relied on the principle of competition to organize their economic life. And, at base, this is a principle that denies the importance of broad social connectedness. It is a Darwinian principle that justifies the survival of the fittest. Whoever enters the marketplace and reaps the largest gains deserves them. The gains are the reward for effort and skill and creativity and luck. The losers deserve to lose. That is the ideology. Bad economic times, like the Great Depression of the 1930s, have forced some modifications of this basic belief. The New Deal of the thirties and the Great Society of the sixties both expressed the idea that all Americans bear some responsibility for one another's welfare. But the old, resilient faith—the belief in the rightness, the necessity, the inevitability, of unregulated competition as a way of economic life—springs up again whenever political efforts to control it are relaxed. And they were relaxed with a vengeance in the 1980s.

In the big law firms, the results were dramatic. As we have seen, the new style of practice offered to those at the top—the senior partners of the biggest law firms—incomes lawyers had not even dreamt of as late as the 1970s. Lured by the loose money available in the newly deregulated markets of the eighties, the top law firms threw themselves into competitive business practices as they never had before. They raided other firms for top lawyers, courted clients aggressively, and added armies of tough young associates to their ranks to provide, on the instant, any service clients wanted. In the process, the competitive spirit fostered but also channeled and controlled by the traditional adversarial system was let loose by the new profit seeking of the 1980s to heighten the tension and pressure on all its practitioners. And the effect on women, especially those carrying direct personal responsibility for others, was to drive them out.

But the pressure on big-firm lawyers was not just a matter of all-encompassing claims on their time and nervous energy. The new competitiveness also exerted intensified pressure on the lawyers' ethics, on the moral core of the profession. To gain big clients and keep them, law firms had to deliver zealous protection of their clients' complex corporate interests, right to the edge of illegality—and sometimes beyond.

For example, in March 1992, the federal government levied a fine of $41 million on the New York law firm of Kaye, Scholer, Fierman, Hayes & Handler for complicity in the illegal activities of its client Charles Keating, Jr., who as head of the Lincoln Savings and Loan Association had profited massively from the widespread illegal lending and fraud that had triggered the disastrous failures of S&Ls across the country in the late 1980s. The firm was accused of exceeding proper bounds in protecting their notorious client's interests, and though they denied culpability, they did agree to pay the fine. Then, in April 1993, another firm, Jones, Day, Reavis and Pogue, agreed to pay the government $51 million to settle a case based on similar charges of aiding Keating's fraud.

The moral dimension of these episodes arises in the paying of their costs. Because the S&Ls' losses were backed by the Federal Deposit Insurance Corporation (FDIC), they had to be covered by the federal government, which is to say by the American taxpayers. The American middle class specifically, bearing the bulk of the nation's tax burden, was paying for a looting of the nation's riches by unscrupulous bankers protected, virtually to the prison door, by zealous big-firm lawyers.

The lasting problem for the legal profession is that it did not withstand, at its places of greatest power, the buccaneering business norms of the period. Rather, its own culture of competition seemed to boost along the aggrandizement of wealth and power by the few with little concern for the effects of their actions on the many.

Given the aftermath of the eighties—economic recession, jail sentences for investment bankers, hefty fines for their lawyers, a shaken financial structure, a widened gap between rich and poor—a long reexamination of legal ethics is due. Something is ethically wrong with a culture that validates tough, aggressive, adversarial practices untempered by a sense of responsibility for their consequences. And something is seriously wrong with a profession that requires its practitioners to think and act as if they were unrelated to other human beings. The ethic of competition in the big firms, undercutting older norms of social responsibility, clearly needs to be curbed. In this situation, the resistance of many women to competitive practices is valuable to the profession as a source of needed criticism.

But I do not take the moral of these intertwined stories—the stories of women leaving the competitive ethos of the big firms and the stories of ethical failures in those firms—to be that women shunning competition should stand, automatically, as the new exemplars. For one thing, not all women did shun the competitive games of the eighties. A number of them were as deeply involved as their male colleagues in the excesses of that era. But, more important, I do not think that women should accept the role sometimes thrust on them of natural carriers of a morally superior approach to professional life. This is the role implied in the idea that the legal profession or any other will automatically improve in moral tone as it includes more women. The belief in the moral superiority of women is just another version of the old dichotomy that requires distinct behaviors from the two sexes and inevitably connects public power to the behavior of men.

What is needed—and what women who are particularly discomfited by untempered competition might start to provide—is discussion that complicates and breaks down the simplistic division between masculine and feminine, tough and soft, in the practice of law. This division, like the mind/body split, masquerades as a natural phenomenon—the way of the world—but is actually a division of power. It is a division of power between men and women and between economic elites and outsiders. To validate toughness within a competitive economic system is to license the use of power by the strong without concern for the way their actions work through the intricate connections of the social system to affect the weak. Taking responsibility for the weak is a "soft" activity assigned to others —mainly women. To strengthen social responsibility within the economic system generally and the legal system specifically, the tough/soft line needs to be erased and the mechanism of competition carefully reconstructed.

Perhaps women, because they occupy the point of greatest conflict between an ethic of competition and an ethic of care, are well placed to bring to the profession this new complication. Out of their mixed experience of legal analysis and responsibility for others, they might bring to big-firm practice the new metaphors called for by the federal magistrate quoted earlier, metaphors that go beyond the winning and losing in sports and war. (I will look at some thinking of this kind in Chapter 7, which examines new models of legal practice being developed by women in various corners of the profession.)

But women are rarely able to apply to the big firms the critiques they develop cut of their particular experience, because, for the most part, they leave the firms before gaining the authority to speak and be heard. And they leave with little recognition gained by their firms of the significance of the conflict that drives them out. In each case, the conflict appears to be a logistical problem, and the leaving a personal choice. The moral dimension of the conflict—the blindness to human need in unrestrained competition—goes unexplored.

6

MEDIA

IN ONE WEEK IN MAY 1992, a woman lawyer was shot in a court-house hallway and another was murdered, albeit symbolically, by her own mother, in two very different TV dramas. Watching this outbreak of serious hostility toward women lawyers, I realized that my examination of cultural attitudes concerning them had to include a look at the media. For several months, then, I watched more TV and all the movies I could identify about women lawyers, and also followed, amazed, the struggles of Hillary Rodham Clinton, the lawyer wife of the Democratic presidential candidate Bill Clinton, to project an image of herself broadly acceptable to Americans. What she had to contend with was a widespread negative reaction against precisely her lawyerly qualities—strength, confidence, articulateness, combativeness—qualities that made her seem harsh and cold. Her struggle intensified when she was indirectly but clearly attacked by Marilyn Quayle, an ex-lawyer and the wife of the Republican vice president, Dan Quayle, who was running for reelection. Ms. Quayle, who had forsaken a legal career for her family, virtually accused Ms. Clinton of denying her essential nature as a woman by practicing her contentious profession.

Further attacks by Republican campaign officials centered on Hillary Clinton's early scholarship, in which she advocated the development of children's legal rights against abusive or irresponsible parents. She had noted in several articles published in the seventies that the usual rationale for depriving people of rights is their incapacity to make decisions about their own welfare, and explained that in such instances, the society allows others to hold authority over the incapacitated group. For children, the protective institution is the family. Other such institutions in the past, Ms. Clinton wrote, were marriage and slavery. Her point, I take it, is that these institutions no longer hold their once-acknowledged authority.

Slavery no longer exists, and married women hold their own rights. And so, she concluded, should children, to some degree.

This was a new but not wildly radical point of view in the field of family law when the articles were published, but in 1992, Republicans jumped on Ms. Clinton's words to picture her, in inflammatory language, as antimarriage and antifamily. She had likened marriage to slavery! And she would give children rights to sue their parents if the kids did not want to help with family chores! One pamphlet on sale at the Republican National Convention called her a "dowdy feminazi" and added that she was the person who "really wears the pants" in her husband's presidential campaign. By way of contrast, the Republicans promoted the image of President George Bush's wife, Barbara, the quintessential helpmate and mother and the nation's plump, lovable, white-haired grandmother.

The apparent response of the Clinton campaign was to soften Hillary Clinton's public image. Even before the stepped-up attacks at the Republican convention, she had begun to wear softer colors and a softer hairstyle. And stories began to appear in popular magazines about her qualities as a good mother. In July, *People* magazine pictured the Clinton family on its cover, parents and twelve-year-old daughter, Chelsea, nestled together, smiling, on their back lawn. The story, accompanied by more pictures of the family at home, included Bill Clinton's statement that Hillary's greatest achievement was to be a "wonderfully successful" wife and mother. And increasingly, Ms. Clinton remained silent when campaigning with her husband, adopting the traditional adoring smile prescribed for political wives and applauding vigorously as her candidate husband spoke.

As the campaign wore on, the media began to note some backlash to the attacks on Ms. Clinton, some substantial sympathy for her, especially on the part of working women, and antipathy for her attackers. But clearly, both before and after Bill Clinton's election, the persona of Hillary Clinton, a self-assured and successful professional woman, a practicing corporate lawyer and political adviser to her husband, did not easily fit into the cultural space reserved for presidents' wives. Professional women have cheered her, but for many, her image in the media has produced ambivalent reactions, a certain nervousness about women in the law, women making the law, women with power. And fictional portrayals of women lawyers in the media seem to reflect that same ambivalence, although in some instances, such as the shootings already mentioned, ambivalence gives way to outright antagonism.

But media representations of real and fictional people do more than reflect social attitudes. They also shape them. Quietly, covertly, media images teach young women entering the law—and practicing lawyers, too—what kind of behavior is acceptable, what manner, what speech, what dress. They convey disapprobation for violations of accepted form —usually more subtly than by shooting. They influence identities and self-understandings. And to the extent that they ratify the social conventions that have confined women to the private sphere—the conventions that Hillary Clinton challenged—the images undermine women's claim to full authority in the law.

And, for the most part, undermining and disapproving *is* what these media images do, although rarely blatantly. The subgenre of woman lawyer stories in the movies and on TV is fairly sophisticated, at least superficially. It is a recent genre, fully developing only in the 1980s following the first noticeable appearance of women lawyers in American life in the 1970s. There were several notable precedents: *The Merchant of Venice*, in 1596 or so, and *Adam's Rib*, with Katharine Hepburn and Spencer Tracy, in 1949. But it wasn't until the mid-1980s that the place and the behavior of women in the law began to be frequently explored.

As of this writing, woman lawyer heroines have been featured in about a dozen fairly prominent Hollywood movies: *First Monday in October* (Jill Clayburgh, 1981), *Jagged Edge* (Glenn Close, 1985), *Legal Eagles* (Debra Winger, 1986), *Suspect* (Cher, 1987), *The Big Easy* (Ellen Barkin, 1987), *The Accused* (Kelly McGillis, 1988), *Music Box* (Jessica Lange, 1989), *Presumed Innocent* (Greta Scacchi, 1990), *Class Action* (Mary Elizabeth Mastrantonio, 1991), and *Defenseless* (Barbara Hershey, 1991). On TV, the most notable series has been *L.A. Law*, a drama set in a small corporate law firm made up of highly attractive male and female lawyers engaged often—and fairly realistically—in contemporary issues of great complexity, as well as in the more usual private agonizings over love and lust. The program went on the air in 1986 and quickly won a large, loyal audience, including mesmerized law students across the country. Other series involving women lawyers that have lasted long enough to note are *The Trials of Rosie O'Neill* (now off the air), *Civil Wars*, and *Reasonable Doubts*, whose heroines are, respectively, a public defender, a divorce lawyer, and a deaf assistant district attorney.

One major theme driving the plots in many of these stories is precisely the negative reaction toward women who defy the mind/body split (as discussed in Chapter 4) that lay behind the attacks on Hillary Clinton. In that ancient tradition, if a woman chooses to live in some significant way through her mind, she places herself at odds with her body, her emotions, her womanliness. And the mind/body stories generally show that a woman cannot cross the line into the world of men without relinquishing something of her womanhood, and suffering for it. Most extreme are the stories of women who eschew all feminine qualities and engage in the male world of power with tough, cold, self-aggrandizing calculation. Such women in movie and TV plots are sure to meet brutal punishment.

An unusual dramatization of stark transgression and retribution is Nancy Barr's *Mrs. Cage*, a seventy-minute, two-character play that was telecast by PBS's *American Playhouse* in May 1992, starring Anne Bancroft. One of the two characters is Mrs. Cage, a conventional, respectable, upper-middle-class housewife in her late fifties who has inexplicably shot and killed a young professional woman she did not know in a supermarket parking lot. (This is the first of the two shootings that set me off on this inquiry about media images.) The other main character is the police detective who, in our stead, is trying to find out why Mrs. Cage did what she did.

The facts are not in dispute. The young woman who was killed preceded Mrs. Cage in the supermarket checkout line, ordered the checker, a high school boy, to carry her groceries to her car, and encountered in the parking lot a man who grabbed her purse and ran. The checkout boy ran after the thief, who shot and killed him and then dropped the gun. Mrs. Cage picked up the gun and shot the woman.

We learn that Mrs. Cage, a few months before, had taken a great liking to the young boy who was killed, touched by his flirtatious smile, his courtesy, and his high-spirited singing of the *Rawhide* theme song as he gathered shopping carts in the parking lot. We also learn that she had instantly disliked the woman whose demands had put the boy in a situation that caused his death. Mrs. Cage had observed her parking in a handicapped space, pushing into the express checkout line with more items than the maximum allowed, and insisting that the boy leave his checkout station to carry her grocery bags. Then when he was shot pursuing the thief, the young woman stood screaming not about him but about her stolen purse. That's when Mrs. Cage shot her.

But fondness for the boy and outrage with the woman would not alone have moved the decent, rational Mrs. Cage to kill. What emerges slowly, circuitously, never wholly spelled out, is that the young woman reminded Mrs. Cage of her daughter, who is, like Mr. Cage, a lawyer.

Mrs. Cage's husband is a criminal-defense lawyer, an upholder of the rights of the accused, but her lawyer/daughter seems to lack any moral framework. She appears to be out for herself, heedless of others. She likes making money. She is divorcing her husband and beginning an affair with a man already divorced and with children. She parks her car anywhere she wants and pays off hundreds of dollars in fines at the end of the year. She is thoughtlessly contemptuous of her mother's domestic skills, which include the perfect ironing of Mr. Cage's shirts. Nothing that Mrs. Cage holds dear—marriage, constancy, long-term giving, courtesy, and concern for others—seems to be valued by her daughter, or by the pushy young woman in the supermarket.

The policeman presses Mrs. Cage as to whether she feels remorse. She says that she does, although it is clear that she was struck with remorse only when she heard that the dead woman's mother had been notified. It hadn't occurred to her, until then, that the woman would have a mother. She was remorseful about the mother, not the daughter.

As Mrs. Cage, Anne Bancroft is so honest and appealing, so full of pain and integrity, that she compels helpless sympathy from the viewer, but what are we supposed to sympathize with? Are we supposed to ratify her act? And what does the act, the killing, mean? Is it an ultimate condemnation of women who leave the traditional place of their mothers and enter their fathers' world? Do such women violate their nature so badly in that world that they become moral monsters, spreading death around them? Or do they, by crossing the mind/body boundary, threaten the right order of males and females? Does their appropriation of the masculine role squelch the joyous, exuberant male energy represented by the supermarket boy? Or was the shooting, perhaps, an act of anguish over the plight of mothers, who live by the principle of love and then relinquish their children into a society that lives by the hard principles of contract represented by the law, principles that kill spontaneity, generosity, sweetness, affection, caring, and joy? Or did Mrs. Cage shoot in murderous protest against her own entrapment in the "cage" of an unwanted, unneeded role, relieved only by the dream of freedom represented by the singing boy? Did she kill the "daughter" who was the heedless killer of her dream?

We don't know. Mrs. Cage doesn't know. But we are left, nonetheless, with a mother symbolically killing a daughter who has entered a lawyer father's world. And the sympathy the mother commands from the police detective and from the audience suggests, at the very least, tremendous ambivalence about the place of the daughters in the law. We do not ratify the killing, but we sympathize with the mother and shrink from the daughter.

Mrs. Cage is a complicated story, delicately told, that asks questions it does not answer about the conflicts and confusions surrounding the movement of women into places of power. But while Mrs. Cage condemns her daughter's coldhearted professionalism, her story also presents a bleak picture of the conventional alternative, the woman at home. The viewer is left unsettled, does not know where to turn. But in most TV and movie renderings of coldly ambitious professional women, we are not left in moral doubt. Such women are monstrous and meet horrible deaths, richly deserved.

A classic case is the fate of the power-seeking prosecutor played by Greta Scacchi in the film version of Scott Turow's novel *Presumed Innocent*. Her gruesome murder actually opens the story, which then centers on the struggles of the hero (played by Harrison Ford), a deputy prosecutor of great personal charm and professional virtue, to clear himself of charges that he killed her. As he fights to prove his innocence, details of the woman's life accumulate, in recollection and flashback, until we see her virtually as a demon inhabiting the body of a stunningly beautiful woman. We see someone whose mind is bent so utterly on power that she coldly, repeatedly, uses her gorgeous body to gain whatever advantage she needs from hungry, vulnerable men, including the hero. An obsessive affair with her has been his one fall from grace, but we are asked to sympathize with this transgression because he has an unhappy wife (played by Bonnie Bedelia), an intellectual embittered by her inability to make it in the academic world. Eventually the charges against the hero are dismissed, but it is not he so much as the dead woman the story asks us to judge, and it asks us to judge her harshly. In case we are in any doubt, we learn that the hero's sidekick, a tough but lovable police detective, thinks the hero did kill the woman in a moment of fury provoked by her betrayal of his passion. But, the detective assures his friend, she deserved it.

I should add that it is somewhat difficult to extract the mind/body moral from the general misogyny that pervades the plot of *Presumed Innocent*. Almost all its women characters appear as victimizers of men. In addition to the monster/seductress, we see or hear of a mother who tortures her young son by squeezing his head in a vise, a judge's wife who abandons her deserving husband, driving him to drink and bribe taking, and, of course, the hero's wife, whose unhappiness drives her husband into the arms of another woman (and drives her to horrible acts I will not reveal here). The only woman who appears in a positive guise is a disabled lawyer confined to a wheelchair. Presumably she is granted a license to use her mind without disapprobation because her body has already been compromised.

Perhaps the most blatant warning to women that the excessive use of mind will curdle their womanhood and make monsters of them was delivered by *L.A. Law* in the story of Rosalind Shays, the only really powerful woman lawyer among the half dozen or so who have been regular members of the cast. Shays (Diana Muldaur), a middle-aged attorney with a string of large corporate clients, was brought into the show's firm as a partner to shore it up financially at a point when its fortunes were shaken. Beautiful, formidably competent, quietly manipulative, icily realistic, and completely committed to making money, she saved the firm but in the process so irked her mellow partners that in a series of episodes in the 1990–91 season, they forced her out. However, she returned to the story, first waging a successful sex-discrimination suit against the firm, and then, despite that hostile act, settling into a romantic interlude with the firm's founder and patriarch, Leland McKenzie (Richard Dysart).

In the course of their affair, Rosalind declares her love for Leland and asks him to marry her. Flattered but confused, he declines, telling her that he values her companionship but does not love her.

In a later sequence, while waiting for an elevator in the firm's office tower, the two quarrel mildly about business matters, and Leland chides Rosalind for holding out on some minor point out of resentment over his rejection of her. She protests that this is not the case, and he says that it is, that he, after all, has said he does not love her. At this precise point, the elevator door opens and Rosalind steps in, only to plummet down an empty shaft to her death. And as if this were not horrible enough, we learn that her body, entangled in cables at a point of limited access to the shaft, cannot be retrieved for a day or so.

Except for Leland, no one grieves. Several lawyers joke about the accident. The message seems clear. Women who enter the world of men, follow male rules, and win male rewards in power and money are somehow monstrous. They deserve to lose their positions. They do not deserve love. And they deserve to die, horribly.

In many film and television stories, the mind/body split, and some form of punishment for a woman opting for mind, appears in less obvious, less exaggerated form. Often, the woman lawyer is portrayed as a competent professional, tough, perhaps, but not egregiously so, sharp and competitive, and yet attractive and capable of winning love. But still, something is usually missing—children, or a husband, or both. We see the woman lawyer as incomplete.

In the movies and TV shows I've looked at, there are, altogether, twenty women lawyers who are main characters, and only five have children. One (Glenn Close's character in *Jagged Edge*) has two; the rest, including Rosalind Shays, have one. But Rosalind's daughter, we are not surprised to learn, does not speak to her monstrous mother.

Another of the *L.A. Law* regulars, Ann Kelsey (Jill Eikenberry), not only has a child, but its begetting and birthing, more or less on camera, occupied most of one TV season; that drama was preceded by the attempted adoption by Ann and her husband, Stuart Markowitz (Michael Tucker), of a baby girl who was reclaimed at the last minute by her birth mother. Ann and Stuart fought the reclamation in court, but lost. So motherhood plays a large part in Ann Kelsey's story, but she is unusual among her fictional peers in that respect, and also with respect to marriage. The only other married woman among the group is Amanda Bonner (Katharine Hepburn), in *Adam's Rib*. Eleven of the twenty are divorced; Ann is the only one who is both married and a mother.

One other among the group directly discusses the compatibility of motherhood and professionalism, although in distinctly odd terms, and that is Ruth Loomis (Jill Clayburgh), who becomes the first woman Supreme Court justice in *First Monday in October*. On her nomination to the Supreme Court from a judgeship on a federal court of appeals, Loomis appears for the requisite hearing before the Senate Judiciary Committee, where the senators try to fathom how her sex is related to the law. In reply to their clumsy questions, she informs them that it is entirely possible to have both a uterus and a brain, and she goes on to say that she hopes that her womanhood *will* influence her decision-making. Men are influenced by being men, she says, and for two hundred years, that has been the only influence on the Supreme Court. It is time, she proclaims, that the majority of the people, women, were represented by at least one Supreme Court justice. Then, when one senator mentions the fact that Loomis has no children (she is a middle-aged widow), she replies that she has had hundreds of children in the form of her court opinions and her writings. She sends her opinions out into the world, she explains, and they are full of ideas that grow, change, develop, and affect people, taking on a life of their own, like children.

The senators are suitably silenced by her feisty replies and approve her nomination forthwith. But the viewer is left to wonder where the uterus comes in. No doubt Judge Loomis has one, *and* a brain, but she has given birth only through the brain. The *First Monday* plot, carrying out the cultural mandate to enforce the mind/body split, does not allow her to do both.

Nonetheless, most of the women lawyers who have begun to appear as dramatic or comedic heroines do not appear to suffer from their childless state. They may talk about it from time to time, but the issue does not seem to dominate their lives. What we see most often as evidence that some price has been paid for their shift into the man's world of the mind is that something is unstable, awry, in their emotional lives, more or less permanently. They are beautiful, professionally successful women who have been wrenched from their emotional base, and they are somewhat at sea, somewhat off-balance. The public defender heroine (played by Sharon Gless) of *The Trials of Rosie O'Neill*, for example, appeared at the beginning of each show in her psychiatrist's office. Her husband had left her for another woman. She was happy at work, unhappy at home. The woman divorce lawyer (Mariel Hemingway) in *Civil Wars* is herself divorced, and seems, at least through 1992, to spend her nonwork time either at home with a book or involved with some utterly unsuitable man.

The emotional lives of the women on *L.A. Law* are constantly troubled. Grace Van Owen (Susan Dey), a moody character who was usually greatly affected by the traumas of her clients, was often involved in some passionate love affair that ultimately ended unhappily. However, when Dey chose to leave the series at the end of the 1991–92 season and Grace had to be written out of the script, the device used was to have the character, on a sudden impulse, throw over her work for love. She abandoned her partnership in the L.A. firm in order to follow Victor Sifuentes (Jimmy Smits) to New York. Previously, she had renounced Victor, who had abandoned her after her pregnancy, by him, ended in miscarriage, but who, through therapy, had come to understand that he wanted and needed her. In choosing love, Grace had presumably stabilized her emotional life at last, but with what effect on her career we will never learn.

Abigail Perkins (played by Michele Greene) divorced an abusive husband, shied away from the advances of a number of men, had an affair with a married man, and explored a lesbian relationship for a while. She seemed fragile, permanently on edge.

Jill Eikenberry's Ann Kelsey gets it all together eventually—work, husband, baby—but she is almost always in an emotional dither that is usually resolved by her reasonable, easygoing, well-balanced husband. Shorter than she is, and chubby, he is also the softer, more maternal character of the two. Odd plot developments in the 1992–93 season change the relation between them, but in the show's heyday Stuart's continuing task was to bring Ann back to an emotional center.

The cheeriest of the L.A. women, Amanda Donohoe's character, C. J. Lamb, was outside the usual frame entirely. English, punk, and bisexual, she broke all the rules with charming insouciance. But apparently she went too far for many viewers, as she was dropped from the show after several seasons.

As for the movie lawyers, when plots focus on their personal lives, it is definitely to explore emotional imbalance. Glenn Close's character in *Jagged Edge* and Barbara Hershey's in *Defenseless* both sleep with male clients they are defending in criminal cases, believing the men to be innocent. Trouble, not surprisingly, ensues. The *Defenseless* heroine, talking to herself in her kitchen, laments her repeated involvement with men who use her. "Why do I do it?" she cries. Up against a world of violence and viciousness in her work, she seems vulnerable in her private life to the overtures of any strong, worldly man who offers love.

Another variation of imbalance to be found in women living through the mind is emotional and sexual repression. We see this in the character played by Ellen Barkin in the *The Big Easy*. A prosecutor investigating police corruption in New Orleans, she encounters a charming Cajun police lieutenant (Dennis Quaid) who is ostensibly responsible for providing police cooperation with her inquiries. His actual purpose, however, is to obfuscate the facts, which include his own involvement in a well-established police "protection" system. Realizing that the beautiful attorney, while intellectually acute, is sensually underdeveloped, the lieutenant sets out to rectify the situation, to teach her how to live.

They go to a Cajun restaurant, where he introduces her to the delights of exotic food. When she says she can't dance, he teaches her how. At his apartment, when he begins to make love to her, she says she can't relax. His tutelage continues, and he brings her to orgasm.

For her part, she leads him to uncover corruption that offends even his easy standards, with the result that she makes an honest man of him while he makes her a real woman. The movie ends at this point, so we don't know what happens to her mind once her body has been brought to life. But the last scene, in which she's wearing a sexy wedding dress and being carried across the threshold, suggests that the body, surrounded by tradition, prevails.

These plots all contain powerful messages warning women against living through the mind. Developing the mind for public work means curbing, quieting, distancing the body and its attendant emotions and senses. This, the stories say, is difficult and unnatural for women. If women move away from their bodies, they pay a price. At worst, they become monstrous and unlovable. At best, they find themselves emotionally adrift, lonely, childless. What we see in the media messages is tremendous resistance to the idea of women healing the mind/body split, joining the professional world and still living joyously through their emotions and senses and reproductive powers.

As I have argued earlier, the resistance is strong because the wholesale entry of women into public life, on their own terms, would force a wholesale reordering of the public and private spheres, which is to say a massive redistribution of power between men and women. It is this resistance that Hillary Clinton aroused, this resistance that sprang up, alarmed, when she walked onto the scene, a symbol of greater change than her husband's or any other presidential programs could ever bring about.

But the media messages about women lawyers carry a second line of resistance against the potential for serious change carried by women lawyers. And that is the practice of casting them, in one guise or another, as handmaidens of the law. These women do not enter the legal profession with different perspectives challenging the legitimacy of settled law. They have no radical agendas for rewriting the law. They may have questions and frustrations and disagreements from time to time, but on the whole they are upholders of established order.

Debra Winger's character in *Legal Eagles* learns her trade as a trial lawyer by patterning herself on the model supplied by her lawyer hero (Robert Redford). She even practices before the mirror the "looks" she sees on his face when he addresses juries. When she tells him this, he says, "You don't develop looks. You just look." Nevertheless, the point is that the looks belong to him. He owns them. To enter his world, she has to learn them, etch them into the muscles of her face, and she does.

Even more closely identified with the law as it stands is the deaf prosecutor played by Marlee Matlin in the TV series *Reasonable Doubts*. Except for lipreading and the occasional articulation of simple phrases, she communicates only through an interpreter, a male assistant proficient in sign language. She is completely integrated into the system, speaking literally with the voice of a man.

In *First Monday in October*, Jill Clayburgh's Ruth Loomis seems more combatively positioned, and spends much of the movie in pitched ideological battle with fellow justice Daniel Snow (Walter Matthau)—she a conservative, he a liberal. But at the end she remarks, "You know something? You and I make each other possible." And he replies, "Damn right we do." He had earlier remarked of the conservative jurist she replaced on the Court that the two of them were like buttresses, holding up the roof of Justice. If they were both on the same side, he said, they would push the structure down. In ratifying this view, Clayburgh's character is staunchly upholding the adversarial system, and the justice of its results.

The women of *L.A. Law* assume a similar stance, but their ratification of the system is especially powerful because unlike the comedic *First Monday*, *L.A. Law* is serious. Though the show often includes comic episodes, it has also explored some of the most difficult dilemmas the society faces, and treated them realistically. Looking just at women's issues, it has dealt with sex discrimination, battering, rape, incest, child-custody battles of lesbian mothers, maternal versus fetal rights, and, as mentioned earlier, the conflicting interests of birth mothers and adoptive mothers. Sometimes, the issues as they are argued out in court seem too complicated, too large, for the system to resolve fairly by the legal standards available. But generally, the show's outcomes are satisfying enough to convey full confidence in the law and its processes. The system is made to seem solid, admirable, probably the best we can do. Further, the women lawyers function in this fictional universe more or less on the same terms as the men do, and, apparently, satisfactorily to themselves. They are not questioners of the system.

In a number of these stories, the woman lawyer, rather than ratifying the general health of the system, restores it to health by operating as a moral force that exposes or removes some spot of corruption. As we've seen, this was one of the plot lines Ellen Barkin carries out in *The Big Easy*. So does Glenn Close in *Jagged Edge*. Close's character, Teddy Barnes, is a former assistant prosecutor who has left the practice of criminal law in remorse for succumbing to pressure to conceal evidence in a trial that put an innocent man in prison, where he ultimately committed suicide. Established in a big corporate law firm, she agrees reluctantly, at the request of senior partners, to take on the defense of an important client (Jeff Bridges) who has been accused of murdering his wife. She goes up against the same senior prosecutor (Peter Coyote) who had pressured her in the earlier case, and she is convinced that he is manipulating evidence again. In fact, he is not, but her trust in the system has nevertheless eroded seriously. Finally, Teddy nails all the guilty parties, including the untrustworthy prosecutor, whose incipient political career she effectively quashes with public revelations of his dishonesty.

Similarly, Cher, playing public defender Kathleen Riley in *Suspect*, uncovers the corruption of a federal district court judge before whom she is representing a homeless man accused of murder. Aided by a juror (the charmingly devilish Dennis Quaid, willing, as always, to bend a few rules in a good cause), she discovers that the judge, in a desperate attempt to cover up an act of bribery that had put him on the bench in the first place, actually wants to assure that her client is convicted. Revealing all this in the courtroom, Kathleen ends the crooked judge's career.

In two other stories of lawyer heroines exposing corruption, *Class Action* and *Music Box*, considerable cost is borne by the women for their heroic acts. In both cases, that cost involves the relation of the women to their fathers, who are also associated with the justice system —one is a lawyer, the other is a former police official. Both fathers are flawed men. Both daughters have entered the fathers' world of the law and are trying to stake out moral space for themselves there, but are confused by the morality that requires loyalty to flawed fathers. Both finally resolve their conflicts by allying themselves with the true spirit of the law, the principles of the fathers that transcend the flaws of human beings. They become true daughters of the law—one happily, one unhappily.

In *Music Box*, Anne Talbot (Jessica Lange) dances into the picture in the arms of her immigrant father (played by Armin Mueller-Stahl) at a Hungarian-American social affair, but soon becomes involved in defending him against charges that he committed war crimes as a policeman in Hungary during World War II. The father, who lovingly brought up his daughter alone after the death of his wife, protests his innocence. The daughter believes him. It appears that he is being framed by the then communist government of Hungary for his anti-communist activities directed against that government. The lawyer/daughter's defense efforts are aided by her ex–father-in-law, a tall, slim, elegant patrician (played by the bristly browed Donald Moffat), who is a wealthy pillar of the legal establishment. He taps wartime intelligence connections to produce evidence of the Hungarian government's hand in discrediting its foes in America. But, apparently driven by nagging doubts, the daughter seeks further evidence and finds it, uncovering her father's guilt. The only question is whether she will reveal the evidence and devastate her father's life. Will she act as a loving daughter or as a principled lawyer?

And here the pivotal figure is the father-in-law, representing the law as a force for right. When Anne says that she is not cynical enough to exploit the appeal of her young son by putting him on the stand to testify to his grandfather's kindness, the father-in-law replies, "Yes, you are. You're a lawyer like me." But pulling the heartstrings of a jury and pulling other strings to gain information about a foreign government are not the same as suppressing evidence of terrible crime. The proto-father gives the tormented daughter permission to be a tough adversary, but not to violate the integrity of the law. And she does not. In the conflict between the family father and the fathers' law, she stands with the law, acting as a moral force righting what has gone wrong.

In *Class Action*, lawyer Maggie Ward (Mary Elizabeth Mastrantonio) is at odds with her lawyer father, Jedediah (Gene Hackman), whose world she has entered but whose political values and professional choices she has rejected. He was a sixties radical and in middle age is a plaintiff's lawyer, bringing cases, often class actions, against corporations for various harms done to workers or consumers. His daughter, who learned the law at his knee, has opted instead for a large corporate law firm whose senior partner, a wealthy pillar of the legal establishment, is a tall, slim, elegant, bristly browed patrician played by (who else?) Donald Moffat.

This time, however, it is Moffat's character who is corrupt, who wants to suppress evidence of a client's culpability. His law firm is defending an automobile company that sold cars knowing an electrical defect would in certain circumstances cause the cars to explode. Company officials continue the sales after calculating that it would cost less to pay damages in lawsuits resulting from a predictable number of explosions than to recall the cars. As the movie begins, the company faces a suit in which victims of the expected several explosions are represented by Jedediah. This circumstance pits father and daughter, who has campaigned to get assigned to the case, against each other. Neither knows, at the outset, of the car company's guilt, or of the law firm's suppression of the evidence that would prove it.

The daughter has sought the case, a big, splashy one, to gain notice and credit in her quest for partnership in the firm, and she conducts vicious depositions of the plaintiffs, mercilessly unnerving a man who was crippled and whose wife and child were killed in one of the explosions. Jedediah, disgusted, says to her, "I hope you make a lot of money, because without a heart and soul, that's all you'll ever have."

Soon, however, the daughter discovers the corruption both in her client and in her firm, and following proper legal procedures, she lets Jedediah know about it. The client is obliged to settle the case for a huge amount. Maggie loses her position in the firm in which she had aspired to become a partner, but, repulsed by its corruption, she returns to her father's arms—literally. When last seen, the two are dancing together.

Here, moral standards in the law and filial love can both be fulfilled. The daughter does not have to choose between them. She can integrate herself completely into the law her father stands for. But what exactly does he stand for? Are we supposed to conclude that corporate law firms chronically bend their ethics to their clients' desires, and that the radical father represents true morality because he fights a chronically corrupt system? If this is the case, then the story stands as a strong condemnation of the system as it is, and its heroine stands not as an upholder of patriarchal order but as a challenger of it. However, the movie has nothing of this tone. Rather, the role of the supposedly radical father seems to be to work within the system to keep it honest. He and others like him are keeping pressure on the companies and their legal counsel to stay straight, play fair. He uses the adversarial system as a tool of social justice, and it is this role that his daughter adopts. She is not going outside the system in leaving her big firm. She is simply switching sides within it. She is still a loyal member of the established order and brings a particular sensitivity to corruptions that might threaten it.

Perhaps as a warning to women lawyers who make the wrong choices when confronted with moral dilemmas, a woman prosecutor on *L.A. Law* who followed a superior's directive to suppress awkward evidence, even to the point of lying about it under oath, was shot by an enraged plaintiff as she emerged from the courtroom. This is the second of the two shootings I mentioned at the beginning of this chapter. The lawyer was Zoey Clemmons (Cecil Hoffmann), the little assistant district attorney with waist-length blond hair who generally struggled mightily to do what's right. And she did in this instance too. Leaving the courtroom in which she'd perjured herself, she told her boss she was going back in to withdraw her testimony and tell the truth even if admitting to perjury resulted in her disbarment, because remaining in the profession wasn't worth losing her integrity. But just at this point, the desperate man whose case her testimony had destroyed burst into the corridor with a gun and opened fire. She was not allowed to desert her post as keeper of moral order for even a few minutes. (We learn in a later episode that Zoey survives the shooting but believes that she *was* being punished for her self-serving perjury.)

In the media, then, most women lawyers stand foursquare behind the system. But sometimes the fit is not exact. Occasionally a dissonant perspective appears around the edges, and the woman lawyer in some way poses a challenge to the status quo. The most directly subversive of the lot is Amanda Bonner, Katharine Hepburn's character in *Adam's Rib*. She and her husband, Adam (Spencer Tracy), are both lawyers—she a solo practitioner, he a prosecutor. They end up on opposite sides of a case brought against an aggrieved wife (Judy Holliday) who has burst in on her husband and his mistress and shot at them, wounding the husband.

Adam is assigned the case to prosecute, but Amanda has sought the defense, offering her services to the accused woman for ideological reasons. She is incensed by what she sees as a double standard being applied to the woman, a double standard that does not appear on the face of the law but lurks beneath it.

Amanda is outraged that press stories and street conversations automatically condemn a woman who would shoot her husband for so trifling an offense as sleeping with another woman. The consensus is that she must be crazy. But, says Amanda, if a man whose home was being destroyed by another man pulled out a gun and shot at his wife and her lover, people would think he was within his rights. Not his rights under the written law, but under the cultural law, which says that men can stray but women, especially married women, can't. When Amanda's secretary confirms that this is what she thinks and Amanda asks, Why the difference? the secretary shrugs and says, "I don't make the rules." Amanda snaps, "Yes, you do. We all do." And, she declares, "This deplorable system seeps into our courts of law, where there is supposed to be equality!"

So she goes to trial determined to argue that women should be treated equally, even to the point of escaping the letter of the law if men would. Adam is furious, accusing his wife of having contempt for the law. "It's a disease!" he declares. But utilizing courtroom tactics that are often humiliating to Adam, Amanda demonstrates both that women are intellectually and often physically equal to men, and that they are treated chronically as if they are not. And she wins her case.

Meanwhile, Adam has left her, yelling that he wants a wife, not a competitor, and a number of plot turns are required to get them back together, the last one being Adam's demonstration that men, like women, can fake tears. He is apparently trying to establish that, in important matters, the two sexes are already equal. But the point is, the Hepburn character has revealed clearly and explicitly that the supposedly objective letter of the law applies differently to men and women because unrecognized assumptions about male and female differences get applied along with it. Her radical message, however, did not dissolve the system of cultural inequality, in *Adam's Rib* or in the real world. The same argument proposed by feminist legal scholars in the 1990s still sounds radical. And present-day fictional lawyers don't touch it.

Several, however, wrestle with the inadequacy of the law to deal with complicated and emotion-laden issues of violence against women. One of these is the prosecutor played by Kelly McGillis in *The Accused*;

another is Barbara Hershey's muddled but determined defense lawyer in *Defenseless*.

The Accused depicts the efforts of an assistant district attorney (McGillis) to win convictions of a group of men accused of gang-raping a woman (played by Jodie Foster) in a bar. The difficulty, as in any rape trial, is to overcome the defense of consent, the claim that the woman consented to the sexual acts in question. In this case, the woman's vigorous insistence that she did not consent is undercut by her inability to present herself as a person of high moral character. She has a generally loose reputation. She has a past conviction for drug possession. She was dressed skimpily at the bar, had been drinking heavily, and was dancing provocatively. Foster's character, Sarah, keeps protesting that all this was true, but irrelevant. Or rather she keeps saying, "What the fuck difference does it make? They raped me."

Under pressure from male colleagues not to waste time on a tough case, and reluctant herself to take on a contest she is likely to lose, the prosecutor plea-bargains with the defendants, accepting their guilty pleas to lesser charges with short jail sentences. Sarah, however, who was not consulted, is outraged, because she has been deprived even of the chance to accuse the rapists publicly, and accuses the prosecutor, vehemently, of selling her out. She says that people who recognize her treat her like trash ("Everyone thinks I'm shit") because the prosecutor did not allow her a chance to explain the rape. Officially the men did not rape her, so officially she is a slut, she says. The prosecutor, having first taken the mainstream male view of the case, becomes remorseful and sees that she, as well as the legal system as it conventionally operates, *has* betrayed Sarah. So she sets about to find a way to bring another case that will put the rape on record and allow the Foster character to tell her story. She digs up an old and little-used law against solicitation of felonies and decides to bring this charge against the men in the bar who were egging the rapists on, cheering, pressuring them to continue. It's a weird charge, utterly unconventional, and unlikely to succeed. But one of the men present during the rape breaks ranks and testifies against the others. And the women, lawyer and victim, win.

But it is a victory at the margins. They do not win on the straightforward charge of rape because the law—the written law and the unwritten attitudes surrounding it—works against the victim. And acceptance of this fact is so much a part of the system that even a female prosecutor had become desensitized to the injustice of the results, and it took the untutored, outraged outsider to see and describe clearly, in eloquent profanity, the limits of the protection the law affords to women. Still, while pointing to a dangerous failing in the law, *The Accused* leaves the viewer reassured that the system can deliver a fair measure of justice.

Defenseless enters murkier territory, places where women are subjected to threats the law cannot even adequately define. Unfortunately, while the issues the plot raises are serious, the film is not. It is a melodramatic thriller, one in which Barbara Hershey's character, T. K. Katwuller, like *L.A. Law*'s Rosalind Shays, falls down an elevator shaft. But not to worry, a detective (played by Sam Shepard) rescues her, managing at the same time to shove down the shaft, to his death, the deranged man pursuing T.K. with a gun. This man is the father of a teenage girl who has been performing in pornographic movies produced by the man T.K. is defending against charges of dealing in obscene materials. She is also sleeping with her client, believing that he is *not* a porn producer but has unwittingly rented warehouse space to someone who is. When she discovers her client/lover *is* a pornographer—and that he is married to her best friend from college—she rushes to his office to break off their affair. Then she rushes out, forgetting her keys. Then she dashes back to get her keys, only to find that in the meantime he has been stabbed to death. She calls the police. She becomes a suspect. And so forth. *Defenseless* is not a good film, but it does raise a knot of issues connecting pornography, incest, sexual abuse, and domestic violence, and this it does, on some levels, realistically. It follows, for example, the anguished emotional relations in two mother/daughter pairs caught up in sexual violence beyond their control. Both young women perform in the porn producer's films and have sex with him. One of them is his own daughter. The other is the daughter of the crazed man who attacks T.K. In both cases, the mothers are helpless to save their daughters from the power of the fathers—until the porn producer's wife kills him. It is the only way she can stop him. The law does not seem able to reach him. The young women are under his sway and will not turn against him. The crazed man who is trying to kill him can't find him. And neither the police nor T.K. can fathom what is going on.

In the end, justice is not done under the law. The killer, the wife/mother, is tried for murder, but defended by her old friend T.K. (who once again mistakenly believes that her client is innocent), she is acquitted. T.K. is then charged with the murder, but clears herself by gaining a confession from her friend, who can now not be tried again. In short, the law cannot grapple with this situation. The harms, the abuses of sexual power on the part of the husband/father/pornographer, cannot be reached by the definitions of wrong the law supplies.

At this point, however, T.K., the lawyer who has never had a clear grip on the situation herself, retreats to the law, as it is, to make her final judgment. She lectures the wife who killed her morally monstrous husband, saying that ever since college the woman has blamed others for her own problems. "They don't hurt us. We hurt us!" T.K. concludes sternly.

The viewer is bewildered to be told that the moral of the story, a story of gross betrayal of trust at every turn by a powerful man, is "They don't hurt us." If the lawyer had condemned murder as an answer to violence we might agree, but her insistence that it was the victims who had hurt themselves is incomprehensible. The point of the movie, finally, is that it doesn't make sense. It mixes together the law and a woman lawyer and subterranean forms of sexual violence, and cannot make sense of it all. T.K.'s attempt to wrap it up at the end simply doesn't work. But a kind of existential confusion is as far as the media have gone, since *Adam's Rib*, in presenting women lawyers as anything other than true believers in a system that works justice for women as well as for men.

The reason for this, according to Terry Louise Fisher, one of the creators of *L.A. Law*, is that deep questioning of the established order is not entertaining. Fisher is a lawyer whose own view of the legal system is far darker than the one that appears on TV. She says she has seen, as an assistant district attorney, horrendous cases of crime victims the law could not protect, and has used such material in several unusually tough *L.A. Law* episodes. In one, a leukemia victim who was gang-raped decided not to continue testifying against her attackers because of harsh, accusatory questioning of her credibility by defense lawyers. She did not want to spend the last few months of her life under attack in a courtroom. Fisher says that she was criticized for exaggerating the nastiness of this case on the show but that in fact the reality was worse. The criminal-justice system doesn't work, she declares flatly. But this view does not shape most *L.A. Law* story lines because, she says, the show is entertainment: "People want to be told stories [in which] something bad happened, and the hero comes in and makes it better."[1]

So that is the story that TV and movie lawyers supply. The media

---

1. Michele Kort, "Terry Louise Fisher: How She Dreamed Up the Women of *L.A. Law*," *Ms.* (June 1987), p. 38. For a longer analysis of the *L.A. Law* women, see Diane Glass, "Portia in Primetime: Women Lawyers, Television, and *L.A. Law*," *Yale Journal of Law and Feminism* Vol. 2, No. 2 (Spring 1990), pp. 371–434.

send in the lawyer hero to make things better, thus reinforcing the belief that the hero *can* do it, time after time, or should be able to. A drama might portray a failed hero, but not a failed system, or even a system with chronic, serious flaws. And these views, not created by the media but reinforced by them, are hard on real women lawyers, because Amanda Bonner was right. The justice system *does* work differently for women— sometimes uncomprehendingly, sometimes harshly, sometimes discriminatorily, sometimes cruelly. And yet the images that help to shape the norms for women lawyers portray them as beautiful, competent, forceful, glamorous, *and* operating without any evident sense of dissonance within the system. The problem, then, for real-life women lawyers when they perceive systemic double standards and discrimination is to find a way to speak about them when the norms say that good women lawyers, successful women lawyers, see no such problems.

In short, the media images help to muffle dissonant speech. And, combined with the parallel images that warn women against going too far in reliance on their minds, these images stand in the way of women's authority in the profession by keeping them off-balance. I don't want to exaggerate this point. I don't mean that the media rule our lives with images we cannot escape. I mean only that they matter, that they're part of the mix. And I would add that the images are not all negative. To see portrayals of attractive women carrying out difficult work with confidence and skill no doubt helps young women to form an expanded sense of themselves. That is clear. What isn't clear is the subtle undermining beneath the surface. If women lawyers must worry about a loss of femininity and loss of love should they use their minds as fully and creatively as they might, and if they cannot speak openly and forcefully of unfairness in the system as they see it, they must stifle authenticity in themselves. They must curb their strength, move cautiously, withhold judgments, stay safe. And on those terms, they cannot gain substantial authority. They must remain quiet subordinates.

The next question is, Are these images stifling women's voices so fixed in the culture that they cannot change? Would it matter if the culture of the entertainment industry itself changed, if more women like Terry Louise Fisher were producing, directing, and writing movie and TV stories? Would different perspectives reshape the powerful images the media send out?

The entertainment industry has always been notoriously male-dominated and, more than that, noted for crass, sexist attitudes that assign value to women as sex objects or possessors of body parts—breasts, legs, buttocks, mouths—and nothing more. One interviewee who does entertainment-law litigation for a Los Angeles law firm speaks vehemently on this point. "It's the most sexist industry, bar none, I have ever seen," she says disgustedly. "They talk about secretaries they like because of their 'big cantaloupes.' They're cheating on their wives. They think of women as trash." And she adds that these attitudes make it extremely difficult for women to gain a toehold on the production side of the business. "To include women as equals," she says, "they would have to give up their whole method of operation. They really would have to, you know, not be the assholes they are, and they don't want to give that up."

Others in the industry speak of the added difficulty for women of adapting to a wildly aggressive style of doing business. A lawyer who works in-house for one of the major film studios says that she was taken aback on first arriving to find that "yelling and screaming" was a normal means of negotiation. "I sit there and I observe this thing and I say, 'Whoa, this is really interesting. This is bizarre. People act like this? And they run companies?' " Yet women are gaining some ground in the industry. And authority-challenging woman characters are appearing on the screen.

On television, Diane English's *Murphy Brown* has skewered the Senate Judiciary Committee's ineffectual handling of the Clarence Thomas hearings, as well as then Vice President Dan Quayle's sanctimonious condemnation of single motherhood, which was aimed largely at the (fictional) journalist Murphy Brown, who had had a (fictional) baby out of wedlock. On-screen, Murphy struck back during the 1992 presidential campaign, informing the vice president that a family was properly defined by commitment and love, not by its formal structure. Even more significant, the Murphy Brown character sends out images every week of a strong, smart, tough-minded professional woman who is, nonetheless, attractive and lovable.

In the movies, we have seen (as of 1992) *Thelma & Louise*, depicting two women who defy, albeit unsuccessfully, a justice system that cannot effectively punish rapists but is very likely to punish women who use force against men who attack them. In director Susan Seidelman's *Desperately Seeking Susan*, a woman breaks out of confining conventions, reconstructs her identity, and goes off in search of adventure. And filmmaker Penny Marshall, in *A League of Their Own*, explored the complexities of women's engagement in a man's world of competition. Her arena was baseball, not business or law, but still, the film's heroine suggested subtly the outline of a new competitive ethic—one in which the strongest players, the winners, could also be concerned about empowering the weaker ones.

But so far, the ranks of the new heroines do not include a cadre of dissident lawyers. Where is the new Amanda Bonner, pointing to the laws behind the laws that too often compromise equal justice for women? Perhaps with so many more women in the legal profession than there were in 1949, Amanda's fighting words have become too dangerous. The numbers are there. If the media projected images of women lawyers examining cultural biases in the legal system rather than continually ratifying the status quo, who knows what might happen?

PART TWO

---

*How are women lawyers
using the authority they have
to advance the equality
of women generally?*

7

CHANGING PRACTICES

THE BARRIERS TO WOMEN'S EQUALITY in the legal profession are formidable, and while some women make it through them to gain substantial authority in mainstream practices, most do not. But a number of women, rather than going along with the old rules that work to exclude them, are devising new ones. They are developing new models for the practice of law, models that carry the possibility, at least, of equalizing power between male and female practitioners.

One new practice constitutes a direct and deliberate challenge to the prevailing power structure in the law, and that is an insistence on the principle of diversity. Women are insisting on the need for the deliberate inclusion of outsiders in places of professional authority, and especially in places where the law develops—the law schools and the courts. We have seen earlier, in Chapter 2, the arguments over this issue in law school faculties, the fury aroused over the challenge it raises to the traditional principle of objectivity. The issue is less politicized in the judiciary, less explicitly defined, but still sensitive.

The principle of objectivity, to which judges traditionally adhere, decrees that legal thinking must be done by reasoners who are detached from their personal identities and therefore uninfluenced by them in their judgments of law. It is a direct violation of this principle to grant legal authority to someone *because* of her sex or class or race, to invite her to look at the law deliberately from those perspectives. And few judges would say that as a matter of principle, they approach their work subjectively. Nonetheless, outsiders on the bench, women and minorities, recognize that on many issues their viewpoints do differ from those that have traditionally prevailed. They note that the usual holders of power—mainly elite white men—frequently do not feel, do not see, and do not grasp some of the negative ways the law affects the powerless. And they find it of great importance that the judiciary become more diverse.

A woman who worked as a staff attorney for a federal court tells a story that points to the importance of class in shaping a judge's point of view. She describes sitting in on an argument before a three-judge panel concerning a case in which lawyers were being barred by doctors from access to patients in a state mental hospital. "Here were the three white men sitting up on a high podium saying, 'Well, if the doctors don't think it's good for the patients, then I don't think it's a good idea.' And I was sitting with a black woman who was a clerk for one of the judges, and I said, 'You know, there ought to at least be a requirement that one of the judges on the panel has gone to public school.' I mean, they were so removed from the reality of what a state hospital for psychiatric patients was likely to be like, and the caliber of doctors who dealt with them."

Presenting the same view from the other side, an appellate court judge remarks that her court now includes a black judge who picks up women's issues immediately and, moreover, had once noticed an anti-Semitic element in a case when a Jewish judge had missed it. "Any vulnerable group can see the issues of other vulnerable groups," my interviewee says. She means issues that the powerful tend not to see.

It is demonstrably true that women judges, although they make up only about 10 percent of both state and federal benches, have brought a markedly different focus to laws applying specifically to women. One state court judge I spoke with singled out child support as a matter that has been "drastically affected by the way in which women judges view that issue." Another woman, a state appellate court judge, recalls a child-custody case that came up under a law providing that the parent with custody could not take the child out of state and away from the other parent unless the move was in the best interest of the child. A woman with custody had wanted to move to a distant state to take a better job, and the lower court judge had ruled against it. The woman judge, sitting on a panel of three, the other two being men, was troubled because the lower court had looked at the case only in terms of the father's interest in retaining access to the child. Researching the question, she found a pattern of decisions allowing such moves as in the child's best interest when the *father* wanted to leave the state for a new job. And she persuaded her colleagues to send the case back to the trial judge to look explicitly at both the father's *and* the mother's interests as they affected the child's welfare. She thinks that this kind of shifting focus on such issues occurs often when women enter the scene.

Another state appellate judge speaks of male/female differences in judicial bypass hearings in cases of minors seeking abortions without parental consent. She says that male judges tend to treat such young women as having done something wrong, questioning them sternly, whereas women judges are likely to be sensitive to the women's embarrassment. The decisions of male and female judges may be the same, she says, but their manner is different, the men tending to see the young pregnant women as immoral without making the same judgment about the men involved.

This judge, a woman with long experience on the bench, goes on to talk, wearily, about the differences she has observed between male and female judges on issues of violence against women. "Men tend to think that in a case of alleged rape, the woman asked for it. I read a wonderful article by someone who put the question, 'Does a wealthy man in elegant clothes living in a mansion entice a robber to enter his house?' And men also don't see domestic violence the way women do. Once in court, the man charged with violence is wearing a suit, looks normal, behaves rationally, whereas the woman who has been abused is likely to behave hysterically. I think seventy to eighty percent of men don't believe charges of battering, and all women think it's worse than charged."

Another judge speaks at some length on the same issues. "I'm discouraged by the domestic-violence problem," she says. "The incidence of domestic violence is so high that it just frightens everybody. There's enormous resistance to admitting it, acknowledging it, dignifying it. I remember, when I was being trained as a judge, I was very aware of domestic violence through [a lawyer's group] setting up [a shelter] for battered women—but when we came to the court that handles civil-protection orders, we were told, 'Well, this is kind of boring.' And then we heard in the courtroom major tales of serious domestic abuse. . . . I think the problem is epidemic. Men don't want to acknowledge it *because* it's so widespread. I think child abuse is not nearly so threatening and unsettling a problem as domestic violence. Ninety-nine percent of the people would understand and condemn child abuse, but violence between adults runs up against a cultural norm that says an occasional slap or punch or pushing around or even beating up is okay. They won't acknowledge that it is wrong even *if* there is verbal provocation. And another piece of it—even for those who acknowledge it, men *and* women, it's hard to understand, in your gut, the psyche of a battered woman. . . . There's a big tendency to say, 'Why did she take it so long? Why didn't she get the hell out?' Consequently, you have some measure of contempt for the victim that interferes with your willingness to impose severe sanctions on the batterer. If you haven't been through it, you can't really comprehend the terrorization process. You have to be taught intellectually."

This is why it's so important, she thinks, that women judges are arriving on the scene. "Women on the bench are in a position to notice these issues, raise them, ask for data on matters that their experience in the world tells them must be important and extensive. By having on the bench a group of people who haven't been there before—i.e., women—you bring in the viewpoints and biases that haven't been there before. We make a zillion credibility determinations, for example, and credibility, no matter what anyone says, is the most subjective thing in the world. . . . But certainly the gender-bias studies show that there is a great tendency on the part of male judges to not believe women witnesses, expert witnesses, women particularly in domestic violence cases. Having women judges on the bench, you at least have them there to bring their experience and their view of women as people to kind of put into the hopper in terms of judging credibility. . . . Not that, as a class, women are different or better than male judges, but that they bring different experience and knowledge to the process."[1]

The point these women are making is that excessive detachment from the issues results in only a partial understanding of them, and that it is precisely women's attachment to issues involving the impact of the law on women—an attachment the tradition of objectivity regards as a flaw—that is essential to full and equal justice. The logo of the *Yale Journal of Law and Feminism* expresses this idea graphically. It is a drawing of the mythic female Justicia, complete with blindfold and scales, except that this Justicia holds her scales in one hand while removing her blindfold with the other. An explanation in the *Journal*'s first issue pointed out that traditionally, the blindfold symbolizes objectivity, the detachment that ensures impartiality. But with the blindfold on, the editorial note continued, Justicia cannot see the differences in social power among the litigants before her. She cannot see and take into account any context of disad-

---

1. Quantified studies bear out the differences, reflected in these stories, between male and female judges analyzing women's issues. And as it is mainly state law that deals with women's issues—rape, battering, divorce, abortion, responsibility for children—the differences are most marked among state court judges. The decisions of male and female judges in federal courts, which deal primarily with commercial and regulatory matters, are less differentiated by sex. See Thomas G. Walker and Deborah J. Barrow, "The Diversification of the Federal Bench," *Journal of Politics*, Vol. 47, No. 2 (May 1985), p. 596; and David W. Allen and Diane E. Wall, "The Behavior of Women State Supreme Court Justices: Are They Tokens or Outsiders?" *The Justice System Journal*, Vol. 12, No. 2 (Fall 1987), p. 232.

vantage, and must make judgments according to the standards of those with the power to write them into law.[2]

When the feminist Justicia takes the blindfold off, she looks at rape law, or domestic violence, or sexual harassment, or divorce settlements, or child custody, from the point of view of the victim. This is not to say that she single-mindedly favors women in all cases, but she looks to see whether the law, as traditionally conceived and applied, takes women's experience and perspective fully into account. Again, the idea the new Justicia represents is that women's personal experience of disadvantage, and their awareness of it, and of its relevance to the law, are crucial qualifications, not disqualifications, for their inclusion in the ranks of high legal authorities.

If ever this principle was borne out dramatically in practice, it was in the Hill/Thomas hearings on sexual harassment. Although not an actual judicial proceeding in a court before a judge, the hearings mimicked a trial, with the senators on the Judiciary Committee acting as a panel of judges (although also as prosecuting and defense attorneys operating under rules that seemed straight out of *Alice in Wonderland*). In any case, the all-white, all-male panel clearly could not, or would not, comprehend Hill's story. As noted briefly in Chapter 4, Professor Kimberle Crenshaw has pointed out a number of ways in which the combination of Hill's race and sex put her experience beyond the bounds of what the committee members, or most Americans, could readily see. She notes that the metaphors, the visual images, that commonly represent acts of sexism and racism are the white woman raped and the black man lynched, and she argues that the effect of these metaphors is to erase the experience of the abused black woman from the popular mind.

Black women claiming sexual abuse, from harassment to rape, Crenshaw says, are less likely than white women to be believed, because they are not protected by the same image of purity. They are popularly assumed, at least among whites, to be sexually available and thus to have consented to whatever sexual acts they later complain about. But, Crenshaw adds, black women bringing complaints against black men are also subject to disapproval in the black community because of the strong tradition of racial solidarity. In this tradition, blacks should not expose to the white world the differences among themselves, and any black who

---

2. Ursula Werner, "Dis-Covering Our Cover," *Yale Journal of Law and Feminism*, Vol. 1, No. 1 (Spring 1989), p. 1. See also Patricia Williams's provocative commentary on the dangers of false objectivity in *The Alchemy of Race and Rights* (Cambridge, Mass.: Harvard University Press, 1991).

does so is automatically regarded with suspicion. Anita Hill, therefore, had to struggle for credibility and support against two forms of cultural dissonance. At the same time, Clarence Thomas could, and explicitly did, invoke the powerful protection of the lynching metaphor to ward off probes into his credibility. Once he called the hearings "a high-tech lynching," Crenshaw declares, the all-white committee could not mount the moral strength to challenge him seriously. Its members could not move beyond the bounds of their inherited understandings. Thomas fit a pre-defined role of victim, whereas Anita Hill did not.[3]

As noted earlier, thousands of women throughout the country re-acted furiously to this spectacle of cultural blindness and arrogance on the part of the powerful. Almost immediately, they began to mount un-precedented efforts to support women running for public office. It was, I believe, the first widespread recognition and acceptance of the principle of diversity in lawmaking. That is, many people seemed to see for the first time that without the participation of women and minorities in sig-nificant numbers on the Senate Judiciary Committee, in the Congress, and in public office throughout the country, the actual experiences and the actual disadvantages of outsiders would never be present in the law-making process.

And among women lawyers, awareness of the importance of women and minorities not only in public office, but as formulators of law on the bench and on law faculties was also heightened. At the annual American Bar Association meetings in the summer following the Hill/Thomas hear-ings, a session addressed jointly by Anita Hill and Hillary Rodham Clin-ton, the latter a longtime promoter of women's equality in the law, generated unusual excitement. There was, according to the *New York Times*, "an unmistakable air of exhilaration and anticipation," a sense that Americans "were entering eras in which women mattered more than ever before."[4] Indeed, several months later, when Bill Clinton had won the presidency, he proceeded to assemble a cabinet that for the first time in history was not overwhelmingly white and male. Women were appointed to head the Department of Health and Human Services, the Department of Energy, the Environmental Protection Agency, and—with the consid-erable drama and difficulty discussed in Chapter 1—the Department of Justice.

3. Crenshaw, "Whose Story Is It Anyway?" in Morrison, ed., *Race-ing Justice*, pp. 402–40.

4. *New York Times*, August 10, 1992, p. A10.

I do not doubt, although I cannot demonstrate with certainty, a connection between the trouble surrounding the appointment of a woman attorney general and the deep resistance in the legal profession to the principle of diversity, of multiple perspectives, in the law. The very spectacle of a woman as the nation's chief law enforcement official raises all the old fears of women's emotionalism, bias, and softness undermining the integrity of the legal system. And behind these fears lurk disturbing intimations of radical change in the old order of inequality between the sexes.

Janet Reno, President Clinton's third and successful candidate for attorney general, was well chosen to calm such anxieties. Suspicions of softness were countered both by her imposing physical stature—she is over six feet tall—and by her long experience as an elected state's attorney, a prosecutor, in an undeniably tough jurisdiction, Dade County, Florida. And as a single woman without children, her transgression of the old rules requiring women to take care of their families was minimal.

Nonetheless, signs of a different perspective, a woman's perspective, entering the Justice Department with the new attorney general were apparent at the outset. When asked during her confirmation hearings how she would approach the growing problem of violence on city streets, she replied that much more attention was needed to violence in the home. Young people pick up attitudes and habits of violence, she said, when they see a man beating up his wife, or parents abusing a child. No previous attorney general had identified domestic violence as a serious national problem and certainly not as a basic root of street crime. And several months later in an address to the 1993 Harvard Law School graduating class she delivered other atypical messages, urging the fledgling lawyers to put families before careers, to assume both personal and a broader social responsibility for children, and also to organize family lives so that both parents can achieve professional fulfillment.

But the efforts of the Clinton administration to increase the representation of diverse viewpoints in the law foundered again on the attempted appointment, in the spring of 1993, of a black woman law professor and civil rights lawyer, Lani Guinier, to head the Justice Department's civil rights division. At issue were several law review articles in which Guinier advocated the use of voting mechanisms aimed at increasing the political influence of African-American minorities in localities where they were consistently outvoted by whites. When Guinier was made to sound like a dangerous radical attacking democratic principles—in spite of the fact that some of her proposals were actually in effect in a number of cities and counties—President Clinton withdrew her nomination before confirmation hearings had begun.

Here again was a woman lawyer in no-man's-land. When attacked, she had no powerful protection surrounding her, and the less so as she was explicitly challenging the rules that militate against outsider voices being heard. As a result, not only was Guinier herself excluded from public authority, but national discussion of the rules allocating public authority—in this case voting rules—was effectively blanked out by the power of groups resisting change.

But this story has a paradoxical sequel. At the same time as he was filling positions in the Justice Department, President Clinton was seeking a nominee to the Supreme Court to fill the place of retiring Justice Byron White. And he seemed to have found one in Stephen Breyer, chief judge of the First Circuit Court of Appeals. But, it developed, Judge Breyer, like Zoë Baird, had failed to pay Social Security taxes for a domestic worker, and the issue of a double standard was raised. Could the Senate, in its confirmation process, overlook in a male candidate a legal transgression that had defeated the candidacy of a woman?

The question had no sooner arisen, however, when it became moot with the president's nomination instead of a woman, Ruth Bader Ginsburg—thus raising another question. Did the successive defeat for high judicial office of three highly qualified women—Zoë Baird, Kimba Wood, and Lani Guinier—influence the president when it came to the Supreme Court? Had women's growing insistence on entry into lawmaking positions gained enough legitimacy to exert real pressure on the presidential appointment process?

If so, Ruth Bader Ginsburg herself had played no small part in producing such a result. At the time of her appointment to the Supreme Court, Justice Ginsburg was a judge on the Court of Appeals for the District of Columbia Circuit, appointed in 1980 by President Jimmy Carter. But before that she had been, as the first director of the Women's Rights Project of the American Civil Liberties Union, a leader in the 1970s campaign of litigation for women's equal rights and opportunities. I discuss that movement and she describes her part in it in the next chapter.

But I would add here, as a final twist in the saga of diversity played out in the first months of the Clinton administration, that Justice Ginsburg, while a passionate advocate of equal rights for women, is cautious about the principle of diversity as such. She has not, in her advocacy or her writing, sought mechanisms for the inclusion of women in public life as holders of distinctively female views and interests. Rather, her aim as a feminist has been to *resist* notions of difference between women and men, because historically such notions have hurt women, casting them generically as emotional creatures properly engaged in homemaking activities. And, like other equal rights feminists, she fears that defining women as a sex-based class for any purpose invites a return to invidious stereotyping and discrimination. Still, whether or not she supports theories of difference and diversity, Justice Ginsburg, as the second woman on the Supreme Court, represents the *fact* of change in the ancient tradition of male-defined law.

SEEKING THE INCLUSION of women in places where the law is made does not exhaust the efforts of women lawyers to find ways of organizing the profession on terms of greater equality. Many women who have worked in the big firms and found them seriously inhospitable have tried in various ways to create alternative forms of law practice, organizational forms that allow women to live according to values—professional and personal—that the big firms constrict.

A woman who was in law school during the late sixties, and actively involved then in the civil rights and antiwar movements, subsequently worked both in government and in-house for a nonprofit corporation, then turned in the late eighties to the creation of a small, "fancy" law firm that disdained the eighties emphasis on mega-incomes and aggressive expansion. The new firm, in Washington, D.C., set out to be both commercially successful and humane as a place of work. Its founding members placed higher value on collegiality and respectful mutual relations than on massive billings. In practice, this meant eschewing dependence on grinding out "zillions of hours" from associates. Further, the partners do not require a fixed number of billable hours, as they do not want to equate hours and salary levels. Rather than encouraging hard work, they think, such an equation puts a premium on billing time instead of working efficiently. And with these principles in place, the founding partner told me, the firm finds it can easily compete for outstanding young lawyers, its best source of supply being the big firms whose life-crushing work burdens prompt many young associates to flee.

Another model, getting started at about the same time in another East Coast city, is an alternative firm specializing in commercial litigation. All the founding partners, three of whom are women who graduated from the Harvard Law School in the early or middle 1980s, have had experience both in big-firm practice and as government prosecutors. They are committed to doing a mainstream business, but to do it on their own terms. It is the three Harvard women who tell me about the new venture.

Their principles of organization, carefully defined in a full year's planning process, are equality, collaboration, balance of work and personal lives, and valuing themselves and each other in human, not monetary, terms. They hope also, by targeting small and middle-sized companies as their likely clientele, to operate directly with the management of companies they represent and to deal with issues as part of a company's whole business agenda, rather than as abstracted, fragmented parts. They prize the sense of usefulness that comes from working with the whole, seeing how their work makes a difference to the ongoing life of an enterprise. And they value also the freedom to hone their own litigating styles without the pressure of institutional habits and expectations.

Collaboration began with the first glimmerings of the idea of a firm. They spent a long time, they tell me, hashing out their individual visions and how they could make them mesh, and then they took a year, working with a consultant, to develop a business plan—finding quarters, designing space, buying furniture, defining a shareholders' agreement with buyout provisions should a partner become unable to work, or die. When they opened the firm, they met daily to figure out every little detail of operation. At first, they collectively and directly dealt with everything, from ordering paper clips to coping with the cleaning service. Then, when everyone knew the system, the chores were divided up. As time went on they needed less constant contact, both because many matters became routine and because their shared vision became progressively more defined and commonly understood, requiring less constant discussion. They continued to meet to discuss such matters as whether to take a certain kind of business, or a client with a certain range of issues. And they have found that joint thinking—voicing and exchanging questions, doubts, ideas, and excitements—has produced a depth of understanding and conviction that none of the individual partners had herself previously held.

Their equality is expressed in several tangible ways. All five partners' offices are equal in size, and none occupies that point of prestige in the hierarchical business world—the corner. And the office design in general bespeaks the lawyers' open, straightforward approach to each other and the world rather than the mystery, not to say pretension, of the large establishments. The predominating colors are light blue and white, the furniture is modern, functional, and comfortable, and colorful posters behind Plexiglas dot the corridor walls. Individual office doors are usually left open, and the partners call out to one another to settle small questions.

Apart from equal space and openness of operation, the equality principle governs also the division of profits, and thereby both expresses and, the partners hope, reinforces their relation of collegiality. One speaks for all on this point. "The fact that we work through collegiality, not hierarchy, and have incredible respect for each other as lawyers and people, creates an atmosphere that is unique. . . . It's something you don't see a lot in the professions. . . . People forget how to cooperate. We're trying to set up a situation where cooperation is possible because there is nothing to compete for. . . . You seek clients, you do their work yourself if you want, or if it's not your thing, see who wants to do it, and the money goes to the firm and is divided equally. That may change with time if someone turns out to be a very different kind of worker than the others . . . but even an unequal division of money wouldn't change the cooperative mode of operation. I think if one of us brought in much more money one year and we as a group decided she should get a bonus, it wouldn't make the others feel less valuable, because we don't value ourselves in terms of money. That's a critical factor. We don't measure our self-worth in terms of money."

Collaboration and equality are important principles for relations among the partners, but what of relations to clients? Is there something distinctive that this alternative firm, and particularly its women members, have to offer clients? In a flurry of newspaper stories about the firm's formation, the partners were at pains to describe themselves as "tough" litigators, seasoned veterans of the U.S. Attorney's office, ready to protect and promote a client's interests in the classic tradition of this most contentious of fields. They were proclaiming the absence of significant difference between themselves and mainstream litigators, and in emphasizing toughness, evoked ready images of sharp, aggressive, even flamboyant courtroom performers. But when I ask the women whether they do indeed practice in a high-pressured, pushy, abrasive way, they tell me that they generally do not—that effective litigation does not depend on an antagonistic, macho approach.

One partner says, "You can represent your client without always being on the offensive in an offensive way. It's just as important to listen and observe and figure out what the other side really wants, what people are really fighting about—both clients and lawyers. It's often more important than entering a room and throwing your weight around. Often, people who are doing that miss some of the subtleties that tell you what is really going on. The same thing is true when you're presenting a case to a fact finder. That involves communication, persuasion, subtlety, thoughtfulness, a lot of other things besides power. Pure power is not going to win the day most often. Personality and leverage matter, but not brute force. A lot of people think that if you can't walk in there and take over by dint of your personality, you shouldn't be a litigator—and that's just not true."

Another adds, "You can often see this in taking depositions. If you take a quiet, sympathetic approach, you can often get more out of a witness, because the witness forgets you are the adversary. It seems just like a conversation with a nice, interested person. You can disarm a negotiator the same way—be tenacious but quietly, calmly tenacious. It's very disarming when someone is used to blustering and hitting up against bluster on the other side. They're lost if you don't yell back. What do they do next?"

When I ask if this, then, is what women helping to build a new kind of firm have to offer—a different way of working—the answers are mixed. Many men as well as women employ a quiet style, my interviewees agree, and some women litigators are vigorously aggressive. But they agree that on a stylistic continuum from quiet subtlety to loud antagonism, there is a gender breakdown at the extremes—quiet women, loud men—with an overlap in the middle where you find the counterexamples in both sexes. Still, adds one, "You do see a gender difference if you have two women. And the nicest thing . . . We've been in situations where the two lawyers are women and the judge is a woman. Then the court works differently. There's less dueling going on. People don't have their swords out. People aren't . . . It's not a pissing contest. It's more getting to the heart of whatever it is they're supposed to be doing. . . . When there are only women in there, there's a level of communication that goes on from the beginning, so they don't get to the point where [the judge] has to *announce*, 'I'm in charge here, you fools. Stop carrying on like this.' That just all happens by itself real fast."

Says another, "We've had clients tell us that they thought they were spending a lot of money on male ego, men showing off, wasting time. A lot of bluster and showmanship is not necessarily in the client's best interest."

So why don't these women market themselves as different—subtle, psychologically astute, sensible, time-saving, wise? Why talk about being tough? Everyone laughs and shrugs. Because, they tell me, there is no available language to describe the alternative qualities credibly within the necessarily adversarial tradition of litigation. The risk is too great that to describe themselves as different in this context is to convey that they are soft, weak, second-class, not to be trusted. One of the women says of the model of difference they've described, "I don't think there's ever been a language to talk about these things. You just have to *be* it, and develop a reputation."

As for balancing work and personal lives, the partners are clear—and tough—on the necessity of placing limits on the claims of work. And this, even in the pressured field of litigation, they regard as well within their power. One of the women is especially adamant on this point. "It's true that when you're in trial, forget personal life, you're doing it twenty-four hours a day. But when you're not in trial, you have a lot of control. To the extent you don't have control or give control away, you've chosen to do it. And if you have chosen to, it may be because you like power, and the more cases you have and the busier you are, the more powerful you feel. Or greed—the more cases, the more money. But if you have other things in your life you value, then in our kind of situation you can control the demands of work. You can't control it in a large firm. That's because litigators in large firms are working on a number of different issues at once, a number of things coming to crisis at the same time, and they have control over none of it.

"All of us value our private lives highly. It's written into the share-holders' agreement that partners can take personal time, sabbaticals, flex-time, family leave. Nobody is willing to give over her whole life to a job, and nobody was going to look at anybody else and devalue her because of giving time to outside things. That's exactly what happens in big firms."

Another partner remarks that even in big firms, people can take more control over their time than they often do. She recalled a classmate's saying at a law school reunion that you couldn't say no to a client, even one who calls on a Friday afternoon and wants something by Monday. "But that's not true," she tells me. "There are ways of getting people through real emergencies. And also, over time, you can teach people not to get into emergencies, and that you're not going to respond to it if it's self-generated. It's a question of control, making choices and controlling your life rather than letting others make choices for you. I really suffered in a big firm from the fact that I couldn't control my life. A partner could schedule me for ten a.m. Saturday morning, and I couldn't say no. I vowed that I wouldn't live that way."

The prior speaker affirms this stand fervently. "It's a matter of self-definition. For some litigators, predominantly men, there's a real high in having an emergency on Friday night. You are one important person if you're busy all weekend. To me, you're a schmo if you're busy all weekend! That's a real difference about what you value. I mean, there's something special about getting there in the locker room first thing Monday morning and talking about how you had to work all weekend, and you had to meet with a client! Relax, folks, it's just really not all that—I mean, if you think about it rationally, there are very few situations in a commercial context that are real emergencies. This is crazy. People are just generating this stuff. . . . The trial is the exception. Once you're on trial, you know it's twenty-four hours a day, seven days a week, till it's over."

And her partner again. "There's no real reason for this crazed approach to work. It happens because it's valued, not because it has to. It gets reinforced by firms giving raises and bonuses for extra work. The only way you can break the cycle is to step out of it."

What is striking in this story is the mix of logistics and values in the choices these women have made. They say it is important to have time for a private life and, like many women, they found the "crazed" demands on time in the big firms unacceptable and have eliminated them in their own schema. But they have done so by eliminating the values that generate the demands. It is the values that prevail in the big firms that they criticize, and not just in personal terms but professionally as well. In stepping out of the big firms they have stepped out of the valuing of work above all else, the constant chase after money, the worship of competition at the expense of cooperation, the pit-bull approach to litigation, and the habitual reliance on hierarchy as a means of organizing work. In short, they have rejected the whole pattern of materialistic and individualistic values that have come to dominate the profession.

Clearly, the equality these women seek is not equality on the professional terms that now prevail. Actually, the implication of their analysis is that the prevailing terms will never produce equality, because their very premises cede the greatest power in the profession to those who are willing to strip their lives of any commitments that stand in the way of top-speed work. And most women, trained from childhood to live through their emotions and relations as well as their intellects, are unlikely to make such a choice.

Another model for change is discernible in a form of practice long regarded in the legal profession as somewhat second-class: the practice of in-house counsel. "In-house" means in a corporation that has its own legal department. Traditionally, large corporations have tended to use their own legal staffs for routine matters, and to rely on outside counsel to handle large financial dealings or issues of legal complexity. Therefore, in-house staffs, drawing up contracts, processing taxes, or keeping their companies in compliance with government regulations on a daily basis, commanded little prestige.

In spite of its lesser reputation, this work has long been attractive to women because its regularity allows its practitioners reasonable and predictable hours. In-house lawyers typically follow normal eight-hour workdays and can get home for dinner without feeling derelict in their professional duty. But the stories told me by women doing in-house law disclose attractions to their work that go beyond the practical matter of logistics to the deeper question of values.

Like the women in alternative law firms, many in-house lawyers take seriously a set of values that run counter to the prevailing traditions in the law. Although they do not as a rule describe themselves in this way, they are nevertheless practicing values that challenge directly the warrior ethic by which the profession derives its core identity. The warrior-hero in the law is the litigator whose combat, traditionally, uncovers the truth, the distinction between right and wrong. He works as an adversary, battling opponents over each detail until confusion and falsity drop away. He carries out with words the purifying mission that since the time of ancient Greece we have assigned to the soldier. Most in-house lawyers, on the other hand, perform an essentially cooperative function, aiding the smooth organization and operation of usually complex business or non-profit enterprises. And unlike the litigators' battles, the in-house lawyers' work contributes to results—their company's product or services—that are often tangibly useful to the public.

As one woman who works in-house for a major airline says, "You can see what you've done. I work on the financing of a terminal, and I can see my terminal and walk through it. I have a real sense of pride about it." She also says that she likes being part of a company where the people for whom she provides legal services are colleagues she works with continually. "You're working *with* them," she stresses. "You work on a deal from the beginning. You help structure it."

The large question is whether the choice of in-house work by many women reflects a general preference by women for cooperative rather than strongly adversarial functions. My interviews suggest that the answer is yes, and so do the studies conducted by various feminist theorists who have looked at distinctions in male and female approaches to problem solving.

Carol Gilligan's *In a Different Voice* first set out the now familiar argument that men tend to solve moral dilemmas by applying rules or principles, and women by seeking to retain and reinforce relationships among the parties involved. Other theorists have ratified and refined these ideas as they apply to the work of the legal profession. Rand and Dana Jack, studying male and female lawyers practicing in Washington State, found almost stereotypical distinctions down the line—men focusing on competition and winning, women favoring cooperation and compromise; men interpreting issues as conflicts of rights and duties between individuals, women seeing issues as conflicts of responsibilities in a network of relationships; men reasoning formally and abstractly, women reasoning contextually and holistically; men trusting hierarchical authority, women looking to decentralized consensus.[5]

The characteristics the Jacks found in the work of women lawyers appear clearly in the story of another in-house lawyer who has thought a great deal about the values that guide her work and the choices they have led her to make. Most striking is her desire to find and strengthen threads of moral connectedness in the society, a purpose she formed before she even reached law school. As an English major in college, she focused on American literature and was particularly touched by the period between the two world wars, by authors grappling with issues of alienation in a society becoming technologized, "searching for meaning in a world they weren't sure had much meaning."

A native Californian, she prefers the East Coast for its rootedness, its "sense of continuity with the past." A longing to see the places of the past was one reason she applied to Harvard when she decided to go to law school, and on arrival she felt immediately "at home" in Cambridge. "Coming from California, it was just amazing to walk down the street and see gravestones from the 1600s. . . . One of the first days in law school, I remember walking down to the Square and passing the graveyard at that church right on Mass. Ave. and seeing graves there from the 1600s and 1700s, and I wrote to my parents. I was amazed. This wasn't something that was preserved. It was something people walked by every day and didn't take any particular notice of!" She dragged her boyfriend to Amherst to see Emily Dickinson's home, to Walden Pond to visit Thoreau, and around Boston to see the buildings where the Revolution was plotted.

She says that she found the physical presence of the nation's past reassuring, not because she wanted to be stuck in tradition but because

---

5. Rand Jack and Dana Crowley Jack, *Moral Vision and Professional Decisions: The Changing Values of Women and Men Lawyers* (New York: Cambridge University Press, 1989). Carrie Menkel-Meadow develops similar ideas in a series of articles, including "Portia in a Different Voice: Speculations on a Woman's Lawyering Process," *Berkeley Women's Law Journal*, Vol. 1, No. 1 (Fall 1985), p. 39.

she was looking for firm ground from which to move onward. Apparently, this is what she hoped also to find in the law—a usable past and a vital, social connection to the present. Although she had no clear sense of professional direction, she viewed the law as importantly related to the political issues she most cared about—the environment, women's issues, and child care.

After graduation, she married her law school boyfriend, and both started off by working in big firms. By this time her interest had settled on health law, and although she was disappointed that her firm did less of it than she had expected, she was able to work on a series of Medicare/Medicaid payment issues along with general corporate work focused on commercial lending. But her lack of interest in strictly commercial transactions and an increase in the firm's annual billable-hour quota to two thousand convinced her to leave in less than three years. "I was not willing to do that at all. I very much have other interests outside of the office. I wanted to be involved in the community. I wanted time to see my husband. I wanted time to read. I wanted time for friends. I just felt I was not leading any kind of a balanced life. . . . I'm just not willing to give up that much." She considered going into another firm, one with more reasonable hours and a substantial health-law practice, but instead found a good in-house position with a company that supplies temporary health-care personnel and runs training programs on health and safety procedures. Eventually, she says, she would like to be more involved with health policy, perhaps in a nonprofit advocacy group or in the government, but she makes it clear that her in-house job is vastly preferable to the one she left.

"I feel a real sense of connectedness with the people I work with. I get calls from field offices, for example, saying 'We have a nurse who's been accused of taking drugs, the hospital's just sent her back to the office, what should I do?' And I feel like I do things that are important to people and that are very helpful to them, that they really need me for, and that I'm interested in. In fact, to me that's a much more interesting issue than some of the financing deals I did when I was at the law firm. You know, intellectually it's interesting to figure out how all the pieces got together, but I did not care whether that particular bank was making a ten-million-dollar loan to this particular company, where I *am* interested in resolving those issues of balancing the nurse's rights—to a fair hearing and a chance to tell her side of the story and to be treated fairly—against our interest in protecting patient safety. I'm interested in some of the regulations that are coming down. There are new regulations I'm working

on right now to establish compliance programs for the disposal of hazardous waste, and I'm working with our nursing department to implement
procedures to train our people in how to comply and to make sure that
we have contracts with waste-disposal companies. That's interesting. . . .

"And I'm also involved with the same group of people, which I like.
We're a fairly small subsidiary, and I have a real rapport with a lot of
our field offices. . . . I've built up a lot of trust with them. And it's very
rewarding to sort of be able to work as part of a team instead of in a law
firm . . . particularly as law firms are going more into transactional work.
In the old days, a particular bank would go to a particular law firm. They
would do all their work. Lawyers who handled that account would know
those people in the bank very well, the upper-level people. Now more
companies are getting in-house counsel to deal with the more routine
matters, and they go to the law firm only when there's a major deal
involved, or a major piece of litigation. And so a lot of times [in a law
firm] you find that you're working for clients whom the firm has never
dealt with before. They don't have any long-standing relationship with
you. You get to know them fairly well over the course of the deal . . .
but you really don't have a sense of their business except for what you
learn on the transaction. You have no idea what their strategy is for the
future, what they've done in the past, what their relationships are with
the people in that new corporation. . . . You know, it's just 'We want to
do a merger, this is the company we want to buy, we want you to draw
up the documents.' I'm enjoying very much the opposite, seeing where
we've been, where we're going, where our financial plans are, having a
chance to anticipate legal issues and say, 'We really need to start doing
some research in this area. There may be a whole lot of regulations that
we may need to comply with in this area. . . . We need to get compliance
plans together.'

"And having a relationship with our businesspeople. Businesspeople
generally hate lawyers . . . and I think because they sort of see me as
their own lawyer, I'm okay. And they listen to me. They disagree with
me. We fight a lot. But they will listen to me, and if I can convince them
that what I'm telling them is right, they will do it. And I like that
relationship."

Where we've been and where we're going. Health. Community.
Trust. Relationships, as opposed to isolated transactions between
strangers. The key word is *community*. This woman wants to be part of
and contribute to a society whose members acknowledge moral connections—which means acknowledging both the weight and imprint of

history and the conflicting claims and interests of the present, and being willing both to struggle with the trouble all this generates and to maintain responsible relationships with others, including antagonists, who are part of a complex social function. The hit-and-run approach of singular, sequential transactions leaves her cold. And nothing she says suggests that she conceives of herself as a warrior. She may fight with her clients, but she is not trying to defeat an opponent, as a litigator must do, in a contest that can produce only a win or a loss. Rather, like other in-house lawyers, she is solving problems in a process that merges legal rules with social priorities, financial calculations, and other open-ended elements, to produce not victories but choices.

The story of another woman, drawn from a big law firm into the legal department of a multinational corporation, also exemplifies the desire to know how all the parts of a complex institution fit together. But this saga suggests, too, some of the reasons why many women like and do well at collaborative work, and why in-house practice values it in ways that law firms tend not to. And it suggests also that the corporate world, which would seem to be an unfriendly environment for women, may actually be more open to outsiders than is the more tightly structured world of the firms.

This woman, a divorced mother of two, went into law from a career in special education that included work with emotionally disturbed children. Having been repeatedly passed over for promotions to administrative positions in her school system, she hoped a law degree would provide a credential that would help her crack the heavily male world of education policy. But once in law school, she became intrigued enough by the law to be diverted from this course and into a large law firm immediately on graduation.

She found her niche in the corporate department of the firm after spending six months trying out litigation, which she hated in spite of the fun of traveling all over the country with senior lawyers, taking depositions in a big case. "I can't deal with the psychology and dynamics that go on in litigation," she says. "It's a fight. People are nasty. And they play games. And for what? I can't relate to it at all." But corporate law is different, she found. "There, at the end of negotiating a deal, you shake hands. You have to be a tough negotiator so that you protect your client, but at the end you want to have a deal that both sides can live with, so that they can go on and work with each other."

She was also deeply curious about how the private sector works generally, how companies make decisions, how money moves around.

She found it all fascinating. It was as if she had landed on another planet. "How I got from sitting on the floor with five-year-olds saying 'This is a fish' to doing public offerings of stock for a big law firm still amazes me," she remarks. But after several years, she became frustrated by the obstructed and fragmented view of the business world that her vantage point in the law firm afforded. She could see into the corporate system only as it intersected with the law, and she wanted to see more. "I wanted to get into the boardroom," she says.

Then she found that her view of the business world was being further obstructed by a subtle form of sex discrimination in her firm. That is, on the theory that business executives are more comfortable dealing with male lawyers, she was occasionally excluded from direct talks with clients even when she was the principle associate on the matter under discussion. After one egregious incident of this kind, she blew up at the partners involved. "The funny thing is that this guy who didn't include me, he has a daughter who's a lawyer. . . . And I brought that up at lunch, talking about the kind of thing that I was experiencing. He denied it all the way. He came up with rationalizations why I wasn't included. But that was the end for me. I knew I was going to leave the firm. I just don't let that happen to me." So she looked around and moved in-house, into the heart of the mystery she wanted to solve.

The culture of the company she had joined, she soon discovered, was strictly hierarchical, highly contentious in a macho style, and very hard on women who do not like operating through loud exertions of will and power—and also hard on those who do. "Some women try to play the game," she says. "They think they're equal players if only they follow the rules, but they're not. They don't have a clue that there are two games—the young ones especially—until reality comes crashing in on them."

But she does not rely on power-brokering in her own phase of the operation—a law-and-business function involving the worldwide licensing and distribution of her company's product. Instead, she has created for herself a valued role based partly on special expertise and partly on skills that maintain working relations among people whose unequal power within the business structure produces chronic resentments and potential for internal warfare. "They think I'm good with people," she says. "What I do is make it work, come out with a product you can be happy with, and get the people to do the job. That's the best I can do as a lawyer. I mean, it's not ultimately what I'd like to do, but that makes me happy for now."

And she's learning how all the pieces fit together. "I know how you manufacture stuff all over the world. I know how you put the money out. I'm learning all these secrets. It's not this great mind game that all the guys like to think it is, so difficult. You peel the onion and there it is— it's not such a big deal. It's harder to raise children. That is much more difficult than anything I do at work. Men don't want to hear that, but it's the truth. It's difficult to raise young people, and if I were doing it full-time it would be just as difficult as doing my job full-time. So women who are home with kids, you think, Well, they don't have the skills. They're not allowed to go into the boardroom. Once you get into the boardroom—and I haven't been the number one player yet, I've been a minor player, but I've watched a lot—it's just not that magical or that mystical or that hard. It's hard. But once you get the education, there really is no mystery."

In fact, she found that what the closed door of the boardroom hides is often incredible irrationality. "I love going to these meetings and sitting there watching the dynamics, because all that you think goes on doesn't," she declares. "Decisions are made on such an arbitrary basis for huge, huge amounts of money. And it's really interesting. I had to peel away that onion to see, and now I know. I thought the public sector was pretty weird, but this is really weird!"

Clearly, it continues to bother her that the operation of big business is widely considered to be a male occupation for which women are some-how unsuited. Having seen from the inside the nuts and bolts of a huge enterprise and found it all comprehensible, if not rational, she remarks with a shrug, "They're all afraid the women are going to get in there and say, 'Ha ha, this isn't so difficult. I can do this.' "

She goes on to say that the interaction she had with people when working as a teacher of emotionally disturbed children gave her skills which she uses in business working with people all over the world, getting their efforts coordinated. "It's harder to work with emotionally disturbed kids and parents who don't have any money," she concludes.

Hers is a story of an outsider wanting to see the inside, getting there, and then finding, like Dorothy, that the Wizard is not all he's cracked up to be. Business is not necessarily "a mind game." It's a power game, with hierarchies, shouting, and sex discrimination, all operating against the inclusion of outsiders. But it also involves tangible functions that require coordination and the meshing of people with different personal-ities, interests, and status. And here, the woman in question has skills that the enterprise needs. She is "good with people," and she is vitally interested in making all the parts of a highly complicated, internationally operating process come together and work. Within a harsh and alien culture, she has found a way of working well and usefully and being recognized and rewarded for it.

The skills that she brings to her work came in part from education, as she says, but also from her experience as a mother and a teacher. And though she does not develop this last idea, does not explain how working with children relates to the functions of business, others have. Carol Gilligan first popularized the idea that women's social responsibility as primary caretakers of children and families requires that they focus on the intricacies of ongoing relationships and the importance of maintaining wide webs of connection in the community. And in doing so, Gilligan found, women tend to develop values and skills grounded in relatedness that they carry over into broader social thinking. Carrie Menkel-Meadow, proposing a "Research Agenda for the Feminization of the Legal Profession," expands on this idea and urges women lawyers to "stop focusing only on the opposition of the roles of mother and lawyer as if they must inevitably be in conflict" and start thinking about the application of relatedness and collaboration to their legal work.[6] And Sara Ruddick, in a series of articles amalgamated in her book *Maternal Thinking*, develops this idea at length.

Ruddick insists that *because* women who raise or work with children learn much about the complexities of human emotions and development, these women are particularly well equipped to deal with the complexities of the public world. For example, through a mother's immersion in daily detail, her close connection to a multifarious reality, she is likely to learn the futility of attempting exact control of a situation through power. She also comes to know—again, through close connection—the refractory complication of human beings. A powerless person—a child—can be prevented from doing specific things, can even be destroyed, but can rarely be fully controlled. Knowledge of this kind, Ruddick thinks, breeds over time a habit of humility, teaching people with seeming power to stay close to the mess of reality they deal with, not to allow themselves the comfort of abstract analyses that render problems neatly solvable by leaving messy pieces out.

I would stress that Ruddick is talking about knowledge, not about innate nurturing capacities in women. She is talking about problem-

---

6. Carrie Menkel-Meadow, "Exploring a Research Agenda for the Feminization of the Legal Profession: Theories of Gender and Social Change," *Law and Social Inquiry*, Vol. 14, No. 2 (Spring 1989), p. 289.

solving skills developed in situations of extreme difficulty and stress, about experience that teaches how to keep people working with each other even in situations fraught with conflict.[7]

The former teacher, on entering a multinational corporation, had to learn its peculiar culture, both to understand the processes of the business and to protect herself against hostile uses of power. And she had to learn how the basic functions of the company worked—"how you manufacture stuff all over the world . . . how you put the money out." But once she knew the basics, she could draw on a reservoir of understanding about people and social systems. As she describes it, her special value to the enterprise derives from her ability to keep people who have good reason to be endlessly suspicious of each other working cooperatively and well. This is difficult, she acknowledges, but she already knew a lot about it from sitting on the floor with small children and working with parents who had an emotionally disturbed child and no money.

The traditional devaluation of women in the law—they are not tough enough, they have their children on their minds, they avoid arenas of fierce competition—completely misses the value to the law of what women do know through their social training and their connections to children. And it may be the disparaged in-house practice that is most likely to provide space in which women's particular knowledge can develop, and women's influence as institutional organizers can grow.

Still, the potential for professional growth in the in-house space is necessarily limited by the very fact of its low status. The prevailing legal culture continues to place primary value on contentious, rule-based problem solving, and lesser value on collaboration and reinforcement of working relations. It continues to recognize the warrior-lawyer, the hero working heroic hours, as the model for professional prowess. And given the continuing migration of women out of the big firms that are the hero's habitat, keeping the old model preeminent keeps women out of professional power. And out of political power as well.

One of my interviewees, a tax lawyer interested in public policy, worked for a congressional committee during the Carter presidency and participated in a number of technical but satisfying changes in the tax code, only to find herself stymied politically by the Reagan administration and its massive shift in policy away from a progressive allocation of tax burdens. She left government for several ultimately unsatisfactory positions in New York firms and finally settled on an in-house position with

7. *Maternal Thinking: Toward a Politics of Peace* (Boston: Beacon Press, 1989).

the realty department of a large investment firm. Like others working in-house, she finds it satisfying to engage in a deal from the first proposals to its closing, rather than to be called in only for specific tax matters, as she would be in a law firm. For example, she says, if her company wants to diversify its real estate holdings in downtown San Francisco, she works on identifying alternatives, such as mortgaging property or bringing in an investment partner. She then helps to identify potential investors, seeks and reviews offers, and helps to negotiate the terms of the deal as it emerges, all of which gives her a stimulating role with a lot of decision-making power. But she's still not entirely comfortable with the position she's in.

Partly, she seems dogged by the lack of prestige of the in-house position. The people in her field who are held in the highest regard are partners in law firms, and because she isn't a partner, she "feels behind her law school peers." She acknowledges that she is not behind most women, and in salary she is not behind most men who are tax partners, but in "recognition and prestige," she insists, she is behind. She worries that she uses being a woman as an excuse for lack of achievement, al-though, demonstrably, it's a good excuse. Very few women from her law school generation—the early seventies—are partners in New York firms.

But beyond prestige, although connected to it, is the issue of public policy. She would like to reenter government and enlist again in the battles over taxes. "Where the money is, is where the issues are," she says. But you need the status of partnership, she thinks, to have a shot at good federal appointments. "It's a badge of eligibility for public policy."

This is a perilous situation—for women and for the society: for women because as long as they feel compelled to leave the big firms, their route to political authority as lawyer-advisers is effectively blocked by reliance on the partnership credential; for the society because that cre-dential generally excludes those whose experience of problem-solving is nonheroic. Yet skills in collaborative decision-making, close-up experi-ence with the day-to-day dealings of an enterprise, perspectives grounded in rich personal and social as well as professional lives, are crucial ingre-dients of a healthy society. Political rule-making as well as corporate rule-making are enriched by them. Without them, with excessive reliance on adversarial thinking, on competitive displays of capacities to control, the very ingredients of a humane democracy are in jeopardy.

How is it possible to counteract the professional norms that have the continuing effect of devaluing the particular skills and perspectives that many women bring to the law? How is it possible to revalue the work in the private sphere that enriches the professional lives of many women and that challenges the primacy of the traditional ethic of competition? How can women themselves bring about change in the values that dominate and constrict the working of the profession?

Professor Christine Littleton of the UCLA law faculty thinks a crucial step is a new round of consciousness-raising among women lawyers. "My theory of social change at this point," she says, "is that when you have a structure that has been exclusionary and you're going through a process of trying to infuse the excluded into it, there are roughly three reactions that can occur. One is a sort of allergic reaction. The structure and the excluded person can't communicate at all. In the legal profession, a lot of women in law firms find it so alien, and the men in power in the firms find those women so alien, that there is no communication. And those women either leave or are forced out. They leave to go into other forms of practice, or they leave law altogether and the law firm goes on its merry way thinking this person was not really a good lawyer.

"And then there's another class of women, who look so similar to —or can make themselves look so similar to—the old guard, that they do get some credibility, get some voice. But they may have very little to say in it, in that new voice, having assimilated so thoroughly. In fact, part of the tragedy of those women is that at some point or other it's always noticed that they're really women. At some point or another, the guys catch on! '*Oh no!* It's really a woman. Get her away from that partnership or get her away from that judgeship!' And this is a real betrayal of the rules of the game, which are 'Be like us and we'll let you in.'

"The third group is a very important part of the process, too, and that is those women who can talk the lingo enough to be seen as potentially credible lawyers but are always uncomfortable and are always making the guys uncomfortable. I mean the ones who hang in somehow, who don't leave, but who see that the system is exclusionary and find ways to criticize it.

"What we don't have and what we need is to find a way in which all three groups can operate together. There has to be some form of communication between those who open the doors, and those who keep the doors open, and those who see how small the door is. And it's hard. But if there's enough communication among all three groups, among all three positions, then you can get the benefit of all three perspectives. What is difficult is to maintain communication. Not just communication, but a real serious critique of each other in a supportive and loving fashion. One of the things that I've been thinking a lot about is the question about how we develop a model that allows for criticism *and* support in which neither one is trivialized. Usually, we have feminists trashing each other, and we have feminists supporting each other in uncritical ways, and it's very difficult to be both supportive and critical. So that's another thing I struggle for. We'll never run out of work, right?"

She is certainly right about the gulf among the groups. Those women who simply leave the firms as unlivable places tend not to theorize about what they're doing but, rather, to see their departure in purely personal terms. Therefore, they're unlikely to join activist attempts to bring about changes in the system as a whole. The second group, the women who decide to make a run for partnership by following men's rules, cannot publicly challenge the rules, and many of these women find it difficult to do so even after making partner, for fear of losing the respect of male colleagues. And the third group, the critics of the status quo, can easily come to feel serious hostility toward women lawyers who seem to accept the present system uncritically or who play it for individual advantage without apparent concern for its effect on other women.

The outlines of one possible model for bridging these gaps in consciousness, interest, and politics among women lawyers emerge from the story of another professor, Charity Scott, who moved from the world of big-firm law to a small firm with a strong civil rights focus and then to the faculty of the Georgia State University College of Law in Atlanta. A leitmotif in Scott's story is the practice of conversation, by which she means talk that ranges across personal and professional concerns. This concept of conversation does not seem remarkable on its face, but it is remarkable in the context of women working in a male world of high prestige. There, as other stories have made abundantly clear, women are not supposed to talk about their personal lives, their babies, their houses, or their children's schools. If they do, they risk not being taken seriously. They are under pressure to disprove the suspicion that their minds are taken up with matters irrelevant to their work.

From the beginning of her career, however, Scott refused to play this game. Interviewing at law firms in the early eighties, she made a point of talking about her baby and asking partners about real estate agents and school districts, even though such talk tended to produce an air of discomfort. She tells me that a woman partner at one firm simply shuffled her feet and gave no straightforward answers to questions about how women there accommodated work and family.

"No one would even address the issue. It was 'not done' to talk about it," Scott says. "Overall, I'm glad I did," she adds. "The discourse had to start somewhere." But she was not engaging in these conversations as a matter of ideological conviction. Rather, it simply did not seem sensible to her to divide the sphere of work completely from the sphere of family. It did not seem right for a person who went home to a family to talk and act as if families were insignificant—as if what mattered in a family had no relation to what mattered at work. Later, as a law professor, she began to see the broader point of what she had felt impelled to do as a young lawyer, and she began deliberately to foster among her colleagues an ongoing conversation that makes personal experience and personal values relevant to legal work.

She finds that Georgia State provides good ground for such conversation because it has a far greater percentage of women in its ranks than do the highly prestigious law schools, or law firms. "This is the first time I've been in a situation where there is a critical mass of women," she says. "And it is delightful. The women here are happy to talk and to talk about instantly personal things. . . . Maybe it's a level of friendliness. Maybe it's a level of intimacy. You know, if you're working with men, they often have a pattern of discourse. I keep coming back to conversation. I keep coming back to relationships. I am happy to establish close bonds, male or female. But traditionally, men don't establish as close bonds. I mean, you go to lunch and you talk about baseball. You have all of these impersonal kinds of things you talk about, and I'm more interested in What ages are your children? What are they doing?—your personal concerns or relationships. It's a matter of not having to watch your p's and q's, not thinking that you're being evaluated and put down if you even mention children."

Shortly before our interview, Scott had taken steps to advance the conversation of her faculty a step beyond the informal stages she has just described. With another woman, she had organized a faculty-wide seminar on feminist legal theory, circulating beforehand Robin West's article "Jurisprudence and Gender,"[8] which sets out a theory of pronounced gender differences both in basic values and in approaches to the law.

West argues that women have a distinct nature which is grounded in the fact of their literal connection to others in the act of intercourse, in pregnancy, in breast-feeding, and in the care of children. Therefore she thinks a central issue for women is intimacy, with most women valuing it and some regarding it as invasive and burdensome. Men, on the other hand, West says, lacking the experience of literal connectedness, focus

---

8. *University of Chicago Law Review*, Vol. 55, No. 1 (Winter 1988), p. 1.

on issues of autonomy, either as an ultimate value or, in the form of alienation and isolation, as an ultimate fear. The point for American law, West says, is that it reflects mainly the values of autonomy and protection of the individual against destruction by other autonomous individuals. Neither the law nor the market economy it organizes, she concludes, values nurturant, intimate labor. Nor do they identify the separation of the individual from family, community, and children as a harm to be protected against.

Scott tells me that she had not intended to jump into the question whether women's perspectives would change the law, but simply to raise the issue whether women have a different perspective at all. And she thought that the West article might lay the subject out as a quick introduction. But, she says ruefully, "It was too quick for some." A number of faculty members disliked the article because it seemed to set women against men. And some male faculty members in particular saw it as inflammatory because the words describing women seemed more positive than those describing men.

However, Scott adds, "People did talk. It was a good discussion. I tried to set it up so that differences weren't labeled in pejorative terms, but it's a tough subject. Raising it is like going around and talking at law firms about babies. That's not what you do."

Clearly, though, she is going to go on doing it. What she is seeking is conversation that allows the whole person to enter, that makes whole lives relevant to professional functions. And here, I think, is the beginning of a process with the potential to dissolve the boundaries of groups now insulated by silence. Somehow, unlimited, ongoing conversation among women about their whole lives should be able to include the women who are opting out of the law, the women who are trying valiantly to play by rules that do not fit their lives, and the women who analyze and criticize the profession of law generally.

The purpose of such conversation would be to advance a shared understanding, in concrete, daily terms, of conditions that block what women—as women—want to do as lawyers. What's needed is clarity about the commonalities that lurk in the welter of differences among women lawyers with widely varied skills, ambitions, values, and personal lives. Women lawyers need to recognize themselves as a class—a class of daughters—that suffers disadvantages due to ingrained social structures that define women's place as subordinate. They need to recognize also that the legal profession, and others, operate according to norms that downgrade values and social tasks associated with women—that part of the systemic disadvantage that professional women encounter is the perception by male authorities that women are not "serious" about their work or do not want to "work hard" when they involve themselves in nonwork relationships—usually, with children.

To counter their disadvantage as a class, women need to learn not how to conform but how to refuse to conform, how to seek change in the attitudes and structures that protect the presently privileged. They need to talk, to protest, to dissent, to resist, to organize new structures to accommodate their values and visions. And to do this, they need a voice. In spite of their increasing numbers, they do not have a sufficient voice in the profession to make their common interests heard. They need to speak their interests and values, not hide them.

As to where women's conversations could best take place, how women's voices could most effectively be raised, it is possible that the process might best develop in the places where it is already strongest—the less powerful, less prestigious places where the numbers of women are relatively high. Charity Scott remarks that among the many women faculty members at her small public law school, she feels freer to speak about things it is "not done" to mention than in any other professional setting she has been in. "I find it's changing among men, too. I find conversations are opening up among both men and women." Perhaps the conversations need to begin and gather force on the periphery, wherever there is "a critical mass of women," before moving to the centers where women's voices are still easily drowned out.

8

EQUALIZING POWER

BEYOND THE QUESTION of equalizing power between men and women in the legal profession is the larger question of equalizing power between the sexes in the society generally. And for women lawyers, or the activists among them, the further question is how they can deploy the law as an equalizing instrument.

For many women, the original attraction of the law is what they see as its power to define right and wrong and therefore to bring about change by identifying and reforming social wrongs. What they tend not to see clearly, as idealistic law students and young lawyers, is the function of the law as conservator, as protector of the status quo, as the carrier of the values and interests of the power holders in the society, and, therefore, as a force constantly resistant to equalization. In fact, many lose their focus on social change while in law school because, as one activist reformer puts it, they are barraged in most of their courses with the message that the law, far from being a protector of the powerful, is actually a "nonvalue system." That is to say, students learn that the overall system of law works objectively, and, therefore, it does not matter what side you represent. You are not harming the society by working in a large firm for Fortune 500 clients, because someone else is representing the other side, and the overall system produces fairness. Once they accept this idea, the reformer concludes, young lawyers lose their ability to see where the system does not work fairly and they become fair game for the lure of high-salaried law. They convince themselves that by serving the legal system on its own terms they are serving the cause of fairness generally, for women and for everyone else.

But those who retain a critical vision see the inner tension in the law, the inner contradiction between a requirement that the law maintain a system of inherited order and a promise that the law deliver justice, equally, to all. Activist lawyers must press their vision for reform within a system that is, at the same time, profoundly radical and profoundly conservative. They must invoke the values of fairness inherent to the law while remaining ever wary of the rules and procedures that would defeat those values. Still, walking this uncertain line, lawyers seeking equality for women have achieved some remarkable results.

Reform lawyers work, necessarily, from the margins. They are to be found, for the most part, in public interest agencies, in government agencies and prosecutors' offices, and in law schools among the developers of new critical legal theories, including feminist jurisprudence. In all these places, the critical mission of the inhabitants, their distance from the establishment, meets the eye—and ear—immediately. Where the interiors of the big firms are swathed in rich materials and their carefully groomed lawyers dressed in quiet colors that match quiet voices, the milieu of the reformers is usually unadorned and noisy.

In public interest agencies, people may be dashing about as in private firms, but they're wearing jeans, not suits. And they do not work in quiet, separated spaces. They sprawl behind battle-scarred desks. They clatter along uncarpeted floors past walls hung not with staid prints or modern art but with newspaper clippings and cartoons recording victories or defeats in whatever cause the agency pursues. In small, crowded, busy offices in Chicago, the el rattles past third-floor windows every few minutes.

In New York, the prosecutor in a sex-crimes unit works in a building that horrifies her lawyer father. When I was there, one winter morning at nine o'clock, hundreds of people, mostly poor, mostly black, formed a line nearly a block long, two- and three-deep, moving slowly through metal detectors into a cavernous, drafty, dingy lobby. These were the accused and the accusers, their families and witnesses, and they were quiet, glum, probably frightened. The guards running the detectors were mostly white, uniformly unsmiling, and wary. The elevators and the upstairs corridors were bare-floored and starkly lit. Warrens of offices were carved out of high-ceilinged, dark-wainscoted rooms. Nothing was freshly painted, nothing was upholstered. But the staff was brisk, polite, and cheerful, and so was the young attorney I met. Small, slim, dark-haired, vibrant in a bright red dress with matching shoes, she seemed poised for whatever demands the day might bring.

Morale seemed high, too, among the lawyers working in one big-city municipal office building that had seen much better days. Built in the Progressive Era, this majestic structure expresses huge confidence in solid good government, but now displays scars from many lost battles. Too little cleaning for too many years has left the marble lobby soiled around the base of its walls and the brass elevator doors dull. The press of urban problems requiring more officials and more offices has sliced grandly high rooms into two levels, each topped with flimsy ceiling tile and bars of fluorescent light. Or sometimes tall ceilings have been left intact but the floor space partitioned into offices higher than they are wide. And instead of the polished woods, rich brocades, and mirrored elevators of the law firms, one finds battered desks and tables, faded drapes, and Progressive Era plumbing. But the lawyers I visited were working overtime, oblivious of their surroundings, designing new procedures to control corruption in city contracting.

Law school offices are quiet and well equipped. The furniture is newer than in public service agencies, and computers are plentiful. But the style here, too, is generally ascetic, utilitarian, with books and papers piled high, spreading everywhere. In the midst of these mountains of ideas, casually dressed professors work in chronic tension between internal goads and the external demands of classes, meetings, deadlines.

The contrasting styles of the two legal worlds, the mainline firms and the reform sites, demarcate the dual nature of the law. The one, ringed with signs of wealth, protects the established order, and the other, marked by conspicuous nonconsumption, challenges it. But both work under a single rubric of rules. Both seek to construct a good order for the society through common rules applicable to all. The question then is, What rules have the feminist activists sought to construct, from the margins, to further their project of equalizing power between men and women? And how have they done it?

The most ambitious efforts have been those mounted by public interest groups that have raised money to support long-term programs focused on change in some specific area of law. These may be lobbying campaigns directed at legislatures, such as the long and finally unsuccessful effort to add an Equal Rights Amendment to the federal Constitution. Or they may be battles carried on in the courts through litigation posing feminist challenges to prevailing interpretations of the law. Going this route, feminist activists seek out cases that raise the issues they want to contest and provide lawyers for the side they want to support. And they also keep a close watch on other cases raising important issues, and join in the argument by submitting briefs as amicus curiae ("friend of the court"). Then, even if the lawyers actually arguing such a case do not raise or thoroughly discuss the issues in feminist terms the activists want to press, the amicus briefs bring the missing arguments to the attention of the judges deciding the case and writing the opinion.

The best-known feminist fight in the courts has been the long battle over abortion rights. Cases backed by local civil rights groups arguing a constitutional right to abortion were making their way to the Supreme Court in a number of states when *Roe v. Wade*, from Texas, got there first in 1973. And since then, determined efforts by the American Civil Liberties Union (ACLU), the National Organization for Women Legal Defense and Education Fund (NOW/LDEF), the National Women's Political Caucus (NWPC), and the National Abortion Rights Action League (NARAL), among others, have been vigilant in their resistance to strongly mounted efforts to overturn *Roe*. But lesser-known, less-politicized campaigns to broaden women's basic rights and protections have also had impressive results.

Notable among them was the effort carried on through the 1970s by the Women's Rights Project of the ACLU to gain new readings by the Supreme Court of the Fourteenth Amendment equal-protection clause. That clause prohibits the states from denying to their citizens the equal protection of the law. Passed immediately after the Civil War, the amendment was designed to protect the rights of former slaves in southern states but has since been taken to apply to any group that might be subjected to discriminatory standards. However, a long history of interpretation established that the courts would take race discrimination more seriously than other forms, giving such claims "strict scrutiny" while applying to other groups, including women, the more lenient standard of "reasonableness." Under this latter standard (discussed briefly in Chapter 2), state laws could treat men and women unequally if the purpose of the distinction was reasonable, which meant, in practice, if the state supplied almost any reason at all.

Historically, the most galling forms of sex discrimination practiced by states were restrictions on women's employment. While the stated reason for such legislation was to protect women's health and safety, the actual effect was to protect a male monopoly on better-paying jobs. Similar restrictions imposed by the federal government, to which the equal-protection clause also applies, are the limitations on activities open to women in the military. Applying the reasonableness standard, the courts would accept the stated reason for such laws and not scrutinize their actual discriminatory effect. It was this standard—which affected a wide range of issues in addition to employment—that the Women's Rights Project was formed to challenge.

As noted earlier, the first director of the Project was Supreme Court
Justice Ruth Bader Ginsburg, then a Rutgers law professor. As Justice
Ginsburg recalls it (she was still on the D.C. Court of Appeals when we
spoke), the equal-rights litigation sprang up at first out of its own mo-
mentum, the pressure for it taking her and the ACLU almost by surprise.
"At the end of the sixties the women's movement came alive, and I was
not out in the forefront of it by any means," she says. "I was tugged into
the effort by two forces. One pull came from students at Rutgers who
wanted to have a seminar on women and the law. And the other came
from the local ACLU. I was teaching procedure and I had never worked
full-time for a law firm. The one way I could respectably get litigation
experience and have my faculty tolerate it was to be a volunteer lawyer
for the ACLU. I signed on as a volunteer for the New Jersey Civil Liberties
Union, not for any ideological reason but simply to do real lawyering
work. The Union began to get sex-discrimination complaints, raising
issues that were unfamiliar to the staff, so they referred the complaints to
the woman close at hand. Two kinds were the most frequent in those
early days. One kind came from pregnant workers, principally school-
teachers, who were told they had to leave at three months, four months,
surely by the time the pregnancy showed. These were people who wanted
to stay on the job, to continue teaching in the classroom, and didn't want
to be forced out on what was then called 'maternity leave,' which was a
euphemism for 'You're out, and if you want to come back, then we'll
consider whether we want to take you back.' That was one kind of complaint. Another raised in the early days concerned women who worked
in factories and wanted to subscribe to family coverage under the health
plan at their factory because the family coverage at their plant was better
than the coverage offered at their husbands' plant. Family coverage, at
that time, was often available only to a male worker. The female worker,
because it was assumed she would quit after marriage, or surely after
childbirth, could cover only herself. This was late sixties.

    "And there were a variety of other interesting challenges. Princeton
University was running a summer-in-engineering program for sixth-grade
children, a marvelous program. It introduced ghetto children to math and
science early on and followed up their progress in junior and senior high
school. But this fine program was for boys only. The local chapter of
NOW supported the parents of girls who wanted a chance to gain admission to the program. Then the Supreme Court took the *Reed* case
[which challenged a state law automatically making the father of a deceased
child the administrator of the child's estate when both parents sought the

appointment (404 U.S. 71, 1971)]. I had asked Mel Wulf, then the legal director of the ACLU, if I could write the *Reed* brief, and the two of us ended up writing it together."

It was when the Supreme Court ruled unanimously in favor of the mother, Sally Reed, that the ACLU recognized the importance of the emerging issues of sex discrimination that the women's movement was defining, Justice Ginsburg says. From that point on, it tried carefully to choreograph a succession of cases for ultimate judgment by the Supreme Court.

Culling cases that arrived in ACLU offices around the country, the Women's Rights Project raised issues that included, among many others, lower veteran's benefits for female veterans, the effective exclusion of women from juries in some states, differences in property-tax exemptions and Social Security benefits for widows and widowers, as well as the ubiquitous state and federal laws restricting women's employment for supposed reasons of safety.

Underlying most such discriminations were unexamined conventional assumptions about the social and economic roles of men and women. Men were assumed to be breadwinners, women homemakers, and the logic of this view, written into the laws, tended to confine men and women to their stereotyped roles. It was that barrier, the confining stereotypes, that the lawyers in the Women's Rights Project were aiming at. They wanted the Supreme Court to read the equal-protection clause of the Fourteenth Amendment as prohibiting legal distinctions based on sex as strictly as it prohibited distinctions based on race. In this, they did not fully succeed, but the line of cases they brought did produce a far stricter reading of equal protection applied to sex by the end of the seventies than had stood at the beginning of the decade. The Court finally discarded the reasonableness test and replaced it with the rule that "classifications by gender must serve important governmental objectives and must be substantially related to the achievement of those objectives." Otherwise, a law treating men and women differently was a denial of equal protection, and unconstitutional (*Craig v. Boren*, 429 U.S. 190, 1976).

Perhaps more important, the debate surrounding the cases helped to raise the issue of sex discrimination into public sight. Such talk became part of the effort to dismantle sex stereotypes that has since opened large areas of the work force to women—not yet an entry on equal terms, as is obvious in the legal profession, but wider than it has ever been.

Another feminist campaign, under way in the middle to late 1970s, was the concerted effort by several feminist legal organizations to develop the law of sexual harassment, the campaign referred to in Chapter 4. This is a story of a few women being in the right place at the right time and using the opportunities they had, while they had them. The right time was the four-year period, from 1977 to 1981, when Jimmy Carter, a president genuinely committed to equal opportunity for women, was in office. And the right place was Washington, D.C.

In the mid-seventies, complaints about sexual harassment began to appear in the offices of activist lawyers, who brought them to court on the then novel theory that sexual harassment was a form of sex discrimination prohibited by Title VII of the Civil Rights Act of 1964. In the first round of cases, heard by several federal courts around the country, the new theory was dismissed. But in 1976, the District Court for the District of Columbia reversed this trend and decided that sexual harassment *could* be considered sex discrimination. And, in 1977, several of the earlier cases were reversed as appellate courts, including the Court of Appeals for the District of Columbia Circuit, also accepted the new concept.[1]

Instrumental in pressing the breakthrough cases in the District of Columbia was the Women's Legal Defense Fund (WLDF), founded in Washington, D.C., in 1971 by activist lawyers who had come to the capital during the reform period of the sixties and who converted their intense involvement in the civil rights movement to an early commitment to women's rights. The WLDF consisted of a tiny staff and a corps of volunteer lawyers who stood ready to take on legal tasks for feminist causes. A WLDF volunteer handled *Barnes v. Castle*, the first case in which the District of Columbia Circuit Court of Appeals recognized sexual harassment as a violation of Title VII, and thereafter the organization filed amicus briefs in all subsequent harassment cases that came before that court. But just as important as the appellate briefs they filed were the informal discussions going on among the WLDF lawyers and those in other advocacy groups concerned with harassment law, and the multipronged efforts of the women's rights community to move the issue along. Donna Lenhoff, then a new staff attorney at the WLDF and later its director of litigation, recalls a continuing round of phone calls among WLDF lawyers and those at the ACLU Women's Rights Project and at NOW/LDEF, both in New York, as well as activists at the District of

---

1. *Williams v. Saxbe*, 413 F. Supp. 654 (D.D.C. 1976); and *Barnes v. Castle*, 561 F.2d 983 (D.C. Cir. 1977). Catharine MacKinnon's influential book *Sexual Harassment of Working Women* (New Haven: Yale University Press, 1979), reviews in detail the early case law on sexual harassment.

Columbia Commission for Women; the lawyers at the EEOC, including civil rights lawyer Eleanor Holmes Norton, its chair in the Carter administration; and friendly members of Congress, including Representative Patricia Schroeder.

After gaining their initial legal goal, to bring the sexual-harassment issue under Title VII generally, the lawyers of the WLDF and the other interested groups began to push for a legal definition of sexual harassment that would encompass what they considered its most insidious forms. The early cases had involved women who lost jobs or suffered other clear-cut setbacks when they rejected the sexual demands of employers or superiors. But the next step was to reach chronic kinds of sexual pressure that did not carry the threat of reprisal but, rather, made working conditions for women constantly miserable. What was needed was a clear, broad definition of sexual harassment by the EEOC as the enforcer of Title VII.

A willing party to the process of gaining the needed definition was the House Committee on Post Office and Civil Service, which was co-chaired by Democrats James Hanley of New York and Morris Udall of Arizona and included among its members Patricia Schroeder, Gladys Noon Spellman, Geraldine Ferraro, and Mary Rose Oakar. The Post Office and Civil Service Subcommittee on Investigations held hearings on "Sexual Harassment in the Federal Government" in October and November 1979. Donna Lenhoff, representing the WLDF, asked that federal agencies issue explicit directives on the subject, and passed on to the subcommittee a draft model for such directives.

The draft language defined sexual harassment as "any repeated or unwarranted verbal or physical sexual advances, sexually explicit derogatory statements, or sexually discriminatory remarks made by someone in the workplace which is offensive or objectionable to the recipient or which causes the recipient discomfort or humiliation or which interferes with the recipient's job performance."[2] The virtue of this definition, Lenhoff says, was to identify the harm of harassment in terms of the personal suffering of its target whether or not reprisals were involved.

Armed with this and other testimony on the seriousness of the problem, the committee asked the Merit Systems Protection Board to initiate the survey on sexual harassment in the federal government already referred to in Chapter 4. But even before the survey was completed, government agencies began to take action. In December 1979, the director of the

2. Hearings before the House Subcommittee on Investigations of the Committee on Post Office and Civil Service, 96th Cong. 1st sess., October 23, November 1, 13, 1979.

Office of Personnel Management issued a statement recommending that all heads of departments adopt strong management policies on sexual harassment. And in November 1980, Eleanor Holmes Norton for the EEOC issued the definitive guidelines on sexual harassment quoted in Chapter 4, adopting the general concept, if not the exact language of the definition the WLDF had given the House subcommittee.

By 1980, therefore, the sexual-harassment law sought by feminist lawyers was on the books, but it was still subject to challenge in the courts. Employers charged with harassment under the new guidelines could and did defend against the charges in court by arguing that the EEOC was imposing on them an incorrect interpretation of sex discrimination under Title VII. One such case was *Meritor Savings Bank v. Vinson*, which came up through the D.C. courts accompanied by amicus briefs from the WLDF spelling out the issues at each step along the way. The Supreme Court took the case in 1986 and in a unanimous opinion written by Justice Rehnquist approved the EEOC guidelines word for word.[3]

This was a spectacular accomplishment for the advocacy groups. But what the Rehnquist opinion adds to the story is that it was not feminist activism alone that produced the law on sexual harassment. It was the inherent fairness of the principles involved—antidiscrimination, equal opportunity in employment—that impressed themselves on judges throughout the federal court system, up to the Supreme Court. But it was without question feminist activism that got the principles into the courts in the first place, and moved them through the appellate process until their merit was officially recognized.

But the story does not stop there. Litigation has continued for the purpose of further specifying and broadening the meaning of sexual harassment under Title VII. A crucial issue is the question of perspective. In the usual case of male harassment of a female employee, the question is, Whose perspective should determine whether or not the behavior in question is "offensive" within the meaning of the EEOC guidelines? The usual legal standard is the perspective of the "reasonable person." But who is that?

The "reasonable person" has arrived in the law only very recently. For centuries, judges applying a reasonableness standard conjured up the judgment of the "reasonable man." And although this man was, supposedly, a generic figure representing both sexes, his explicators were

---

3. The final guidelines were published in 45 Code of Federal Regulations 74676 (1980). The *Vinson* case is also cited in Chapter 4.

virtually all men, and his point of view tended to be male. It was to correct this tendency that lawyers and judges, in response to criticism from feminists, converted the reasonable man into a reasonable person. But with the bench still heavily male, the viewpoint of the person continued to look very much like that of the man—which in some cases mattered little, but in cases of sexual harassment mattered a great deal.

As Lucinda Finley has pointed out in her article "A Break in the Silence," sexual behavior in the workplace that is regarded as normal kidding by men is often seriously offensive or frightening to women.[4] The problem is that deep-rooted social conventions direct men to be the sexual initiators and pursuers, and also teach them to interpret women's resistance to their efforts as coyness (no means yes, or maybe). As a result, many men are likely to engage in harassment in the full belief that they are not out of bounds. And male judges, as a long line of cases makes clear, are likely to agree with them. Therefore, feminist legal organizations have continued to press cases contesting the standards by which harassing behavior is judged "normal."

One such case, *Robinson v. Jacksonville Shipyards, Inc.*, backed by the NOW Legal Defense and Education Fund, produced a breakthrough. In a 1991 decision, a federal district court in Jacksonville, Florida, found that subjecting women workers to pornographic pictures of women, such as a photo of a nude body with "U.S.D.A. Choice" stamped on it, and to sexual remarks such as "Hey pussycat, come here and give me a whiff," constituted sexual harassment. And it did so even though most of the workers at the shipyards were men, and most of them regarded the pornography and the continual practice of directing sexual remarks at women workers as normal. The court, however, found that what the men regarded as normal was unreasonable behavior adversely affecting the conditions of work for women within the meaning of the EEOC guidelines approved by the Supreme Court in *Vinson*. And to arrive at its conclusion that the behavior was unreasonable, the court explicitly adopted as its measure the standard of the "reasonable woman." Would a reasonable woman, the court asked, find the pornography on the walls and the sexual remarks made by male workers so offensive as to affect the conditions of her work?[5]

The decision placed feminist lawyers in a quandary. They applauded the court's rejection of a male viewpoint as the standard of normality or reasonableness but fell into disagreement over the replacement of the

---

4. *Yale Journal of Law and Feminism*, Vol. 1, No. 1 (Spring 1989), p. 41.
5. 760 F. Supp. 1486 (M.D. Fla., 1991).

reasonable man by the reasonable woman. Some approved on the grounds that only women can know the effects of harassment on them, that the effects *had* to be measured from a woman's point of view. Others, including the WLDF, were concerned that setting up a separate women's standard for legal judgments could open the way to a return of sex stereotypes—women are delicate, sensitive, psychologically fragile, emotional, unable to deal with the stresses of the workplace. And such stereotypes could legitimize—again—the exclusion of women from certain types of work. In an amicus brief to the Court of Appeals for the Eleventh Circuit, to which the Jacksonville Shipyards had appealed the lower court's decision, the WLDF proposed a gender-neutral reasonable-*person* standard, but one that would explicitly take into account the sex, race, and other conditions of vulnerability of the "person."

NOW/LDEF lawyers in amicus briefs in *Robinson* and also in a subsequent case, *Harris v. Forklift Systems*,[6] argued against the adoption of *any* reasonableness standard for judging sexual harassment. They insisted that asking what degree of offensiveness was too much for a reasonable woman *or* person necessarily resulted in sex stereotyping. Further, they pointed out, such standards led some courts to conclude that egregiously offensive sexual behavior was not unreasonable in the workplace because it was the norm in the larger society, or that a woman who had not suffered a nervous breakdown or other severe psychological injury had not been unreasonably harmed by offensive behavior. The proposed NOW/LDEF standard is a test that focuses not on the mentality of the person claiming harassment but on the sexual conduct in question and its impact on conditions in the particular workplace.

At the time of writing, these issues remained unresolved, as the Eleventh Circuit Court of Appeals had not decided the *Robinson* case and the Supreme Court had not yet heard *Harris*. But in any event, what emerges here is the dual difficulty feminist advocacy groups confront in cases of sexual harassment or the violent abuse of women. One is the necessity to move away from supposedly objective but actually male standards of reasonableness. The other is to define new standards that include a woman's viewpoint but do not fall into subjectivity or stereotyping. This problem surfaces in a number of legal issues that I will discuss later in this chapter and in the next. It is a problem of profound significance for feminist jurisprudence, raising as it does the general philosophical ques-

---

6. 976 F 2d 733 (U.S. Court of Appeals for the Sixth Circuit, 1992), accepted for argument before the Supreme Court, October Term, 1993.

tion, Can the two sexes ever see their relations from a single reasonable viewpoint?

The impact that feminist thinking and organization have had on the development of new law can also be seen in *California Federal Savings and Loan v. Guerra*, decided by the Supreme Court in 1987. This case, too, involved the question whether women in the workplace must function under gender-neutral standards or whether they might claim the protection of special rules for women. The specific issue was not harassment but maternity leave. California had passed a law requiring employers to allow pregnant employees unpaid maternity leave, meaning that such employees would have a right to return to their jobs after a specified leave period. The law was contested when a bank, California Federal Savings and Loan, refused a receptionist her old job when she returned to work after a maternity leave. The employee, Lillian Garland, protested, claiming protection under the state maternity-leave law, but the bank claimed that the state law was invalid because it conflicted with a superseding federal law.

The federal law in question was the Pregnancy Discrimination Act, which prohibits employers from discriminating against employees on grounds of pregnancy. The bank's argument was that the state law, by giving pregnant women special rights, was forcing employers to discriminate on grounds of pregnancy.

Even though such reasoning sounds paradoxical, it was hard to refute in the face of the decade-long effort that feminists had mounted to wipe off the books distinctions based on sex. Ever since the early seventies, when Ruth Bader Ginsburg and her cohorts had argued that equality under the law should mean gender neutrality, some feminists have insisted that workplace rules must apply in the same literal way to both men and women. Their fear has been that if employers could make any distinction at all between the sexes, the distinctions would inevitably turn against women. And the California maternity-leave law clearly applied different rules to men and women. It gave women benefits it did not give men.

As the case made its way through the federal courts in California— the state, representing the employee, lost in the district court, then won in the Court of Appeals for the Ninth Circuit—the feminist legal community was in a state of tension and disarray. The case had pushed to the surface a growing body of feminist thought that was critical of the 1970s' "sameness" standard for measuring equality. The proponents of the new approach argued that achieving equality for women depended on recognizing the differences between men and women, and especially the differences imposed on women's lives by childbearing and child care. They asserted that laws providing for restrictions or benefits of various kinds might have to treat men and women differently in order to produce equal results, because men and women started from different conditions and situations. The maternity-leave law was an obvious case in point because women's work lives are physically disrupted by childbirth in a way that men's work lives are not, and the law attempted to remove the disadvantages to women produced by that difference.

The sameness/difference debate over the *Cal Fed* case (as it came to be called) caused particular trouble in the ACLU, whose Women's Rights Project had won the 1970s victories for the sameness standard. When California Federal Savings and Loan, having lost at the appellate level, appealed to the Supreme Court, the southern California branch of the ACLU wanted to file an amicus brief in support of the California law, making some form of a "difference" argument. But this move was over-ruled by the national ACLU, which had decided to file a brief supporting a strict sameness standard, even though, in this case, the result would diminish benefits a state law gave to women.

The southern Californians, however, could not accept the sameness position in this case. Blocked from addressing the Supreme Court in the name of the ACLU, a group of them quickly formed an ad hoc organization, the Coalition for Reproductive Equality in the Workplace (CREW), to sponsor the "difference" brief they wished to send to Washington. Supporters of the venture included Betty Friedan, Planned Parenthood, the International Ladies Garment Workers Union (ILGWU), the California Federation of Teachers, and 9 to 5, the clerical workers' advocacy group, as well as Hispanic groups that wanted to retain the protection of the maternity-leave law for minority women working in unorganized job situations.

A major organizer of this effort and the author of the "difference" brief was Professor Christine Littleton, of the UCLA Law School. Littleton, as a student at the Harvard Law School in the early eighties, had published in the *Harvard Law Review* a note called "Toward a Redefinition of Sexual Equality." Her short article set out the basic idea that the law had to take some account of the differences in the biological and social situations of women and men in order to put the two sexes in positions of equal power. Later, as a professor, she developed that thesis into a longer, more complex argument in her article "Reconstructing

Sexual Equality," published by the *California Law Review* in 1987. Drawing on her theorizing, the brief of the ad hoc activists argued that granting women the right to pregnancy leaves was not so much treating women differently from men as attempting to put them in the same position as men who need not choose between having children and keeping their jobs.

Littleton tells me her version of the *Cal Fed* story, gleefully, some two years after the event. She flew to Washington to hear the oral arguments when the case was presented to the Supreme Court. Sitting with Betty Friedan, she hung on every word the lawyers spoke but was disappointed when the attorney for the state of California, defending the maternity-leave law, did not include in his presentation her argument about the need for a broadened concept of equality. Rather, he stayed on safer, more technical ground. But when the decision came down some months later, Littleton was stunned and overjoyed to find that Justice Thurgood Marshall, writing the Court opinion, had picked up and used the full logic of her thinking. "By 'taking pregnancy into account,' " Justice Marshall wrote, "California's pregnancy disability leave statute allows women, as well as men, to have families without losing their jobs."[7]

Littleton says that she had mentally aimed the argument at Justice Marshall "because he understands that equality has to be interpreted in the light of women's concrete experience," and she was exultant in the success of her strategy. Because of the time difference between the East and West coasts, she learned of Marshall's opinion from a reporter, before she had seen the morning paper. "The first thing I knew, I got a phone call," she recalls. "It woke me up. A Los Angeles newspaper wanted a quote. I didn't even know the opinion had come down. I was so relieved when I heard it was Marshall! Then, when I saw the opinion . . . !"

The issue, however, is far from settled. The Court in *Cal Fed* split four ways. A majority of six was divided into a plurality of four, for whom Marshall spoke, and two separate concurrences based on other grounds. Three justices dissented. And since 1987, conservative justices appointed to the Court have further reduced support for Marshall's reasoning. And the case still worries feminists who think that women are best served by sticking with a literal equal-rights standard. But on the whole, the women's rights activists of the eighties and nineties are generally headed, as was

7. *California Federal Savings and Loan Association v. Mark Guerra, Director, Department of Fair Employment and Housing*, 479 U.S. 272 (1987).

made clear in their actions in the *Robinson* case, toward complicating gender-neutral standards to take into account the different circumstances of men's and women's lives.

Another site of activity by women lawyers pressing for the equality of women is the prosecutor's office. Particularly in state court systems, which deal with crimes of violence against women, young prosecutors work heroically to resist long and heavy traditions that discount the seriousness of such crimes. Though the police decide whether or not to arrest a crime suspect, it is a district attorney, typically an elected official, and a staff of appointed assistants, usually not long out of law school, and seeking trial experience, who decide whether or not to bring the suspect to court. They also choose *how* to prosecute, whether to file the most serious charges possible and risk defeat because the burden of proof would be heavy, or lesser charges bearing a lighter burden. And given long-standing public skepticism about women's claims of violent harm—"She asked for it" or "She started it" or "She deserved it" or "She wanted it"—elected officials are unlikely to expend much political capital on such claims. And their assistants are unlikely to risk defeat by bringing a heavy charge like rape, for example, rather than aggravated assault. Or, rather, the assistants are unlikely to invest great energy in crimes against women unless they are moved by a conviction that women are not receiving adequate protection from the law. This is where the young women prosecutors come in.

One such woman went straight from law school in the early eighties into a big-city D.A.'s office and was placed, fairly soon, in the felony sex-crimes department, which deals with sexual attacks on both adults and children. She had not sought the assignment. She does not define herself as a feminist activist. She was probably put there, as women often are, because male lawyers tend to be uncomfortable with sex crimes. Once in the job, however, she became intensely engaged in the issues.

In sex-crime cases, she says, complicated emotions and frustrations come into play. No one wants to believe that a husband will hurt his wife or that a young man will rape a woman, and there is still great resistance to accepting the seriousness of rape when the people involved know each other—the phenomenon of date, or acquaintance, rape. Juries and judges tend to believe that the woman in some way acquiesced to having sex, if she didn't invite it in the first place—a response classically enacted in the 1991 rape trial of William Kennedy Smith, who was found not guilty of charges that he had assaulted a woman who, on casual acquaintance, had accompanied him to his family's beach house in the early hours of the morning. And the young assistant D.A. has found that accusations of sexual abuse are often withdrawn by the victims. She had one case of a pregnant woman who had been repeatedly stabbed by her husband with knives and forks, and yet dropped charges halfway through the proceedings.

Even if the victims are willing to proceed, many judges, older male judges particularly, resist treating sex crimes seriously. The gender-bias studies discussed in Chapter 4 testify to a continued cultural undertow opposing a clear, unbiased confrontation with the deeply serious, deeply dangerous social fact of sexual violence. And the persistence of prosecutors—bringing the cases, making the arguments, standing up to the resistance, taking the defeats, and coming back again—sets up pressures for change, however slow-working they may be. It is the attitudinal base behind the law that is crucial here, and it is against that base that continued charges, argument, and publicity have their slow effect.

Behind the prosecutors and the activist litigators, contributing crucially to the effectiveness of both in furthering women's equality through law, are the theorists. As was the case in the *Cal Fed* decision, where Christine Littleton's difference theory moved from the pages of a law review to a Supreme Court opinion almost overnight, new conceptions of law argued in a courtroom often have their roots in academe. Indeed, many of the legal scholars developing the new feminist jurisprudence are themselves active as litigators or advisers to groups engaged in litigation campaigns, so their ideas pass quickly from research to places of public debate. And feminist theorizing, while still typically presenting minority or oppositional views, has had a clear effect on a range of issues beyond those already discussed.

In most states, rape law, for example, has been considerably rewritten and reinterpreted in the last twenty years to make convictions of rapists more feasible, if still extremely difficult. One element of the crime that has changed is the definition of consent, usually the main defense against a rape charge. In the old days, courts would accept a defense of consent unless a woman claiming she was raped could show, through bruises or ripped clothing or the testimony of someone within earshot, that she had struggled against her assailant or screamed. Now, with the accumulation of evidence from feminist scholars that women dealing with a rapist may not be able to struggle or may choose not to in order to avoid injury, courts no longer assume that the absence of struggle means that a woman consented to sex. Evidence that she said no is generally sufficient to establish lack of consent—although that evidence is likely to consist only of her word, which leaves the problem of convincing a jury she is telling the truth, absent signs of a struggle.

Also, in the old days, the victim had to make a "fresh complaint," a report of the crime soon after its occurrence, or her charge would lack credibility. But, again, feminists have since amassed evidence showing that women are often too shocked or frightened or humiliated to rush to the police immediately after a rape, and most rape laws no longer require this. Another rule overturned by feminist pressure is the admissibility of evidence of past promiscuity on the part of the victim to show that the act was consensual. Rape-shield laws now exclude such evidence, except in unusual circumstances.

Perhaps equally important, public discussion of all these issues has begun to change the attitudes of the police and medical personnel dealing with rape victims, the judges and juries hearing rape cases, and the rape victims themselves. Slowly, the assumption that women are playing some mating game that implies consent to sex unless they keep themselves at a secure distance from men is losing its force. Translated into the laws concerning rape, this change in attitude has produced a widening willingness to recognize that women are entitled to refuse sex and to have that refusal respected—even if they are dressed in body-revealing clothing, even if they are drunk, even if they have agreed to be with a man in a car or apartment or some other secluded place, even if they are generally promiscuous, even if they are prostitutes.[8]

But to point to changes in the law and in attitudes affecting its application is not to say that the crime of rape is on the wane with the greater likelihood that a rapist will be convicted. Rape is still a vastly underreported crime because the ugliness and emotional pain of rape proceedings, in which the accuser is effectively put on trial in efforts to undermine her credibility, deters many women from going to the police. And many are deterred, too, by the shame that clings to the victim, a vestige of the days when the reigning assumption was that a woman abiding by the rules of propriety would not be raped. Again, the knot that feminists seek to untie is the intermingling of legal rules with social rules inherited from a time when the relations of men and women ran on avowedly unequal terms.

A tight knot of legal and social rules protecting inequality is the

---

8. The work of many scholars lies behind these changes. See, for example, Susan Estrich's *Real Rape* (Cambridge, Mass.: Harvard University Press, 1987), and Catharine MacKinnon's *Toward a Feminist Theory of the State* (Cambridge, Mass.: Harvard University Press, 1989). Both include cogent analysis of the law and extensive reference to other scholarship.

object also of feminist work on the issue of domestic violence. As Elizabeth Schneider, a professor at the Brooklyn Law School, points out, domestic violence harms a wide variety of people. Its victims include children and elders, men assaulted by women, women assaulted by women in lesbian relationships, and men assaulted by men among gays. But by far the most common form of domestic violence is attacks on women by their husbands or boyfriends—or their former husbands or boyfriends. And it is precisely these attacks, especially if they involved no weapon other than fists, that the public, the police, and the courts alike tended until recently to regard as normal behavior. Many assumed that it was a man's prerogative to use some force to keep a woman in line, and believed that if the force seemed excessive, the woman had provoked it, or deserved it.

The first contribution of feminists toward change in the legal response to domestic violence was to name it as a clear wrong—"battering." A victim, then, became not just a woman whose husband punched her in the eye but a "battered woman." The term did not create a new tort or crime, but it helped many, including the victims of violence, to focus on the nature of the wrong. And as scholarly research turned to close examination of battering, its epidemic proportions, as well as its common patterns, became more clearly visible—such as the chilling fact that a woman is in the greatest danger of severe injury or even death at the point when she tries to leave her batterer.

In spite of the risks, however, vastly increased numbers of women have turned to the law for protection, seeking restraining orders or, more seriously, criminal proceedings against their batterers. But in bringing such charges, they themselves face the accusation that they must be exaggerating the violence they describe, because, typically, they have continued to live with the accused batterer for long periods of time. Judges still frequently ask the accusing woman why she didn't leave, why she remained for years with a man she now claims beat her continually.

The answer of feminist scholars to that question is a behavioral pattern called the battered-woman syndrome. They have found that many women who are subjected to violence by men they love tend at first to deny its seriousness, then try to manage the situation by avoiding occasions of trouble, and, finally, come to believe that they themselves are at fault, that they are worthless, that the punishment is deserved. In this state of mind, reinforced, often, by economic dependence on the man in question, they submit to the violence for far longer than people outside the situation see as reasonable. Because of this syndrome, scholars argue, the credibility of a woman bringing charges of domestic violence should not be discounted simply because she has remained for a long time with the man she accuses.

The plight of women who kill their batterers has also led legal theorists and advocates to rethink traditional concepts of self-defense. In the law as it stands, the plea of self-defense can be invoked only when the person accused of a killing could have reasonably believed that her life was imminently threatened. And "imminent" in present law means at the time of the killing. It does not allow for a reasonable fear of death the next day or the next week in a context of long-standing battering and death threats. What feminists have proposed as a defense of battered women charged with murder or manslaughter is an adaptation of the post-traumatic stress disorder that has been identified in combat veterans. The disorder consists of irrational fears and possibly violent reactions triggered by some severe threat to a person who has been subjected to terrifying threats to life in the past.

The courts have increasingly accepted this defense, and several state governors have reviewed the cases of women convicted of killing batterers before the defense was established, and have commuted the sentences of those to whom it would have been applicable. Governor Richard Celeste of Ohio was the first to take this step, in December 1990.

But in spite of their success in introducing the concepts of battered-woman syndrome and post-traumatic stress disorder into the law, some feminist legal scholars have become unhappy with the limitations and implications of these ideas. Christine Littleton is concerned that courts will misperceive the battered-woman syndrome as necessarily pathological or irrational behavior. She is concerned that battered women will be seen always as helpless victims of a wrongdoer when they are often women reasonably and valiantly trying to keep their families together, trying to keep a violent man quiet, trying to hold on to economic lifelines, and, should they end up killing the batterer, acting on the justifiable belief that their lives or those of their children are in danger.

If courts and legislatures held this more-complicated picture of battered women, Littleton thinks, they might devise better remedies than the crude and fairly ineffective one of keeping the batterer at bay with restraining orders on pieces of paper. They might instead emphasize supports for a changed relation between the partners—one not reliant on the power of fists. Littleton proposes, for example, a requirement that the batterer go into therapy as a condition for returning home, and increased support for communal homes where battered women can live until they can organize their lives in conditions of safety. The greater irrationality, Littleton declares, is not in a battered woman's response to violence, but in a social system that validates inequality between men and women and thus encourages unstable men to assert, violently, what they regard as their rightful power.

Elizabeth Schneider carries this basic argument to the further point of proposing that the defense of women who kill their batterers should not be limited to post-traumatic stress disorder. The problem, she emphasizes, is that the trauma defense requires such women to be seen as overcome by irrationality, when the reality is that they may have been reacting, rationally, to real and serious death threats. Schneider argues that a claim of self-defense should be available to such women even if its traditional definition—requiring a reasonable fear of *imminent* death— does not apply. The problem, she says, is in a tradition that conceives of threats to life as occurring man-to-man and that does not allow for such distinctive forms of threat as domestic violence that escalates over time, making it difficult to determine when a threat to life has become "imminent." Reasonable assessments of a threat to life, she points out, might well be different in a barroom brawl and in a domestic fight with a history of violence behind it.

Schneider acknowledges that there are problems, too, with proposing a set of different standards of reasonableness for different people. This, again, is the issue that arose in the *Robinson* case. Whose perspective determines a reasonable fear of imminent harm? The reasonable person's? The reasonable woman's? The reasonable battered woman's? The insistence on a woman's standard in cases of battering as well as harassment, Schneider warns, could end up defeating its own purpose, because old biases cast women as unreasonable to begin with, or equate reasonableness in women with passivity. To see forceful action by a victimized woman as reasonable requires overcoming old notions of normal female behavior, and the difficulty of doing so creates great risks for the woman who turns to violence.

Other feminists fear the lengths to which a separate standard for victimized women might go in excusing a variety of harms done by the women themselves. Professor Jean Bethke Elshtain cites the case of an abused woman whose thirteen-week-old infant starved to death, uncared for by the woman or her husband. Both parents faced criminal charges, but the woman's lawyers claimed for her a battered-woman-syndrome defense. They argued that her state of mind, as she was a victim of abuse herself, relieved her of responsibility for neglect of the baby—a defense not available to the baby's father. Elshtain contends that standards taking women's particular experience into account are necessary but can become "pernicious . . . when taken to exculpatory extremes."

Elizabeth Schneider, on the other hand, points out that battered mothers are often held *more* culpable for failure to protect their children from abuse by violent men than are the abusive men themselves. Nonetheless, she, too, seeks a middle ground on the question of separate standards for battered women who kill. She urges keeping a single standard of reasonableness, broadened by "bringing to it the wealth of different experiences of both men and women." But, she says, the basic problem remains a social focus that is "still on the woman, and her individual pathology, instead of on the batterer and the social structures that support the oppression of women and glorify violence."[9]

In yet another legal arena, feminist efforts to promote change have even more squarely raised issues of inequality built into prevailing law, and in doing so have touched off furious debates well beyond judicial precincts. This is the arena of family law, which includes, among others, issues of abortion, fetal rights, divorce reform, homosexual marriage, children's rights, parental rights of unwed fathers, surrogate motherhood, and the regulation of reproductive technology.

At stake is the inherited family structure that assigns to men the primary role of breadwinner and to women the primary responsibility for the physical and emotional care of the family. Such a structure produces and reproduces inequality because women's commitment of time and energy to the family restricts their range of activity outside the home and severely restricts their ability to earn independent income.

Women's economic security, in this lopsided system, depends either on a responsibly operating and lasting marriage, a career conducted on top of labor devoted to the family, or a career conducted outside the family structure—no marriage and/or no children. And beyond the issue of their economic power, women's traditional family role also limits their ability to fulfill individual talents, ambitions, and interests other than the nurturance of families, and it severely limits their participation in public life and rule-making.

Equality for women depends on changes in these conditions, changes

9. Christine Littleton, "Women's Experience and the Problem of Transition: Perspectives on Male Battering of Women," *University of Chicago Legal Forum* (1989), p. 23; Jean Bethke Elshtain, "Battered Reason," *The New Republic*, October 5, 1992, pp. 25, 29; Elizabeth Schneider, "Particularity and Generality: Challenges of Feminist Theory and Practice in Legal Work on Woman-Abuse," paper presented at the Feminist Literary Theory and Culture Seminar, Harvard University, May 14, 1992 (published in *New York University Law Review*, Vol. 67, No. 3 [June 1992], p. 520).

in the inherited social assignments, and changes in the laws that protect those assignments. It means equalizing responsibility for unpaid household labor, which, in turn, depends on reorganizing workplaces to allow both men and women time for families. It means shifting to employers or taxpayers the need to support—through child care, elder care, and hospital or hospice care—some of the family work now done, unpaid, by women. It means equitable divorce, child-custody, and child-support practices. It means women's control over the question of having a child.

Rethinking the old structures, imagining new ones that would support the health of families while supporting the equal power of men and women, and proposing new rules that would bring about change—these are the tasks that feminist legal scholars working on family law struggle with. And the difficulties they face—in number, depth, and range—cannot be exaggerated. First, the emotional as well as economic investments in the prevailing system are so large that any attempts at change meet intense and anguished resistance. Recall (as described in Chapter 6) the storms set off in the 1992 presidential campaign by the modest proposals for children's rights Hillary Rodham Clinton had advocated nearly two decades earlier.

But there is the further, chronically vexing problem of imbalance between the scope of the issues involved and the capacities of the law to shape them. The nature of the family, and the relation of the family to the individual, to the society, and to the society's political system, raise issues of incredible complication. And one major question for feminists is whether law is an adequate tool for addressing such complexity.

Specifically, the problem for feminist lawyers is that the most powerful doctrinal ground available for challenging traditional family structures and the laws protecting them has been the tradition of individual rights. To take the best-known example, feminists of the 1960s and 1970s, seeking to make abortion legally accessible in an era when most states had laws prohibiting it, doubted that they could gain their ends through general political debate. State legislators, most of them men, were not then subject to organized political pressure from women, but were from strongly antiabortion religious groups. The more promising avenue for feminists, then, was the judiciary. There they could challenge state abortion laws with the Bill of Rights, claiming that the states were denying women their personal rights without due process of law. And this was the argument the Supreme Court accepted in *Roe v. Wade* in 1973, relying on the concept of a right to privacy, which the Bill of Rights does not spell out explicitly but which the Court found to be implied there. Specifically, the Court found that states could not regulate matters that were properly the private business of the individual, and that the decision to terminate a pregnancy was such a matter.

Since that time, of course, the privacy doctrine applied to abortion has become the target of religious and other conservative groups seeking to protect traditional family structures and the traditional roles of women within them. And these groups, minorities within the larger society but large enough to command political attention, succeeded in persuading Presidents Reagan and Bush to appoint Supreme Court justices who do not support broad abortion rights. The result was a series of Supreme Court decisions—most pointedly *Webster v. Reproductive Health Services*, in 1989, and *Planned Parenthood v. Casey*, in 1992—narrowing the scope of *Roe v. Wade* by allowing the states not to prohibit abortion but to impose increasingly broad restrictions on it. For abortion-rights advocates, these cases presented the possibility that the protections of *Roe* would be nibbled away until there was, practically speaking, nothing left.[10]

But such a result would be the consequence of reliance—necessary as it has been—on a form of protection that was narrowly based to begin with. With the abortion issue structured in terms of individual rights alone, feminists have been forced into the defensive posture of arguing about it almost solely in terms of an individual confronting the state, rather than a woman confronting the social responsibilities of family life. They have been forced to draw a false line between the interests of a woman as an individual and her interests as a member of a family, as if the two interests were opposed, and they have thus drawn charges that feminists are antifamily. Perhaps most serious is that feminists, forced to defend women's access to abortion under the rubric of individual rights, have not been able to make this issue part of a broader concept of equality that takes into account the complexity of families, and women's part in them. Discomfited by this situation, a number of feminist scholars are attempting to cast into a broader context the abortion question and the entire net of interrelated family-law issues.

Patricia King, a professor of law at Georgetown University Law Center, said in an interview that a serious problem inherent in the current debate is that the focus on individual rights gives the proponents of legal abortion no way to talk about the fetus. She thinks that the discussion should not treat the fetus as if it were nothing, nor as if it were everything.

10. *Webster v. Reproductive Health Services*, 109 S.Ct. 3040 (1989); *Planned Parenthood v. Casey*, 112 S.Ct. 2791 (1992); *Roe v. Wade*, 410 U.S. 113 (1973).

And while she supports abortion rights—she thinks the issue is far too complex to be regulated politically—she is trying to move the focus of discussion from individual rights to family decision-making. "It should be looked at as a choice in which a variety of people are concerned, the woman and child or woman and fetus, other children, the woman's partner," she says. "The decision has to do with how the whole group is affected." A focus on the family, she adds, brings into the discussion responsibility for prenatal care and for services supporting the family, not just the delimited moment of abortion.

In *Rights Talk: The Impoverishment of Political Discourse*, Mary Ann Glendon of the Harvard Law School faculty mounts a broad-scale argument against what she regards as the tyranny of individual rights as the basis for social policy. With respect to abortion, she points out that the virtually unrestricted right to privacy set out in *Roe* gives a woman the option of abortion but nothing more. The state assumes no responsibility for her welfare and, unlike most European countries, provides no economic, social, or professional supports for carrying the baby to term should a woman want her child but lack the resources to care for it. What Americans need to do, Glendon thinks, is what they did not do in the 1970s, and that is to conduct a wide-ranging, soul-searching political debate about abortion in the larger context of family life and the connected issues of health care, day care, education, and employment outside the home that allows time for families.[11]

Catharine MacKinnon, a professor at the University of Michigan Law School, also faults the feminist reliance on individual rights, both with respect to the question of abortion and, more broadly, as a means of promoting equality for women. But her premises and purposes are radically different from Mary Ann Glendon's. The basic threat to the equality of women, and to their ability to control childbearing, MacKinnon says, is that men control sexual relations in the society. She further argues that prevailing sexual codes prescribe male domination of women, and that the interest of men in controlling sex on terms of dominance takes precedence over any competing social values. Therefore, she concludes, winning for women a right of privacy that guarantees them freedom from interference by the state accomplishes little, because it does not touch the basic reasons for women's inequality. Freedom from state interference in the bedroom, she says, simply leaves women where they

11. Mary Ann Glendon, *Rights Talk: The Impoverishment of Political Discourse* (New York: Free Press, 1991), p. 65.

have always been—dominated, in private, by men. Any basic change in the situation requires addressing a highly complicated web of social relations that runs far beyond the reach of the Bill of Rights and into the psychological and cultural roots of sexuality. In MacKinnon's view the law should be used as a tool for reshaping cultural values that, in turn, shape sexual practices. To this end, she argues, abortion should be cast not as an issue of individual rights but as an issue of equality—and so should sexual harassment, rape, and pornography (about which much more in Chapter 9).[12]

Similar problems with the scope of individual rights as a means of equalizing the position of women run through a variety of family issues —surrogate motherhood, for example. Should feminists support the right of a woman to contract to bear a baby for an infertile couple because it expands the woman's options for available work and income? Or should they insist on placing surrogacy in an economic context that identifies the transaction as exploitation of poor women by rich couples, and that calls, therefore, for state regulation of such contracts, if not for their prohibition or unenforceability?

And divorce. No-fault divorce laws, which swept the country from the 1970s onward, seemed a boon for women trapped in traditions of inequality. But the no-fault concept treated couples as if they had entered a marriage as equal parties to a contract and then had chosen—again, as equal parties—to end it. And divorce settlements also tended to treat the two as equal contracting parties, dividing property equally and presuming that both husband and wife would henceforth support themselves. A broader view revealed, however, in most cases, wide economic inequality. Typically, the wife, having spent considerable time raising children, could not earn anything like her husband's income, if she could find work at all. Therefore, postdivorce, the income of former husbands rose steeply, while the former wife's fell, often to levels of poverty.[13] In other words, analyzing a couple's situation in terms of equal rights could not take into account and measure large economic inequalities imposed by sex-specific social roles. The challenge for feminists, then, has been to devise legal rules for divorce that can identify and remedy the social inequality of

12. MacKinnon, *Toward a Feminist Theory of the State*, chapters 8–12.

13. See Lenore J. Weitzman, *The Divorce Revolution: The Unexpected Social and Economic Consequences for Women and Children in America* (New York: Free Press, 1985); and Martha Fineman, *The Illusion of Equality: The Rhetoric and Reality of Divorce Reform* (Chicago: University of Chicago Press, 1991).

women without reinforcing and reifying the stereotypes that support the inequality.

This is the basic dilemma that feminist legal scholars face, not only in family law, but in all areas of law touching women's lives. How can the law, designed to keep order according to given definitions of right and wrong, deal with wrongs that are outside those definitions? And how should lawyers representing outsiders help them to gain the protection of the law against trouble and suffering that prevailing standards cannot recognize? Should lawyers try to fit women's outsider experience into the old standards, making it somewhat recognizable to the powers that be in order to improve chances of at least partial gains? Or should they mount frontal challenges to the legal system, setting out radical criticism of prevailing rules and insisting on radical change? At what point in this process do they function not as lawyers but as political theorists, advocates, and organizers seeking broad, equalizing redesigns that the law alone cannot produce?

These questions constitute a chronic ethical dilemma for the reform lawyer. The lawyer implicitly promises her client that using the instrument of law will help significantly with the problem at hand. But where the problem—divorce, rape, job discrimination—is shaped by inequality and powerlessness, and the law does not fully recognize inequality and powerlessness, the lawyer's implicit promise will necessarily be compromised. At its starkest, the question is whether anyone seeking radical change should invoke the law at all, or whether the conservative drag of the law is too likely to produce flawed results and to betray the hopes of those who have trusted it.

The *reason* why prevailing law does not recognize the experience of the powerless is that, by definition, people without power have no role in shaping the law. Lucie White, a professor at the UCLA Law School, seeks to remedy this exclusion by devising new procedures by which outsider groups can participate in shaping principles that will apply to them. And she assigns to lawyers a consciousness-raising and teaching role in this function. She says that "change-oriented lawyering" can help subordinated groups to understand the difference between their interests and those of power holders in the system. Lawyers can clarify the manner in which social norms work to define as right and proper the differentials in power among various groups and the serious subordination of some. They can encourage the members of subordinated groups to work together to seek specific change. And they can bring to collaborative efforts to change the law their insiders' knowledge of the way the legal system works, its mechanics, rituals, and procedures.[14]

White's proposal deepens and broadens the issue of perspective that runs through much of the reform enterprise. It is an excellent practice for theorists, advocates, prosecutors, and judges to devise new legal standards by imagining what the experience or perspective of women in certain situations might be. But it is not enough. The voices of battered, raped, harassed, divorced, pregnant, professional, employed, unemployed, lesbian, straight, black, brown, and white women, with and without children, need to be heard directly in the processes of making new law.

That, finally, is the meaning of equalizing power.

14. Lucie White, "To Learn and to Teach: Lessons from Driefontein in Lawyering and Power," *Wisconsin Law Review* Vol. 1988, No. 5 (Sept.–Oct. 1988), p. 699, and "Subordination, Rhetorical Survival Skills and Sunday Shoes," in Martha Albertson Fineman and Nancy Sweet Thomadsen, eds., *At the Boundaries of Law: Feminism and Legal Theory* (New York: Routledge, 1991), pp. 40–60.

9

REWRITING THE RULES
OF GENDER

ONE DAY IN THE EARLY 1980S, a Harvard Law School professor was startled on entering his classroom to find that students had usurped his place in order to present a skit in honor of his birthday. And he was even more startled when a black-robed, big-busted, loudmouthed, man-bashing Mae West impersonator sauntered sassily across the stage as the first woman Supreme Court justice. According to the ebullient young woman, now a lawyer, who played Mae West that day, the skit had no plot. It was just a series of sexy one-liners about the law. The joke was in the visual outrageousness, the sheer improbability of finding Mae West, neutered by robes, hedged in by precedent, and contained by logic, on the highest court in the land. The extravagant breasts, the aggressive sexuality, do not fit the image of the courtroom. The larger point, then, the subtext of the skit, was: women's bodies do not fit in the law; the law does not fit women's bodies.

On a more mundane level, women entering the law wonder from the start how their bodies will fit into the profession. The students I spoke with in 1990 kept returning to the subject of their imagined futures, and they said they did this incessantly. What emerged from their intent speculations were serious concerns about the possibility of uniting, expressing, and enjoying their woman selves, their lawyer selves, and their community selves. How can you be a lawyer who performs work that is worthwhile for the society? How can you be a lover, a wife, a mother, a cook, an enjoyer of life, and a lawyer? Where can you find men who want to share their lives with women who want these things? They talked about their husbands or boyfriends with affection, but also with exasperation. The range of their goals—those of the women and their partners—did not fully coincide. "I'd love to marry someone if he could be another female student," said one. "That's what we keep saying." They wished that they could find men who had all the social and moral attributes of their female friends—their complications, their resistances, their purposes, their understanding of each other, their easy cooperation, and their good-natured humor about it all.

They also talked, with some confusion, about clothes, about how to dress, because what they wanted to express about themselves, what they wanted to do and be, seemed to have no clear correspondence in the professional and social worlds they were about to enter. They did not want to slip into the roles already defined for them, to don the appropriate costumes and follow the preset grooves. They saw the ease with which their male friends had fit into the grooves and found wives or partners willing to accommodate the demands of a lawyer's life, but they also grasped the confinement of those accommodations, and did not want to get stuck in them. They saw all this, and they thought they had a chance of doing things differently.

But they were worried, too. They saw a professional world in which the bars to women were down, but in which femininity was still suspect. At least that was the message they received at school: being a woman in the law is something to worry about.

The source of the conflicts besetting these students and all women lawyers is gender, the way the society defines femininity, its requirements and restrictions. The entire tradition of femininity works against women's being able to freely define who they will be, how they will live, what work they will do. If a woman seeks serious professional work and a heterosexual family structure, she must find a man who accepts her commitment to work, who finds it heartening, not threatening, that her job may yield as much prestige and income as his, and who is willing to forgo claims on her time as a support for his career. In short, she must find a man who accepts something like equality in role and power between husband and wife, an acceptance that flies in the face of the traditional rules of gender. According to those rules, a wife's role, while modernized to include significant periods of salaried employment, still remains primarily supportive of a husband's emotional needs and his work.

The gender rule of natural subordination poses the further problem for professional women that tradition requires women to marry *up*. "My pool of potential life mates is small," a pretty, smiling, energetic woman in her early thirties remarks. A litigator in a medium-sized, busy firm, she says she has no prejudice against dating men less educated than she is or who make less money, but that most men can't tolerate such a situation. Her male colleagues, she notes, can date anyone—their professional coequals, secretaries, flight attendants, students—but she is effectively restricted to high-status professionals. This is a particular problem, a black female law professor tells me, for highly educated black women. She says that she feared all the way through college and law school that she would end up with nobody, or nobody black, to marry. "Had I priced myself out of the market? I made too much money. I had too much education." She did ultimately marry a highly educated black man, but, she says, the odds were against it.

Another woman found, to her astonishment, that she was better able to work out a whole, balanced life after her divorce than while married. "I really discovered in getting divorced that it was a relief not to have one more person that I was accountable to or responsible for," she says reflectively. "My children were little enough that I could flat out make the decisions for the family without discussing them with anybody"— she laughs—"and now that they're getting a little older, of course they have to participate in decisions, too. But I often wonder if I really could include a husband and also have a job and also have the children and also have any sense of personal fulfillment or growth outside of just being a mother and a lawyer. I think the only way to do it, really, is to rely on the fact that people live longer these days . . . and maybe marriage can come once I'm finished with the child-rearing. It's too hard to pile them all together. . . . It's an awful lot to cram into one life."

A somewhat younger woman, a late-seventies law school graduate, describes a similar dilemma, but with a definite twist. She had been unhappy in a big, established law firm, and also in the legal department of a large, bureaucratized corporation, but six years out of law school, she finally found a job she loved. She joined, as general counsel, the founding team of a small high-tech company that grew in six years to a thriving enterprise with twelve hundred employees and $200 million in sales. The other members of the team were men who from the beginning treated her naturally, directly, and equally, with none of the constraint and awkwardness she had felt in her previous jobs.

As part of the management team, she works as a businesswoman as well as a lawyer, and loves doing it. When she works on the legal aspects of a deal, she participates also in the surrounding discussions and decisions on the company's business policy. And as an in-house lawyer, she works more or less normal business hours, not the crazed schedule of the big law firms.

So her work life is just where she wants it to be, but her personal
life is not. She says that until she was thirty she deliberately put work
first, then sought long-term relationships but seemed always to love men
who could not accept commitment. And by her mid-thirties she was facing
the implacability of the biological clock. At age thirty-six, after several
relationships with men who wanted mothering and resisted the mutually
responsible shared life she wanted, she decided she would start a family
on her own and hope to find a mature man later. She has had one child
by artificial insemination and, at the time of our interview, she is trying
to have another. She had found, she tells me, that she had a strong desire
to be a mother, preferably as part of a couple, but that finding a good
partner could wait whereas having a baby could not.

Asked how her friends and colleagues have responded to her single
parenthood, she says, "Everyone but my mother is delighted." She adds
that even the older, more conservative men in her company have warmly
embraced her new-style family configuration. She finds herself accorded
more respect as a parent than she'd received before, as if she were now
a grown-up, now serious, having made a commitment—in her case, with
great deliberation and risk—to somebody else, for life.

But where are the younger men with whom this woman can share
her life? She has the balance worked out—satisfying job, reasonable work
hours, desire and time for a family. It's all fine, except for the blank in
the family picture where she would like the "mutually responsible" hus-
band/father to be.

I read this story as a search for equality: equality at work, where
she emphasizes being accepted naturally, not awkwardly, as a full member
of the management team; equality in love and family life. She speaks of
ending a relationship, after her baby was born, with a man who wanted
to be part of her life but also to remain independent and involved with
other women. She snapped at him that she already had one baby and
didn't need another.

I read the *lesson* of the story to be that professional equality, while
rare and hard to win, is attainable, but that equality in emotional relations
and social roles is, if anything, more elusive. Women seeking equality as
whole selves, insisting on it in all parts of their lives, may be driven to
extraordinary lengths in their quest.

The problem lies in the cultural definition of gender and, to some
extent, the reinforcement of that definition by the law. Therefore, feminists in the law, seeking to disrupt and dislodge the hold of the old
cultural rules, are trying to rewrite the legal structure that helps to prop

those rules up. But in doing so, they come face-to-face, at some point, with the toughest of philosophical questions about the sexes. If the old rules have it wrong, what *is* the difference between men and women? And given that difference, what does equality mean? What relations between men and women can produce and assure equality? And then the easy question: Once we've decided what equality means and requires, how do we get there from here?

Legal scholars addressing these questions are engaged in a great debate, which parallels and sometimes enters the wider debate among feminists over the goals that succeeding generations of women have been pondering and refining since the American suffragists set off the crusade for equality in the 1840s. And the range of thought is wide, the disagreements stark.

Some theorists argue that the only differences between men and women are their different reproductive capacities, and that these are not so significant over a lifetime as to require ongoing "difference" standards in the law. In this view, equality means gender neutrality, the same standards applied to both men and women. For example, feminist theorist Wendy Williams proposes, as a gender-neutral approach to the question of pregnancy benefits raised in the *Cal Fed* case, casting these as disability benefits available as needed to *all* workers. Some scholars, notably Sylvia Law and Herma Hill Kay, advocate gender neutrality for most purposes but would make exceptions for laws relating directly to reproduction, such as paid or unpaid maternity leave, because reproductive differences clearly exist and clearly affect men and women unequally. But the main concern of these theorists is to break out of the long history of gendered views that depict women as different and lesser, naturally different and naturally subordinate. And the only way to do this, they argue, is to insist that the rules for men must also, for the most part, be the rules for women.[1]

Zillah Eisenstein, in *The Female Body and the Law*,[2] begins her argument with a healthy respect for the dangers to women of moving away from gender neutrality but nonetheless believes that something more

1. Wendy Williams, "The Equality Crisis: Some Reflections on Culture, Courts and Feminism," *Women's Rights Law Reporter*, Vol. 7, No. 3 (Spring 1982), p. 175, and "Equality's Riddle: Pregnancy and the Equal Treatment/Special Treatment Debate," *New York University Review of Law and Social Change*, Vol. 13, No. 2 (1985), p. 325; Sylvia Law, "Rethinking Sex and the Constitution," *University of Pennsylvania Law Review*, Vol. 132, No. 5 (June 1984), p. 955; Herma Hill Kay, "Equality and Difference: The Case of Pregnancy," *Berkeley Women's Law Journal*, Vol. 1, No. 1 (Fall 1985), p. 1. For a wider equal-rights argument, see Wendy Kaminer, *A Fearful Freedom: Women's Flight from Equality* (Reading, Mass.: Addison-Wesley, 1990).

2. Berkeley: University of California Press, 1988.

is needed. Like Sylvia Law and Herma Hill Kay, she would make exceptions to neutral rules to take into account the physical facts of pregnancy and childbirth. But she would extend the exception to take into account the social fact that women assume the main burden of child care as well. As long as the culture decrees this division of labor, she urges the passage of laws that seek to equalize the economic status of men and women by recognizing and compensating in various ways for women's work at home. She knows she is courting old-fashioned sex-stereotyping by seeking legislation specially designed for women and, moreover, designed to recognize women's special role in child-rearing. But unlike the scholars opting for gender-neutral laws, she is willing to run that risk in the hope that open political debate can produce distinctions between laws aiming to construct equality for women and laws aiming to keep women in subordinate maternal roles. The legislation she has in mind includes paid pregnancy leaves, child-care leaves for both parents, leaves for the care of sick children, comprehensive day-care programs staffed with well-trained, well-paid caregivers, and access to abortion for all women who want them, including the poor.

Christine Littleton, too, seeks equality for men and women without insisting that their differences are insignificant. Her theory acknowledges that women's maternal role casts their lives into forms vastly different from those of most men, and she does not argue that women should drop or change this role. But she does not argue either that the maternal role is a given in women's nature, or that it cannot or should not be changed. She remains agnostic on this point and instead starts her analysis with the present *fact* of women's primary responsibility for child-raising. Her concern is with the consequences of that fact, which are economic and political inequality. And she wants to employ the law to alter these consequences. She argues that the law should take notice of the different family responsibilities of women and men, and should render the differences "costless." If, to take the *Cal Fed* example, women assume responsibility for infant care and men do not, the law should make this difference costless by guaranteeing that women do not lose their jobs because of it. And she urges a use of law that applies this calculation to gendered differences across the board. She calls her approach "acceptance theory." Her premise is that "eliminating the unequal consequences of sex differences is more important than debating whether such differences are 'real,' or even trying to eliminate them altogether."[3]

3. Littleton, "Reconstructing Sexual Equality," p. 1296.

But whereas Littleton gives the possibility of natural differences between men and women little weight in her legal theory—maybe the differences are biological, maybe they're not—other theorists assign this issue primary importance. If men and women are naturally different, they argue, then designs for equality must respect that difference. This is a much tougher position to work out than either gender neutrality (men and women are essentially the same and will become equal if the same rules apply to both) or gender agnosticism (men and women may be different, but the law can even out the consequences of their difference). To posit built-in, significant sexual differences is to throw into question whether discrete rules, such as guaranteed maternity leaves, could ever be sufficient to organize relations of equality. The problem for anyone starting with these assumptions is to imagine a social scheme that encompasses deep difference *and* equality.

Robin West faces the problem head-on with her assertion that women are profoundly different from men in their pleasures and in their philosophical/political values because their bodily experience of life is different. She believes that the physical experiences of vaginal intercourse, of pregnancy, and of nursing a baby transmit to women deep delight in connection and deep pain in separation, and that this personal measure of sensation provides a basis for broader social values as well. Women are unequal under the law as it stands, she argues, because the law does not recognize women's values. It does not recognize connection as a good and separation as a harm. Rather, the premise of prevailing law is that individual autonomy is the major good and that the destruction of one individual by another, physically or economically, is the major harm. Living under laws valuing autonomy gives women some protection against such wrongs to the individual as sex discrimination in employment or rape. But where autonomy is the highest goal, the law cannot support a social system organized to promote social responsibility and care. And for that reason, the law cannot treat women who want such a system as equal citizens, only as strangers. In short, West seeks a major, literal rewriting of the ethical premises of American law, taking sexual difference into account.[4]

Drucilla Cornell adopts something like the same position in *Beyond Accommodation: Ethical Feminism, Deconstruction, and the Law*,[5] but at the

---

4. The major statement of this position is in West's "Jurisprudence and Gender," cited on p. 201; but see also "The Difference in Women's Hedonic Lives: A Phenomenological Critique of Feminist Legal Theory," *Wisconsin Women's Law Journal*, Vol. 3 (1987), p. 81.

5. New York: Routledge, 1991.

same time, she adds an important variation. In an analysis that owes much to deconstructionist and postmodernist theories, she shifts the focus of reform from the community at large to the individual. She seeks not so much legislative and judicial action that reorganizes public life as psychic change that reorders the thinking and behavior of each person. Like Robin West, she thinks that the complexity of women's bodies and their particular reproductive capacity give women an experience of the world that is necessarily different from that of men. But, she believes, the nature of this experience, and what it might mean for a new form of social relations, are both unknowns at present because women do not have the means to express or even think about and name their own knowledge of themselves or their connections to others. To explain this blockage, Cornell draws on contemporary French feminist theory, which is, in turn, based on the work of the psychoanalyst Jacques Lacan, the philosopher Jacques Derrida, and the political theorist Michel Foucault.

The basic premise of this complex set of theories is that semiotic systems, especially language, construct all that we know—that we cannot reach any reality beyond these constructs. A further premise is that our language systems tend to be formed on a grid of opposites, in which one thing is defined as not being the other. Thus we are drawn by language into thinking dichotomously—man/woman, black/white, animal/human, mind/body. But what the dichotomies are and what values they carry depend on who controls the language, who is doing the naming. And throughout history, men have controlled language. In Lacanian terms, language represents the law of the Father. Therefore our grasp of reality is a representation of the world from a male point of view. The distinctions between things that are the same and things that are different, including the distinctions between men and women, are distinctions drawn by men.

The awful consequence, for women, is that they are trapped by language in a male view of women's nature. And, according to Lacan, this view is a projection of men's doomed nostalgia for the perfect all-giving, all-loving mother whose womb, breast, and body the male child is forced to reject, to separate from, in order to become a separate person and a man. That is, women are trapped in a male fantasy of women's maternal nature. And they are trapped also in the system of values that inheres to the language describing their nature—carnal, not intellectual; emotional, not rational; tender, not tough; and, overall, properly subordinate. What women's sense of their own nature might be, what their sense of their own maternity might be, what their bodily feelings and sexual desires might be, are all unknown, even to women, because women have no uncontaminated language through which to name and understand themselves.

But the trap is not completely tight. If language constructs world-views that reflect the understandings and values of those who hold power, techniques of linguistic deconstruction can detect and decode the connections between words, values, and power. Deconstructionists can spot breaks in a text—written or spoken—that signal the suppression of an opposing idea. They can break apart the text and expose the system of values that it carries. Feminist deconstructionists can, therefore, clarify the prevailing system of ideas about women that seem straightforward and natural but are actually laden with values that express a male desire for female subordination. For some feminists—Cornell draws particularly on Luce Irigaray—another escape from the trap consists of self-expression by women through poetic, emotive ("semiotic") forms of language. The idea is for women to define themselves, to explicate their own nature, not in terms of their difference from men but in terms of their own self-understanding. To do this, Cornell believes, women need to employ language not laden with the law of the Father. They must employ metaphor and myth to draw knowledge from the unconscious. They must allow the usual forms of language to collapse, and draw out fragments that correspond to their inner convictions. She notes as models of this self-redefinition Christa Wolf's *Cassandra* and Toni Morrison's *Beloved*.

Ultimately, the escape from the tyranny of language, for feminist deconstructionists, is the creation of new language, and the use of new language to create a new reality. As Drucilla Cornell carefully points out, this does not mean discovering, finally, what "woman" really is. Rather, it is a substitution of a women's identity imagined by women for a women's identity imagined by men. In short, women move from subordination to equality through changed language and changed consciousness. And this means that the power to bring about change lies not in the state and its laws but in the individual.

Not surprisingly, other feminist legal scholars disagree with the deconstructionist emphasis on the shaping power of language. Robin West, in particular, argues that women's identities and values are most importantly and most directly shaped not by words but by their bodies. She says that women's "non-discursive, woman-bonded, creative, erotic and quietly rebellious self" is not clearly apparent because it is suppressed by patriarchal institutions. But she also argues that these institutions can be changed by politics and law. Decentralizing power to individuals creating new discourses is not enough, she says. Rather, what is needed is a redesign of governmental power. It need not remain in its patriarchal "dominating, positing and delimiting" mode. It can be recast to allow for and support a wide variety of connecting and caring relationships.[6]

Perhaps the most vigorous critic of feminist deconstructionism is Catharine MacKinnon, who is equally scathing in her assessment of Robin West's essentialism and the various equal-rights analyses. For Mac-Kinnon, most feminist theory is insufficiently radical. Either it denies that any significant difference divides men and women, when in her view social rules relentlessly push the sexes into two spheres, one powerful, one powerless. Or it proclaims sexual difference, defining and celebrating a distinct women's nature, when, she insists, any characteristics common to women have been constructed by male rules. For example, MacKinnon argues, if women are "caring," as Robin West claims, it is not due to their essential nature but to male rules that praise and reward women's caring qualities because men benefit from them. And MacKinnon is certain that the rules are not produced mainly by language.

MacKinnon's own social theory rests on one clear principle: The *sexual* exploitation of women by men is the ruling relation of the sexes in patriarchal society. The difference between women and men under patriarchy is that men are the sexual dominators and women are the objects of sexual domination. They are unequal by the definition of the relationship, and cannot be equal until the basic relationship changes.

The MacKinnon prescription for change is as clear-cut as her analysis of what is wrong. The relationship between men and women must be changed, and can be changed, she asserts, by women's gaining political and legal power equal to that of men and rewriting the rules. In part, she means the social rules that convey to people what is right, and expected, and praiseworthy—the rules, for example, that tell women to dress in ways that display their sexuality pleasingly to men. Mainly, though, she seeks change in the formal laws that regulate sexual relations, including the laws on rape, domestic violence, sexual harassment, abortion, and pornography. Through litigation and legislation, she has sought to increase the power of women by redefining the law in all of these areas in terms of equality. Rape is wrong not just because it inflicts physical harm but also because it enforces inequality, she argues, and the law of rape should be cast in these terms. And in her book *Sexual Harassment of Working Women*, MacKinnon argues that laws prohibiting harassment enhance

6. Robin West, "Feminism, Critical Social Theory and Law," *University of Chicago Legal Forum* (1989), p. 59.

women's equality both by improving conditions in the workplace and by subverting the assumption of rightful male domination.

Following the success of the campaign to formulate laws against sexual harassment, and employing the same theory and general strategy, MacKinnon has turned next to a crusade against pornography. In the prevailing law of most American jurisdictions, pornography is subject to legal restraint only if it is "obscene," and obscenity, as defined by the Supreme Court, is measurable by its patent offensiveness to the moral standards of a particular community. But the harm that concerns MacKinnon in sexually explicit material is not its offensiveness but its promotion and reinforcement of women's inequality. She thinks that images of women enjoying rape, degradation, or humiliation, or being tied, cut, mutilated, bruised, tortured, or penetrated by objects or animals, or simply enacting sexual submission or servility, proclaim inequality loud and clear. These images, published primarily for a voracious male market, carry the message that the male domination of women, even to the point of violence, is natural, and, furthermore, that women like it. In short, pornography suggests, teaches, reinforces, and legitimates the forceful domination of women by men.

MacKinnon further insists that pornography has effects far beyond the immediate sexual behavior of its consumers. Because it casts women intrinsically and primarily as objects of sexual desire, it implicitly denies their intellectual, artistic, economic, and political equality. Its images of sexual subordination reinforce conceptions of women as identified with body, not mind, conceptions that prescribe for women confinement to household work or lesser occupations. The insidious effect of pornography, MacKinnon states, is that "it makes inequality sexy," and her aim is to get rid of it.

Her method, working with the author Andrea Dworkin, has been to draft model antipornography legislation and to lobby for its adoption as city ordinances or state laws. The basic model, first introduced in Minneapolis in 1983, defines pornography as "the graphic, sexually explicit subordination of women through pictures or words," and declares its production and distribution to be sex discrimination. Such laws would not criminalize pornography but, rather, would allow those harmed by it to bring civil suits for monetary damages against its publishers and sellers.

The sting in the model laws comes in the definition of those who are harmed. They include people who have been coerced into performing for pornography, and anyone—woman, man, or child—subject to sexual violence caused by pornography. But they also include, broadly, "any woman . . . acting against the subordination of women." And because the law defines any trafficking in pornography as sex discrimination, and because sex discrimination, as such, subordinates women, the law allows any woman to sue anyone dealing in pornography. The strategy is to make the commerce in pornography, a multibillion dollar industry in the 1990s, unprofitable.

But the antipornography crusade has not met the same success as MacKinnon's campaign against sexual harassment. As of 1993, only one MacKinnon/Dworkin model law had actually been passed, and that one, a 1984 Indianapolis city ordinance, never went into effect, as it was immediately challenged in the courts and declared unconstitutional. In its 1985 decision in *American Booksellers Association v. Hudnut*, the Seventh Circuit Court of Appeals declared that the ordinance was an infringement of free speech as protected by the First Amendment. And as the Supreme Court declined to hear the case, the *American Booksellers* decision still stands as the last judicial word on the broadscale prohibition of pornography.[7]

Among feminists, however, the last word has not been spoken. In the eighties, when the MacKinnon/Dworkin laws were on the ballot in Indianapolis, Minneapolis, Los Angeles, Cambridge, Massachusetts, and Bellingham, Washington, activists on all sides of the issue were thrown into intense discussion and discord. And the debate flared up anew in the early nineties when MacKinnon and Dworkin revised their model somewhat and began submitting it to the legislatures of several states, including Massachusetts. The issue rivets feminist attention because it goes to the heart of the relation between inequality and sexuality. It requires close evaluation of the ways in which unwritten cultural rules regulating sexuality contribute to inequality. For lawyers, the issue demands hard thought about the possibility of bringing about change in cultural rules through the formal rules of law. The antipornography laws raise this debate because they set out a clear theory of cultural oppression and a clear remedy through the use of law. The questions, then, are: Does the MacKinnon theory correctly identify what is wrong, and does the remedy—anti-pornography legislation—cure it?

The central argument brought against the MacKinnon/Dworkin law is precisely the one that defeated it in the *American Booksellers* case, that it violates constitutional free-speech protection. Pornography is a form of

7. 771 F.2d 323 (1985).

speech, the argument goes. The First Amendment rests on the premise that democracy requires free speech, and that if governments control speech, democratic choice is compromised. Therefore, democracies must accept ugly, disgusting, vilifying, hateful, even violent speech as the price of freedom. The appellate court opinion in *American Booksellers* is refreshingly clear on this point. It does not argue that pornography is not demonstrably harmful or that the evidence of its harm is not clear. Rather, it states flatly that the court accepts the premises of the ordinance, and then goes on to specify those premises: "Depictions of subordination tend to perpetuate subordination. The subordinate status of women in turn leads to affront and lower pay at work, insult and injury at home, battery and rape in the streets." But the opinion then goes on to say that this causal connection between ideas and behavior proves the power of ideas. And, it states, it is because ideas are powerful that the First Amendment forbids governmental control of them. Otherwise, the government would become "the great censor and director of which thoughts are good for us."

In any event, the court concluded, the purpose of the antipornography ordinance, which is to change a "culture of power," is better served by free speech than by governmental restrictions on speech. "Change in any complex system ultimately depends on the ability of outsiders to challenge accepted views," the court remarked, and such challenges depend on "a strong guarantee of freedom of speech."

Certainly, it is the specter of restricted speech that throws a chill into the heart of many feminists who feel themselves, as outsiders, already prevented from speaking effectively in public roles. They tend to find the connection between pornography and their own voicelessness too indirect to be alarming, whereas the very idea of infringing speech of any kind, even of a repulsive kind, seems threatening.

Further, some feminists see pornography as a positive force for change. They see it as a means of expressing socially disapproved sexual feelings and acts, and therefore, potentially, as a means of subverting the rigid categories of gender imposed by mainstream culture. The entertainer Madonna, for example, claims to use pornographic images to satirize both puritanical sexual repression and conventional displays of female bodies as sexual objects. And some lesbians argue that homosexual pornography subverts socially sanctioned conceptions of sexuality and gender because the same-sex pairs play both dominant and subordinate roles, confusing, or bending, the usual expectations of male/female relations, and thus exploding the stereotypes. In their own way, the gender benders agree

with the court in *American Booksellers*: the remedy for harmful speech is
more speech.

But the free-speech arguments, as they are generally stated, do not
squarely confront the basic premise of the MacKinnon position, which is
that pornography operates at a place in the culture inaccessible to the
forms of speech protected by the First Amendment. The model of change
through dissenting speech is a political model. Its heroes are Tom Paine,
Thomas Jefferson, the abolitionists, the suffragists, the civil rights activists, and the contemporary feminists confronting discriminatory laws.
Where the government and the law are the oppressive forces, speech is
a powerful weapon for change because governments and laws ultimately
need the support of the people, and speech can erode that support.

But if the oppressive force is, as MacKinnon claims, a system of
irrationally and unconsciously formed belief connected to sexual desire
and economic interest, the power of outsider speech to dislodge the oppression is far less clear. Reasoned speech makes little headway against irrationality. Desire is strongly heedless of any protest. Economic power is
less dependent than political power on the support of the powerless. This
is not to say that speech has no effect on the formation and re-formation
of culture, but its effects are, at best, diffuse.

The other generally unspoken premise for the defense of free speech
as the protector of minorities and outsiders is the integral connection
between free speech and the free, autonomous, self-formed, self-defined
individual. In the liberal tradition that defines the most basic American
beliefs, the ultimate defense against oppression of any kind is the will of
the individual. The ultimate value for Americans is the freedom of individuals to form their own values, establish their own priorities, and
resist pressures from other people or institutions to give up or compromise
the choices they have made. And the freedom to speak, to persuade, to
argue, to resist, is necessary to the pursuit of individual goals. Any governmental restriction on free speech threatens the freedom of the individual, and therefore all such restrictions must be resisted, including
Catharine MacKinnon's.

But here the MacKinnon argument is that individual freedom does
not work for women because the culture defines women generically as
sexual objects, not as individuals. And it does not accord them free speech.
It silences them by assigning them secondary status. Their desires and
opinions do not matter, or matter less, are taken less seriously, than those
of men. Therefore, the protections that free speech is supposed to afford
are not available, or not sufficiently available, to women.

These are the claims that the feminist advocates of free speech as a first priority for women do not adequately answer. Rather, they assert the right of free speech as a historically proven protection for dissenters, and rest on the assumption that it is therefore crucial to women's struggles for equality. But to hold this position they must also assume either that MacKinnon is wrong about the oppressiveness of sexual stereotyping in the culture, that this oppressiveness is not so pervasive as she says it is, or that no matter what oppressions lie in the culture, free speech can root them out. What many do assume, in addition to the curative power of speech, is that any attempt to censor materials dealing with sex will be taken over politically by socially conservative groups whose aim is to impose their own standards of sexual repression on everyone. And conservative standards of sexual relations definitely underwrite the subordinate status of women.[8]

So who is right about the relation of sexuality and equality, Catharine MacKinnon or the advocates of free speech? The Supreme Court of Canada has decided that MacKinnon is. In a 1992 decision in *Butler v. Her Majesty the Queen*, the Canadian court upheld the criminal conviction under a national obscenity law of a shop owner who sold and rented hardcore pornography and who had claimed that the obscenity law violated guarantees of free expression under the Canadian Charter of Rights and Freedoms. Like the appellate court in *American Booksellers*, the Canadian court found that pornography did harm women by portraying them "as a class as objects for sexual exploitation and abuse," but unlike the American court, found that this harm justified restricting the harmful speech. The basic reason for this judgment was the court's concern about the ultimate impact of pornographic speech on women's equality. "If true equality between male and female persons is to be achieved, we cannot ignore the threat to equality resulting from exposure to audiences of certain types of violent and degrading material," the court said.

Far more than the American court had, the Canadian court looked to the purposes of free speech in a democracy and found that when a whole class of people is confined to demonstrable inequality, democratic exchange does not work well. Equality needs to be advanced in order for free speech to serve democracy fully. This was an opinion that Catharine MacKinnon might well have written herself, and, in fact, in some sense she did. She was closely involved with the Canadian Legal Education and

---

8. See, for example, Wendy Kaminer, "Feminists Against the First Amendment," *The Atlantic*, November 1992, p. 110.

Action Fund, an activist feminist group that formulated and presented the arguments the court ultimately adopted in its opinion.

While no cases in the United States come close to adopting the view that governments may prohibit pornography because it undermines women's political equality, several federal court decisions in the early nineties did acknowledge the possibility of restricting it when it caused economic harm. These are cases that test the question whether pornography in the workplace can constitute sexual harassment and thus sex discrimination under Title VII.

The case drawing the most acute feminist attention was *Robinson v. Jacksonville Shipyards, Inc.*, as it raised not only the problem of defining reasonableness (discussed earlier in Chapter 8) but also the puzzle of pornography. The Florida federal district court that heard the case found that pornography posted on the workplace walls and sometimes in the work areas of particular women did, indeed, constitute harassment and ordered it removed. And that finding, as well as the court's adoption of the "reasonable woman" standard for judging the harmful impact of the sexually offensive behavior, provoked the battle of amicus briefs that occurred when Jacksonville Shipyards brought the case to the Eleventh Circuit Court of Appeals.

One participant in the argument was the ACLU, which, true to its long tradition, took a stand strongly protective of free speech. The posting of sexually explicit materials that female employees find obnoxious and offensive, the ACLU brief argued, goes beyond the bounds of protected speech and constitutes harassment only if "the expressive activity is directed at a specific employee, and has definable consequences for the individual victim that demonstrably hinder or completely prevent continued functioning as an employee."

This position was countered by an ad hoc group calling itself "80 Individual Law Professors and Lawyers," whose brief argued for fairly broad limits on pornographic speech in the workplace. For the 80 Professors and Lawyers, the employee does not have to show that displays of pornography hindered or prevented her from doing her job, but only that they caused some injury which, depending on the context in the particular case, "may range from inability to concentrate to generalized anxiety to various physical symptoms typically associated with stress."

The reason for allowing such limits on otherwise protected speech, the brief stated, is that the workplace is not a marketplace of ideas. Employers are legally entitled to control various forms of speech among employees, and they often do. In the *Robinson* case specifically, the shipyards allowed male employees to post pornography on the walls and did not take action on complaints about it from female employees. Further, employees who are targets of offensive speech at work usually cannot avoid it by moving out of range, unless they leave their jobs entirely. And this result, the brief pointed out, is often the purpose of offensive speech directed at women employees, especially those in lucrative, traditionally male jobs such as those in the shipyards in *Robinson*.

In short, the brief of the 80 Professors and Lawyers recognized the power of pornography to cause sufficient economic harm to women to justify restriction on it in some circumstances. And this position was reinforced when, in April 1993, the ACLU itself changed its position on sexual harassment including the element of speech. Abandoning the rule it had followed in its *Robinson* brief, the organization adopted a principle potentially more restrictive of pornographic speech. The new policy stated that sexual harassment could include "conduct or expression" that is "sufficiently pervasive or intense to create unequal terms, conditions or privileges of employment on the basis of sex."

The ACLU policy in its entirety is carefully gender-neutral. It applies to the sexual harassment of men as well as women. But in fact the problem is, for the most part, not gender-neutral. A differential in social power allows sexually offensive male speech in the workplace to enforce old rules of gender to women's economic disadvantage. And new rules allowing broader limits on offensive sexual expression, to some degree, offset that power.

At the time of writing, as noted earlier, the outcome of the arguments in *Robinson* remained unknown, as the appellate court decision had not yet come down. But the divisions this issue provokes among feminists as well as nonfeminists mean that the questions involved will be much litigated before new rules take clear shape.

WHAT COMFORT AND WHAT DIRECTION, then, does the academic discussion of gender offer young women entering the law? What guidance does it give them for shaping their lives as professionals, as sexual beings, as mothers, and as citizens? How do their bodies fit into the world of power and into the tradition of the law? And how can they, as lawyers, help other women, as outsiders, to operate in the larger society on equal terms with men? How can they help women find terms of equality that recognize and make room for women's bodies?

The inescapable questions underlying all the others are, What is the nature of sexual difference, and how should the law account for it in constructing a society of equals? Does the culture so grossly misconstrue women's sexuality, so tightly confine women to sexual roles that force their subordination, that women lawyers must slay the cultural monster before any other battle for equality can succeed? And if this is true, how are they to do it?

Is Catharine MacKinnon right when she says that pornography is the monster's lifeblood and that the battle can be won by suing pornographers to death? Or is Drucilla Cornell right when she says that the monster is even more powerful and insidious than MacKinnon thinks it is—that it is, in fact, language itself? Is she right that women are oppressed not just by pornography but by masculine language generally, language that lies about female sexuality and traps women in its lies? Is she right that the only way out of the trap is through poetry and metaphor, not law? Or at least that law can change little until women have been able to find language to express who they believe they are.

But then there is Robin West's argument that women know very well who they are and have the language to express their identity—if they can find the courage. Women know, West says, that their sexuality and the values that stem from it are misrepresented in the culture and not represented in the law. And maybe West is right that women could, by recognizing and asserting their true nature, provide a new critique of the law and begin to reform it, to add in the values of human connectedness and the harms of separation, as opposed to the values of autonomy and the harms of breaching it.

Or perhaps, after all, the culture is not so oppressive as these theorists, the Canadian jurists, and the "80 Individual Law Professors and Lawyers" think. Perhaps the monster is old and weak and holds only isolated pockets of resistance to women's equality. Perhaps the power of old ideas about women's essential carnality is practically dissipated, and women do not need to regard themselves as an oppressed class. Perhaps they are significantly different from men only when pregnant, and all other differences, such as women's responsibility for children, are merely habits that could be changed if women spoke up and insisted on it. Perhaps women should think of themselves simply as individuals, insisting—except for periods of pregnancy and childbirth—on the same rights and terms as men.

Of all the theories on inequality—its reasons and its remedies—the equal-rights position championing individuality is the most hopeful and, I think sadly, the least persuasive. Women *are* oppressed as a class, socially and legally, by a tradition that defines their nature for them and defines it in sexual terms that deny their full complications, strengths, and talents. For all the changes in women's opportunities and status, for all their new professionalism, for all the lip service paid to women's intelligence or to their artistic and intellectual creativity, the heavy hand of tradition still imposes serious constraints. Lingering on, this close to the twenty-first century, is the suspicion or the accusation that strong intellect and power are at odds with womanliness, with acceptability, with lovableness.

For women to seek professional equality themselves or to work professionally to promote the general equality of women without recognizing clearly the remaining force of cultural oppressions is self-defeating. The unwritten rules must be taken seriously. Professional women must recognize that they are not exempt from them, that all women are affected by them and must work together to recognize, challenge, and resist them in the workplace, in the home, in the community, in the country. Women are oppressed by a false definition of their nature imposed on them by long cultural tradition, and this is true regardless of their differences in class, religion, race, culture, work, age, and physical or mental prowess. They are oppressed as a class and have to act as a class to resist the oppression.

But what women as women have in common beyond cultural oppression I do not know. I don't think anyone knows. We do not know whether women, unoppressed, would form a class or not. We do not know whether women have an essential nature that if recognized and celebrated would generate bonds stronger than their differences in class and race and other kinds of cultural markings. But I don't think we need to know this in order to identify and resist the false commonalities that now distort and narrow and suppress women's potential beings. We do not need to predefine what that potential might become once it was released. In fact I think the effort to predefine that potential is itself oppressive.

Why do we do it? Why do feminists who find the individual-rights tradition inadequate go to the opposite extreme of theorizing female commonalities? Why isn't it enough to notice and resist group oppression? Why do we have to have an essential nature as well?

Partly, I suppose, it is appealing to refute the traditional assumptions of women's inferiority by claiming that the supposedly inferior traits are actually innate strengths. Then there is the irrefutable fact that women do tend to behave similarly in many situations. They tend to speak deferentially, and not to speak in public. They tend to be uncomfortable with power. They tend to be aware of the emotional states and needs of people around them. They tend to prefer consensual and cooperative forms of organization to hierarchical authority. And many feminists are convinced that these commonalities stem from deeper sources than the lessons a society teaches its daughters.

But I think that this drive to find some given qualities in women's nature stems also from a broader force at work in American political culture, a force I have called elsewhere the myth of deliverance from evil. This myth, at work in American public life since the country's beginning, requires that reformers theorize systems of social relations as capable of producing harmony among all members of the society. That is, reform proposals, to be taken seriously in the United States, must identify some fairly clear-cut wrong or evil, the removal of which will liberate naturally harmonious relations among the people. Over the years these evils have included the malefactors of great wealth, the bosses of Tammany Hall, communists, the government on our backs, political action committees, and, most recently, radical feminists—or so I heard from speakers at the 1992 Republican presidential convention. What the myth will not permit is any understanding of society as made up of groups in permanent conflict with each other.[9]

Equal-rights theorists fit into the myth of deliverance easily. They identify the wrong that stands in the way of equality as discriminatory law and practice, both of which they seek to supplant with gender-neutral rules that apply to everyone as individuals. Then, they say, harmony depends on keeping malefactors of great wealth, or PACs, or other illegitimate aggregations of power, from undermining the efforts of individuals to organize their own lives through their own choices.

Feminists who cannot accept this Enlightenment vision of social harmony, who see human beings as identified significantly with social groupings, and who see women in particular as an oppressed group have a potential problem with the myth of deliverance. Their vision comes close to depicting women as a group necessarily at war with others. But this potential conflict is solved by essentialist theory in its various forms, because those theories convert the concept of woman/class itself into a basis for social harmony. Women as a group are in conflict with others only in their efforts to remove the evil of cultural oppression—which includes rampant individualism with its legitimation of greed and exploitation. Once those evils are removed, the war is over, because women's

---

9. Mona Harrington, *The Dream of Deliverance in American Politics* (New York: Alfred A. Knopf, 1986).

nature precludes a relation of permanent conflict. In the essentialist view, women are committed to cooperative connections to others. They are empathetic and peace-loving. They seek and practice harmonious inter-dependence. This is the radical feminist version of deliverance.

But the myth of deliverance in any form, feminist or otherwise, is a dangerous delusion. It always has been, because it screens out of political vision the actual forces in conflict that operate, invariably, to hurt the weak. While political attention stays fixated on specific wrongs and wrong-doers (many completely real), deeper social structures operate to consol-idate and perpetuate the privilege of the strong. This was true in the nineteenth-century era of the robber barons and in the twentieth-century formation of national and, then, multinational corporations, which place enormous concentrations of wealth under the management of a few. And now, in the era of electronic technology, the possibilities for worldwide consolidations and centralizations of wealth are almost incalculable. One current statistic tells us that the world financial markets move around as much money—billions of dollars—in one day as the American Stock Exchange does in two months. Add in to the deep economic structures producing inequality the massive population growth in poor countries, and the question arises whether forces widening the gap between rich and poor are controllable at all.

Certainly, they are not controllable in a state of political delusion. Too much wealth, too much privilege, too much access to political le-verage, too much cultural tradition, too much legal protection, divides the powerful and the powerless for feminists to position themselves in a politics of deliverance. What I would hope for feminists is that they would take the lead in disrupting the blind desire for harmony that prevents Americans from seeing clearly the ever more complicated pattern of oppressions we live with. It is because we cannot see that we cannot act effectively—or even begin to try—and it is that ineffectuality that drives us increasingly toward choices between political alienation and political fantasy. (It was probably inevitable that the nation would fall in love with a movie-actor president who couldn't himself always distinguish between film plots and reality, and who produced the biggest fantasy/policy in the nation's history—a decade of wild economic expansion financed by debt or make-believe money.)

To talk about broad patterns in American political culture dating back to the eighteenth century along with threats to the weak posed by international aggregations of capital seems far afield of the puzzles about gender that feminist legal scholars are trying to solve. And I don't mean to argue here that feminists must address all the interrelated sources of oppression before they can think helpfully about gender. Certainly, I don't mean to argue that compared to the immense seriousness of economic issues, the cultural oppression of women is insignificant, and that attention to it can wait until bigger problems are solved.

I have introduced the wide range of economic and political issues to demonstrate what it is that Americans do not see clearly because of the myth of deliverance, and to urge feminists, in analyzing the oppression of women, to move beyond the confines of that myth. To think that removing some single form of oppression would create a state of sexual equality in society is to start off down the wrong track. Catharine MacKinnon's analysis, for example, seems ultimately to fall into this fallacy.

I think she is right when she says that cultural habits of sexual domination significantly contribute to the denigration of women and also encourage violence against them. I think she is also right to focus on pornography as a powerful medium for perpetuating these habits and harms. And I like her idea of striking the pornography industry at its economic roots, although I think any legislation restricting pornography should define it more narrowly and precisely than the Dworkin/Mac-Kinnon model does. But, agreeing with much of the MacKinnon argument, I still do not see that the male sense of entitlement to sexual domination is the keystone to the *entire* social edifice and that removing it would bring the entire structure of oppression tumbling down. Indeed, if pathological male sexuality were that powerful a force, I do not see how moral and legal sanctions could defeat it.

Rather than targeting overly specific wrongs, feminist analyses of oppression must be multifaceted and multilayered, and tactics of resistance must be multiple and continuous. What we should be imagining is a political model that assumes a perpetuation of conflict among people and groups with divided interests, conflict that cannot be settled harmoniously, with all sides, or even all deserving sides, satisfied. This is a world in which one good often conflicts with another, a world in which losses are often unjust. We have to assume this, and then mount political responses that promote and protect broad social goals, including equality, knowing that the need for political contest, for struggles against power, is ongoing. We need to imagine a model that allows women and other outsiders to identify an oppressive force, and then work to subdue its power or release themselves from it, without their also assuming that the release is the end of the power struggle. We have to remember that it is not possible just to vanquish evil and be done with it.

I cannot myself offer a detailed model of a future feminist politics, only some general principles and thoughts. It should be a politics of active participation by women in all institutions, public and private, where decisions organizing the society are made. I mean that a feminist politics of participation should operate in law firms as well as legislatures, corporate boardrooms, day-care centers, secretarial pools, factories, and city halls. Women need to form groups to explore and testify to their own experience of constraint, to investigate exactly what it is and how it works, and they must remain in the decision-making places in order to resist it. But I imagine that as they engaged in this process and confronted the myriad ways in which the culture falsely defines their nature and bodies and capacities and desires, women would also be defining themselves. They would resist, for example, the old division of human nature into mind and body, a division that distorts both male and female capacities for reason, exaggerating the one, understating the other. At the same time, they would be exploring and examining anew how their female bodies do and do not shape their sense of self, and their experience of life.

Here, I think, it is important to listen to Drucilla Cornell's insistence on the need for women to express an identity derived from inner promptings and not from imposed forms, even the most familiar and innocuous-seeming forms of everyday language. Still, I do not agree that we have no public language at all with which to communicate who we are, that we must start at the most private point of emotional utterance or we will remain trapped in masculine formulations of ourselves. I believe that we can appropriate and use the languages available to us, although with great care to be alert to meanings that carry male perspectives though they seem perspectiveless. Women seeking equality must carry the burden of thinking in two languages. They must hear and speak the public language in all its supposed objectivity, *and* they must carry on a running critical translation that draws out hidden gendered meanings in order *not* to be trapped by the submerged ideology.

Again, the *act* of participation in all the society's institutions is the key to carrying on a doubled dialogue, at once resisting old forms and creating new ones. By engaging constantly in the functions and decisions of all the places of work and service, women would meet, head-on, the biases, the limits, and the injustices that continue to proliferate. And if they are thinking critically, and if they are working supportively with other women, they can question, refuse acceptance, propose change, and insist on change. Then, at the same time, in the process of thinking, criticizing, supporting, and resisting—as participants who bear shared responsibility for the outcome of this action—they will be defining and refining a new sense of themselves.

And here the commentary of theorists such as Robin West is relevant. I do not accept West's insistence that women possess a distinct, essential nature that impels them toward a social ethic of connectedness. But there is no doubt that women's literal experience of connectedness through caretaking has taught them a great deal that can be carried over to public life. Taking care of others teaches thousands of lessons about human needs and power imbalances. And in the process of criticizing the constrictions imposed on women and other outsiders by present social institutions, women may very well draw on their hard-won private knowledge. They may, as West posits, draw lessons from a mother's hierarchical but nurturant relation to her children to imagine ways of retaining hierarchical workplace structures while infusing into them an ethic of empowerment—creating a situation in which superiors use authority to empower subordinates rather than simply to direct or control them.

Suggestions of this sort from Robin West or Sara Ruddick or Carol Gilligan make anti-essentialist feminists extremely nervous. They warn that urging women to look to child-raising as a model for public enterprises implies that women speak out of an essentially maternal nature, or that their knowledge is limited to the maternal. But I think that this nervousness is excessive. Caring is an authentic part of the experience of many women and is directly relevant to criticisms of power-wielding that has become detached from human need. In escaping from the old male conceptions of women's maternal roles, women should not have to pretend that their own experience of caregiving means nothing. What women know and value as caregivers certainly should be on the new agenda of women's social participation if women want to put it there.[10]

Contributions by women lawyers to the design and operation of a feminist participatory politics would be crucial. This is the case because the law stands as the ethical regulator of public life, and yet its ethics, including the promise of a single standard of justice for all, often reflect a tradition that wittingly or unwittingly subordinates women. And the

---

10. See Kathleen B. Jones, *Compassionate Authority: Democracy and the Representation of Women* (New York: Routledge, 1993). She argues the need for a new understanding of authority as a means of rule-making that assumes the connectedness and commitment to caring long associated with women's experience, but does not assume a common, essential, maternal nature.

traces of that tradition in the law are often difficult to see, perhaps particularly so for women and other outsiders who put their faith in the law to be fair. They do not want to mistrust the law. In fact, many want to see it as operating beyond the reach of power, responsive to reason alone, more trustworthy by far than the rough, raw procedures of politics. Against these seductions, feminists must keep a vigilant eye on the language of the law, as they must on language generally. They must work with double vision, seeing and understanding the law in its inherited forms and spotting the places where its forms conceal male perspectives and privileges. And the spotters must give the alarm to the teachers, activists, prosecutors, defense attorneys, legislators, judges, and administrators who can go to work on processes of change.

But perhaps most crucially, lawyers seeking change need to stay alert to the connections between law and politics, the places where, in a democracy, public pressures become converted into rules that guide behavior. Feminists in the law, as Lucie White has said, should be inventing new places for that nexus. They should be imagining and promoting wider openings for the participation of outsiders in the processes that produce public rules. Any constituency affected by a rule should be part of its formulation, and feminists should seek radical rearrangements in the making of rules in all kinds of institutions to allow outsiders in.

The best aim of the feminist daughter is not to take over the father's place, to assume his mantle and his power, but to create new space for new forms of authority. The best aim of the feminist lawyer is to devise multiple places of power where divisions of insiders and outsiders break down not into patterns of harmony but into open questions, open conflict, open discussion, open rule-making.

Index

A NOTE ABOUT THE AUTHOR

MONA HARRINGTON was born in Lowell, Massachusetts, in 1936, and was educated at the University of Massachusetts and at Harvard University, where she received a law degree and a doctorate in political science. She served as a lawyer in the State Department, raised a family of three children, and taught political science and women's studies before turning to writing full-time. A resident of Cambridge, Massachusetts, she has published *The Dream of Deliverance in American Politics* (1986), *Women of Academe: Outsiders in the Sacred Grove* (with Nadya Aisenberg, 1988), and various articles on American political culture, women and power in American society, and gender and international relations.

A NOTE ON THE TYPE

The text of this book was set in Plantin, a typeface cut in 1913 by the Monotype Corporation, London. Though the face bears the name of the great Christopher Plantin, who in the latter part of the sixteenth century owned, in Antwerp, the largest printing and publishing firm in Europe, it is a rather free adaptation of designs by Claude Garamond (c. 1480–1561) made for that firm. With its strong, simple lines, Plantin is a no-nonsense face of exceptional legibility.

Composed by PennSet,
Bloomsburg, Pennsylvania

Printed and bound by Arcata Graphics/Fairfield,
Fairfield, Pennsylvania

Designed by Cassandra J. Pappas